The Sleeping Truth

Ronald Seth

THE SLEEPING TRUTH

The Hiss-Chambers Affair Reappraised

HART PUBLISHING COMPANY, INC.
NEW YORK CITY

1545014

The Sleeping Truth

Contents

Acknowledgements

In the preparation of this book, I have received much help for which I would like to express my appreciation. I am particularly grateful to Mr Alger Hiss who gave me several hours and answered my searching questions with frankness, forbearance and in great detail; to Mr Duncan Norton-Taylor, of *Time* magazine, and Mr Henry Anatole Grunwald, also of *Time*, both of whom knew Whittaker Chambers intimately – and liked him – and gave me the benefit of their knowledge; to Mr Alastair Cooke, who, over some pleasant drinks, talked to me about the case, which he covered for the *Manchester Guardian*; to the authorities of the New York Public Library, who gave me entrée to Room 315-S so that I could research away from the hurly-burly of the main reading-rooms; to Miss Joan Worth, who put at my disposal her copy of the Second Trial Transcript when it was necessary to unravel some garbled notes; to the countless number of unknowns who, having heard that I was making a study of the case, talked to me about it, and wished me success. I must also thank my wife who added to her spousely duties many hours of note-taking in the New York Public Library.

I am grateful, too, to the following publishers for their permission to quote from the books listed:

Alfred A. Knopf: *In the Court of Public Opinion*, Alger Hiss.
Random House: *Witness*, Whittaker Chambers.
Doubleday & Co.: *The Strange Case of Alger Hiss*, The Earl Jowitt

ACKNOWLEDGEMENTS

Alfred A. Knopf: *A Generation on Trial*, Alastair Cooke.
The Viking Press: *Friendship and Fratricide*, Meyer Zeligs.
G. P. Putnam: *Treason in the Twentieth Century*, Margrit Boveri
Farrar Straus: *Room 3603*, H. Montgomery Hyde.

Finally, I must thank most warmly my American literary agent, Julian S. Bach, Jr., who made some suggestions for emendations in the text, which have clarified many points.

The Sleeping Truth

I

How it Began

At eleven o'clock on the morning of the 3rd August 1948, in one of the splendid rooms of the Old House Office Building in Washington used for hearings of committees set up by Congress, a plumpish man of middle height and careless dress went to the witness chair and faced the House Committee on Un-American Activities which was continuing its investigations into 'Communist Espionage in the United States'. When he had taken the oath, he sat down and turned his attention to Robert E Stripling, chief investigator for the Committee, who asked: 'Will you state your full name?'

'My name,' said the man, 'is David Whittaker Chambers.'

'When and where were you born?'

'I was born 1st April 1901, in Philadelphia.'

'How long have you been associated with *Time* magazine?'

'Nine years.'

'Prior to that time, what was your occupation?'

'I was a member of the Communist Party and a paid functionary of the party.'

Chambers then asked for permission to read a statement to the Committee, and this being given, he began:

'Almost exactly nine years ago (1939) – that is, two days after Hitler and Stalin signed their pact – I went to Washington and reported to the authorities what I knew about the infiltration of the United States Government by Communists. For years, international Communism, of which the United States Communist Party is an integral part, had been in a state of undeclared

9

war with this Republic. With the Hitler–Stalin pact, that war reached a new stage. I regarded my action in going to the Government as a simple act of war, like the shooting of an armed enemy in combat.'

(It was clear from this introduction that Whittaker Chambers was a writer of some distinction. Since he had been a senior editor of *Time* magazine, earning thirty thousand dollars a year, this was not surprising.)

'At that moment in history,' he went on, 'I was one of the new men on this side of the battle who could perform this service. I had joined the Communist Party in 1924. No one recruited me. I had become convinced that the society in which we live, Western civilisation, had reached a crisis, of which the First World War was the military expression, and that it was doomed to collapse or revert to barbarism. I did not understand the causes of the crisis or know what to do about it. But I felt that, as an intelligent man, I must do something. In the writings of Karl Marx, I thought that I had found the explanation of the historical and economic causes. In the writings of Lenin, I thought I had found the answer to the question: What to do?

'In 1937 I repudiated Marx's doctrines and Lenin's tactics. Experience and the record had convinced me that Communism is a form of totalitarianism, that its triumph means slavery to men wherever they fall under its sway, and a spiritual right to the human mind and soul. I resolved to break with the Communist Party at whatever risk to my life or other tragedy to myself or my family. Yet, so strong is the hold which the insidious evil of Communism secures upon its disciples, that I could still say to someone at that time: I know that I am leaving the winning side for the losing side, but it is better to die on the losing side than to live under Communism.

'For a year I lived in hiding, sleeping by day and watching

through the night with gun or revolver within easy reach. That was what underground Communism could do to one man in the peaceful United States in the year 1938.

'I had sound reasons for supposing that the Communists might try to kill me. For a number of years, I had myself served in the underground, chiefly in Washington, DC. The heart of my report to the United States Government consisted of a description of the apparatus[1] to which I was attached. It was an underground organisation of the United States Communist Party developed, to the best of my knowledge, by Harold Ware, one of the sons of the Communist leader known as Mother Bloor. I knew it at its top level, a group of seven or so men, from among whom in later years certain members of Miss Bentley's organisation were apparently recruited. The head of the underground group at the time I knew it was Nathan Witt, an attorney for the National Labour Relations Board. Later, John Abt became the leader. Lee Pressman was also a member of this group, as was Alger Hiss, who, as a member of the State Department, later organised the conferences at Dumbarton Oaks, San Francisco and the United States side of the Yalta Conference.

'The purpose of this group at that time was not primarily espionage. Its original purpose was the Communist infiltration of the American Government. But espionage was certainly one of the eventual objectives. Let no one be surprised at this statement. Disloyalty is a matter of principle with every member of the Communist Party. The Communist Party exists for the specific purpose of overthrowing the Government at the opportune time, by any and all means; and each of its members, by the fact that he is a member, is dedicated to this purpose.

'It is ten years since I broke away from the Communist Party. During that decade, I have sought to live an industrious and God

1. From *aparat*, the word used by the Russians for an espionage network.

fearing life. At the same time, I have fought Communism constantly by act and written word. I am proud to appear before this Committee. The publicity, inseparable from such testimony, has darkened, and no doubt will continue to darken, my effort to integrate myself in the community of free men. But that is a small price to pay if my testimony helps to make Americans recognise at last that they are at grips with a secret, sinister and enormously powerful force whose tireless purpose is their enslavement.

'At the same time, I should like, thus publicly, to call upon all ex-Communists who have not yet declared themselves, and all men within the Communist Party whose better instincts have not yet been corrupted and crushed by it, to aid in this struggle while there is still time to do so.'

It was a startling statement. No fewer than four highly-placed former officials of the US Administration had been actually named as secret Communists whose ultimate intention had been the overthrow of the American Government. While reporters rushed to the telephones to give their newspapers the first reports, Stripling continued with his questioning of Chambers from whom he elicited that the network he had mentioned was a group of seven men 'each of whom was a leader of a cell.' The seven were Nathan Witt, Lee Pressman, Alger Hiss, Donald Hiss, Victor Perlo, Charles Kramer (also known as Krevitsky), John Abt and Henry Collins. Chambers also disclosed that 'the head of the whole business,' that is, the American Communist underground, was a certain J Peters, a somewhat mysterious person for whom the Committee had issued a subpoena in 1947, but had as yet been unable to trace.

Chambers gave a brief résumé of the careers in the Administration service of the men he had named, and stated that he had collected from them their Party dues. He told the Committee that they used to meet regularly for discussions in the apartment of Henry Collins until sometime in 1936, Chambers thought, when Peters, believing that some of them – among them Alger Hiss – were 'going places in the Government,' gave instructions that they should have no further part in the activities of the network, lest such activities should compromise them.

He then related how, when he had decided to break with Communism, he had gone to Alger Hiss and begged him to make the break, too. But Hiss had refused, weeping as he did so. 'I was very fond of Mr Hiss,' Chambers said, and added that at that time Mrs Hiss was also a Communist.

At this point in our story, it will be helpful to have a brief description of the House Committee on Un-American Activities. Like all Congressional committees it had almost star-chamber powers. Its proceedings were privileged, as are those in courts of law the world over, but it had no rules of evidence. As a consequence, the members of the Committee might all ask whatever questions they wished, and make any comments that might occur to them, whether sensitive to proof or not, and no matter how prejudicial such comments might be to the witness. The witness, unless he invoked the Fifth Amendment to the Constitution, which gave him the right to refuse should his answer tend to incriminate him, had to reply or risk action for contempt of Congress.

The House Committee on Un-American Activities had first been set up in 1938. Its chairman then had been Representative Martin Dies, by whose name, so long as he retained the chairmanship, it was known. In 1945 it was composed of J Parnell Thomas (chairman), Representative for New Jersey, who had been a member of the Committee since its inception; Richard M Nixon, California; John McDowell, Pennsylvania; Karl E Mundt, South Dakota; Richard B Vail, Illinois; John E Rankin,

Mississippi; John S Wood, Georgia; J Hardin Peterson, Florida; and F Edward Hébert, Louisiana. Though the Administration was Democrat, the 80th Congress was Republican dominated, and this was reflected jn the Committee, the first five members named being Republican, the remaining four Democrat. The Republicans had turned into a major political issue the allegedly soft attitude of the Administration towards Communist infiltration of the Government.

As far as personalities went the members of the Committee were a rather bizarre collection. Parnell Thomas was a man of deep prejudices which he allowed always to be on the surface. He came to every investigation convinced that some Un-American activity or other would be discovered. He was totally irresponsible in the charges he made – always in the most flamboyant language – which rarely had any evidence to support them. In his chairing of the Committee he displayed an utter lack of dignity and an almost permanent vulgarity, two non-qualities which brushed off on to the more reasonable and sedate members. In the then-current series of hearings it became obvious that he was rabidly anti-New Deal, and since Hiss had been one of Roosevelt's most ardent New Deal supporters, in Parnell Thomas's eyes he could be nothing else but a bad man, who, if accused by anyone of being a Communist, must be a Communist. Before the Hiss-Chambers hearings were complete he relinquished the chairmanship of the Committee as a consequence of being indicted for 'padding his payroll', and he was later found guilty of these charges and sent to prison.

Co-responsible with Parnell Thomas for the bad name the Committee acquired amongst decent Americans was John E Rankin. During hearings he seemed to be permanently lost in his own thoughts, from which he would occasionally emerge to make ridiculously irrelevant interruptions. Again and again he demonstrated either that he could not follow the proceedings or could not be bothered to, and this led him to produce arguments contrary to evidence already given. If he did participate in the interrogation of a witness, his bullying attitude invariably invoked sympathy for his victim, often when the victim did not merit sympathy.

Karl E Mundt, who was acting chairman on the 3rd August 1948, was a man of somewhat different calibre from these two. He had had a varied professional background, having been, before his election to Congress in 1938, a schoolteacher, magazine editor and writer, and he had since developed interests in real estate, insurance and farming. He had been a member of the Committee since 1943, was dedicated, but not fanatically so, to rooting out Communism from the Government. With Richard Nixon, he was co-author of legislation designed to curb the Communist Party. Early in 1949 he was elected Senator and left the Committee.

McDowell, Peterson and Hébert were rather colourless individuals, making very little impact on the proceedings. McDowell seemed to be completely out of his depth as the case developed, and could only moan, 'I don't understand, I don't understand!' which he did, several times. Hébert made one or two useful interventions, but he had little or no effect on the outcome. Vail and Wood never put in an appearance.

Of the officers of the Committee, two of the investigators were interesting. Robert E Stripling, the chief investigator, had begun his service with the Committee as its clerk under Martin Dies. The *New York Times* was to describe him as 'a powerful figure . . . always alert for the striking or sensational.' With Richard Nixon he was the dominant force on the Committee. The other interesting character was one of Stripling's assistants, the Committee's director of research, Benjamin Mandel.

In his book *Witness*,[1] Chambers has written, 'Later on I went to the Manhattan headquarters of the Workers Party on 14th Street. There I met a fidgety, kindly man who duly issued to me, in the name of Whittaker Chambers, a red Party book, listing my Party number, stamped with the Party's rubber seal (a hammer and sickle) and signed with the nervous man's name: Bert Moller. I knew Bert Moller for many years and even worked closely with him in the Communist Party until his expulsion (another "incurable right-wing deviationist") in 1929. In all that time I never knew his real name. It was General Walter Krivitsky who first told me, shortly before his strange death in Washington, that Bert Moller was really Ben Mandel. And it was almost a decade after that before I would resume my close acquaintance with Ben Mandel. By then he was the research director of the House Committee on Un-American Activities, and I was a witness before it.'

But by far the most intelligent, rational and forceful personality on the Committee was Richard M Nixon. He had been elected to the House of Representatives from California in the Republican landslide of 1946. Graduating in law from Duke University, he had practised in California for five years before joining the US Navy late in 1942. Demobilised early in 1946, within six months he was elected to Congress. On arriving in Washington, he was appointed a member of the Committee at the very outset of his first term.

His early career on the Committee did nothing much to make him prominent among his somewhat strange fellow members, but early in February 1948 he was appointed chairman of a sub-committee to consider legislation aimed at checking the activities and influence of the US Communist Party. He conducted the hearings with a dignity which contrasted greatly with the conduct

1. Random House, New York, 1955. p207.

of the main Committee under Parnell Thomas, and in addition he planned the hearings well, so that his sub-committee commanded the respect of leading lawyers, scholars and other eminent men, who were asked to testify.

There is no doubt that it was Nixon's legal training that gave him a much quicker perception of what was taking place. His questioning of Alger Hiss demonstrated that he saw immediately the weaknesses of Hiss's story, and each weakness he probed relentlessly. From this aspect of the Committee phase of the Hiss-Chambers case, Nixon emerged with flying colours, particularly when it is realised that Hiss himself was a very brilliant lawyer.

The good impression which Nixon made in the early stages, however, was eventually vitiated by the developing emergence of political as partisanship and ambition. It was these factors, much as his sincere detestation of Communism, which were predominant in his later assaults on Hiss and his efforts to produce evidence of Hiss's guilt.

As the Hiss-Chambers hearings continued, Nixon revealed himself as an outstanding and persistent critic of the Truman Administration. Both in the Committee and outside it, he accused the President, his subordinates and federal officials, of complete laxity in dealing with the whole question of Communist infiltration. His particular target was the Department of Justice, and he carried his campaign against the Department so far as to declare, when the Judith Coplon case broke early in 1949: 'In my opinion this case shows why the Department may be unfit and unqualified to carry out the responsibility of protecting the national security against Communist infiltration.' And a little later still he demanded a public investigation of the Department.

The House Committee on Un-American Activities, Republican dominated as it was, had always been antagonistic towards the

Administration. Under Nixon's impetus this antagonism increased, and its full extent became obvious in a long speech made by Nixon in the House of Representatives in which he reviewed the Hiss case in great detail and with almost every point stressed the incompetence which the Administration had shown in dealing with it.

At some point in the proceedings Nixon switched from sympathy with Hiss to aligning himself with Chambers. It is difficult from the printed record to discern exactly when this happened. When I was carrying out my research in New York I sought an interview with Mr Nixon, but he was out of town.

Had I been able to meet Mr Nixon, one of the major questions I would have put to him would have been: 'What specifically was it that decided you that Chambers merited your support and your subsequent protection, rather than Hiss?' I have read Mr Nixon's account of the case in *Six Crises*, and can find nothing to indicate an answer to this question.

I have digressed at this point so that the reader may understand the vagaries of the Committee's minds as reflected in their lines of questioning, which became evident even on Chambers's first appearance before them. For having described the network and named its members, Chambers was asked a number of questions about other people on whom the Committee's suspicion seems to have fallen; these were followed by an invitation to say what he knew about Alger Hiss's career. Mundt couched the invitation in the following way:

'Mr Chambers, I am very much interested in trying to check the career of Alger Hiss. I know nothing about Donald Hiss; but as a member of the Foreign Affairs Committee, the personnel Committee, I have had some occasion to check the activities of Alger Hiss while he was in the State Department. There is reason to believe that he organised within the Department one of the

Communist cells which endeavoured to influence our Chinese policy and bring about the condemnation of Chiang Kai-shek, which put Marzini in an important position there, and I think that it is important to know what happened to these people after they left the Government. Do you know where Alger Hiss is employed now?'

Chambers replied that Hiss was President of the Carnegie Endowment for International Peace. Re-questioned about the disclosures he had made to Assistant Secretary of State Adolf Berle, when he had reported his information to him in 1939, Chambers said he was fairly confident that he had given Berle all the names in the group. Berle, he added, had been very excited, but apparently the Government had chosen not to act on the information.

There were no more questions, so acting chairman Mundt thanked him for his 'courage and good patriotism,' while Rankin, on behalf of the Democratic minority, said, 'Speaking for the minority, I want to say that the gentleman has made a splendid witness, and I only regret that every patriotic American could not be here to hear his testimony.' Chambers was then dismissed.

A reporter had already told Hiss on the previous evening that on the following day a man called Chambers was going to tell the House Committee that he, Hiss, was or had been a Communist. Hiss, in his book *In the Court of Public Opinion*,[1] says, 'The untruthful charge of Communism had been the lot of many who had been New Deal officials in the Washington of the 1930s and the early 1940s. I had not taken such charges seriously when made against others, and I saw no reason why I or anyone else should pay much attention to a similar fanciful charge that might now be made against me.'

1. Alfred A. Knopf, New York, 1957. p4.

The next day, however, he realised that he would have to change his mind. For as soon as the Committee adjourned, a reporter telephoned him at the Carnegie Endowment and gave him the gist of what Chambers had testified. When he saw the newspaper accounts that evening, it was clear that this was no charge to be shrugged off. So, after some thought, and discussion with friends of what he should do (some of his friends advised him to ignore the Committee) he decided to send a telegram to the Committee, which Mundt read out at the beginning of the next day's hearing. The telegram said :

My attention has been called by representatives of the press to statements made about me before your Committee this morning by one Whittaker Chambers. I do not know Mr Chambers and insofar as I am aware have never laid eyes on him. There is no basis for the statements made about me to your Committee. I would appreciate it if you would make this telegram a part of your Committee's record, and I would further appreciate the opportunity to appear before your Committee to make this statement formally and under oath. I shall be in Washington on Thursday and hope that that will be a convenient time from the Committee's point of view for me to appear.

His request was granted, and on the 5th August 1948 he presented himself to the Committee.

Like Chambers, he had also prepared a statement which he was allowed to read immediately after taking the oath and answering the preliminary questions.

'I was born in Baltimore, Maryland, on the 11th November 1904. I am here at my own request to deny unqualifiedly various statements about me which were made before this Committee by one Whittaker Chambers the day before yesterday. I appreciate the Committee having promptly granted my request. I welcome the opportunity to answer to the best of my ability any inquiries the members of this Committee may wish to ask me.

'I am not and never have been a member of the Communist Party. I do not and never have adhered to the tenets of the Communist Party. I am not and never have been a member of any Communist-front organisation. I have never followed the Communist Party line, directly or indirectly. To the best of my knowledge, none of my friends is a Communist.

'As a State Department official, I have had contacts with representatives of foreign Governments, some of whom have undoubtedly been members of the Communist Party, as, for example, representatives of the Soviet Government. My contacts with a foreign representative who could possibly have been a Communist have been strictly official.

'To the best of my knowledge, I never heard of Whittaker Chambers until in 1947, when two representatives of the Federal Bureau of Investigation asked me if I knew him and various other people, some of whom I knew and some of whom I did not know. I said I did not know Chambers. So far as I know, I have never laid eyes on him, and I should like to have the opportunity to do so.

'I have known Henry Collins since we were boys in camp together. I knew him again while he was at the Harvard Business School, while I was at the Harvard Law School, and I have seen him from time to time since I came to Washington in 1933.

'Lee Pressman was in my class at the Harvard Law School and we were both on the Harvard Law Review at the same time. We were also both assistants to Judge Jerome Frank on the legal staff of the Agricultural Adjustment Administration. Since I left the Department of Agriculture I have seen him only occasionally and infrequently. I left the Department, according to my recollection, in 1935.

'Witt and Abt were both members of the legal staff of the AAA. I knew them both in that capacity. I believe I met Witt in New York a year or so before I came to Washington. I came to Washington in 1933. We were both practising law in New York at the time I think I met Witt.

'Kramer was in another office of the AAA, and I met him in that connection.

'I have seen none of these last three men I have mentioned except most infrequently since I left the Department of Agriculture.

'I don't believe I ever knew Victor Perlo.

'Except as I have indicated, the statements made about me by Mr Chambers are complete fabrications. I think my record in the Government service speaks for itself.'

When he had completed his statement, the extraordinary McDowell, who rarely seemed to be able to comprehend anything that was happening in the Committee, made one of his self-revelatory remarks. 'I have forgotten entirely,' he said, 'what charge was made by Mr Chambers.' Acting chairman Mundt thereupon embarked upon a summary of Chambers's evidence two days before.

What had been puzzling Hiss most since he had heard of Chambers's charges against him, was Chambers's identity. He was absolutely convinced in his own mind that he had never known anyone by that name. He had seen photographs of Chambers in yesterday's newspapers, but these had only served to convince him that he had never seen the man.

It was he who deliberately brought up the matter of Chambers's identity. Angry, so he has said, that the Committee had allowed Chambers, who was unknown to him, to testify before he could confront Chambers, he told the Committee so. After one or two questions, Stripling said, 'You say you have never seen Mr Chambers.' Hiss replied, 'The name means absolutely nothing to me, Mr Stripling.' Thereupon Stripling handed him a close-up of Chambers taken while he was giving his testimony, explaining to Hiss that he had put on considerable weight since 1934. The photograph had been taken at such an angle that it would not have been easy for Hiss to identify a casual acquaintance, let alone someone he had not set eyes on for fourteen years. Hiss told Stripling that he would rather see the man than try to identify him from a photograph, and he asked if Chambers was present today. On being told by Mundt that he was not, Hiss said a little tartly that he had hoped he would be.

In the care which Hiss seemed to be exercising here, we see for the first time the lawyer's caution at work. Later he was to apply the same caution to many of his answers, to so many, in fact, that even a reading of the cold transcript makes us wonder what his real motive was in being so cagey. It is only when we have read on that we realise that Hiss was so dominated by his legal mind that he could not have answered otherwise. At the time, however, he irritated the Committee by what seemed to be his refusal to give a straight unqualified answer to any question that might have embarrassed him. For example, when he was describing how he first came to Washington at the invitation of Judge Jerome Frank, Nixon asked him to name any other Government officials who had told him to accept Judge Frank's invitation. Hiss replied that he would prefer not to do so, since 'there are so many witnesses who use names rather loosely before your Committee,' and would only do so on Nixon's insistence. It was this kind of thing that antagonised the Committee. The Committee's attitude also angered Hiss, as is shown by his retort to Mundt who at one point remarked, a propos of the Committee's difficulty in knowing which man to believe, 'You can appreciate the position of the Committee.' 'I hope the Committee can appreciate my position, too,' Hiss rejoined.

Before Hiss was released he was questioned about the occasion in 1947 when two FBI agents visited him and asked, among other kindred questions, if he had ever been a Communist. He answered all such probings frankly, and volunteered the information that Secretary of State Byrnes had warned him, about the same time, that there was a possibility of his being labelled a Communist, whereupon he had gone at once to the FBI and asked to see its chief, J Edgar Hoover; on hearing that Hoover was out of town he had asked for, and been granted, an interview with the Bureau's deputy chief.

When Stripling referred to Chambers's claim that when he had urged Hiss to break with the Party and Hiss had refused, weeping, Hiss flatly denied being involved in any such incident. At this denial Stripling turned to Mundt and said, 'Mr Chairman, there is a very sharp contradiction in testimony here. I certainly suggest Mr Chambers be brought back before the Committee to clear this up.' Mundt suggested that perhaps Chambers had confused Hiss with his brother Donald. Hiss at once leapt to his brother's defence. Donald, he said, was as unlikely to be embroiled in subversive activity as he himself.

This exchange seemed to impress the Committee, Nixon included, for the latter suggested that it would be best for all concerned if it were arranged for Hiss and Chambers to confront one another in private. No decision was taken there and then, and Mundt thanked him for his co-operation and frank statements, and congratulated him on being the first of all those named by Chambers to ask for an opportunity to deny the allegations.[1] Rankin added his thanks for the Democrats, and the

1. Everyone named by Chambers was then alive except Harold Ware.

hearing was adjourned.

According to Chambers in *Witness*,[1] when the Committee withdrew, in the lowest of low spirits, they tried to decide what to do. Some were for abandoning the case altogether, but Nixon insisted that the present impasse must be resolved, 'and thus made the Hiss case possible.' They must, he maintained, for the good reputation of the Committee, try to discover who was lying. It was Benjamin Mandel, the director of research and former Communist, who eventually produced the solution. Why not summon Chambers again, he suggested, and question him closely in *secret session* in an attempt to discover how intimately he knew Hiss? This could be done by asking him facts about the Hisses' private lives, the houses they had lived in and so on, facts which would only be known to someone who had been on intimate terms with the Hisses. When this had been done, Hiss would be asked the same questions and the two sets of answers could be compared.

Nixon seized upon Mandel's suggestion eagerly, and presently found himself drafted as chairman of a sub-committee composed of himself, Hébert and the permanently confused McDowell. They left for New York next day, and summoned Chambers to appear before them in Room 101 of the United States Courthouse at 10 30 am.

Before going on to this encounter, it will, I think, be helpful to know a little more about the two protagonists.

1. Op cit p556.

2

The Two Men

i. Whittaker Chambers

It would be difficult to find two men of such contra-distinction
as Whittaker Chambers and Alger Hiss, both in the manner of
their lives and in the manner of their living, in their backgrounds
and in their personalities. I know that it is often popularly held
that opposites attract – at least insofar as men and women are
concerned; though this has much to do with sexual magnetism,
for example, Lady Chatterley and Mellors, Charles II and Nell
Gwyn – but I find it increasingly difficult to accept the suggestion, indeed the claim, of the anti-Hiss faction that there could
have been even an intellectual intimacy between these two men;
and since there is a complete absence of a physical sexual relationship, which alone might have attracted them to one another, I
discover myself more and more surrendering in favour of Hiss
the strict non-partisanship which I promised myself to observe at
the outset; a non-partisanship which I may as well reveal here
has been completely destroyed since I completed my researches.

Whittaker Chambers was born on 1st April 1901, to Jay and
Laha Chambers in Philadelphia. Jay Chambers was a staff artist
on the *New York World*; Laha was the daughter of a wealthy
family from the mid-West. Whittaker Chambers was actually
given the names Jay Vivian; he adopted Whittaker, his mother's
maiden-name, as a young man.

On the 26th September 1903, a second son was born and given
the names Richard Godfrey. Early in 1904 Mrs Chambers and
her two sons moved to Lynbrook, New York, which made it
possible for Jay Chambers, who since his marriage had been able

to spend little time with his wife on account of his New York post, to live with his family. According to Chambers in *Witness*,[1] Jay Chambers was his hero. 'I loved my father dearly in those days . . . I would often lie awake listening until I heard him turn the knob of the front door. Only then, sometimes after midnight, would I fall asleep.'

It would appear, however, that his family were not heroes to Jay Chambers, for after a while he left home, and stayed away for two years. The absence brought about a change in the boy's feelings for his father, which was a natural result, for while Jay Chambers was away Laha exerted, though unconsciously, an influence on her sons which drew the three of them emotionally together to the exclusion of the father.

Chambers senior did not entirely shirk his responsibilities. He sent his wife eight dollars a month. 'At the time and place, it was possible to manage on eight dollars, and my mother was a good manager. But, as a child, I knew that we were poor. I knew it by direct experience.'[2]

After primary school, Chambers passed on to South Side High School, Rockville Centre, Long Island, from where he graduated in 1919. He had displayed a potential brilliance, but his performance fluctuated. Uninterested in the sciences, he did well in the arts, his best subject being English.

Chambers left South Side High under a cloud. Having been elected class prophet, he predicted that one of his fellow girl pupils would become a prostitute. On reading the draft of the prophecy, which was to be delivered at the graduation ceremonies, the school principal requested that this and certain other passages be erased. Chambers promised to make the deletions, but when he came to make the speech, he read the full version.

1. Op cit p98.

2. *Witness*, op cit p122.

As a punishment he was not allowed to receive his diploma with the other pupils.

Laha Chambers planned that her elder son should go to college. The family circumstances were such, however, that it was essential he should have a temporary job until the university year started, and his mother found one for him at the Lynbrook National Bank. He detested the work, however, and did not get on with his fellow-employees, so he decided to run away from home.

Making for Baltimore, young Chambers took a room in a cheap hotel and looked around for work. Having consulted the newspaper advertisements he decided to apply for a job as a labourer on the Washington, DC, tramways, which he did in the name of Charles Adams – the first of many false names he was to adopt from time to time throughout his life. After continuing at the work for two or three months, until it came to an end, he moved down to New Orleans.

There he took a room in a cheap lodging-house, where one of the other lodgers was a prostitute called One-eyed Annie, whom he came to know fairly intimately, though it is extremely doubtful whether he ever availed himself of her professional services. In fact, Chambers seemed to have been far more interested in her pimp, Ben Santi, judging by the following passage from *Witness*: 'One-eyed Annie was as ugly a woman as I have ever seen. Ben doted on her. Whenever she was out of the house, he would prowl around restlessly, always in his undershirt. His shoulders were massive and he was tattooed like a head-hunter. He walked noiselessly, and he had a caressing softness of voice and an extreme gentleness of gesture that seemed less natural than the result of some conscious constraint that had settled into a habit ... sometimes he would drift into my room and ply me with the wisdom of the deep slums – a jungle theory of individualism, in which a man was merely a phallic symbol, as strong as his power to attract women, or pull a knife, or a gun, on the rest of life which was his natural prey. Ben liked to talk to me because I never interrupted him.'[1]

I shall have occasion later to go into Chambers's sexual nature in some detail, particularly in regard to his relationship with his brother. At eighteen and a few months, however, he felt uncomfortable in the presence of unrestrained sexuality. Ben Santi and One-eyed Annie often invited him and another lodger, Jules Raden, to their room. 'Often they received us in bed, and I could not help observing that, stripped of Shakespeare's splendour, their grotesque passion was the raw stuff of Antony and Cleopatra. They were quite shameless, so that sometimes I left the room quickly on one excuse or another. Their laughter would float downstairs after me. It was not mean or mocking, but indolent and a little wistful, as if to say that innocence is indeed a worthy thing, but, in the world as it is, such a burden.'[2]

Chambers had arrived in New Orleans with savings from his Washington job. In New Orleans he was unsuccessful in finding work, and when his money eventually ran out, he wrote home asking for more. Jay Chambers wired him his fare back to New York.

His running away had been an act of adolescent rebellion against parental influences. Now back under the spell of these influences, he had for the time being to surrender to them. Agreeing to his mother's plan that he should enter Williams College, while waiting he accepted a post which his father procured for him at the Frank Seaman Advertising Company, New York.

Jay Chambers was manager of the art department of this

1. Op cit pp161 and 162.

2. *Witness*, op cit p161.

company, and according to Chambers, he suggested that they should keep their relationship a secret lest people should suspect nepotism. Chambers agreed, and to make the deception less susceptible to discovery, he took the second of his false names – his grandfather's, Charles Whittaker.

There he remained in this job until he went to college. However, his experience at Williams College was a strange one. 'One or two days on that beautiful and expensive campus told me that Williams was not the place for me, that my parents would never stand the costs of that little Harvard. I saw that I had a quick and difficult decision to make. I took a night train for New York. The next morning, before going home, I entered Columbia University.'[1] He signed the papers for the first time using the name Whittaker, to replace his given name of Vivian. This was in the autumn of 1920.

Whittaker Chambers remained at Columbia University until January 1923, when he withdrew before completing his degree course. During these two years the impression he made on Columbia was a diversified one. On the one hand he acquired a reputation for being unconventional – eccentric and a campus agitator; on the other, a student of considerable literary potential, revealing himself as something of a poet. It was one of his literary activities that brought about his withdrawal from the University in January 1923.

In November 1922 he had been elected editor-in-chief of a university publication called *The Morningside*. In the first number to appear under his editorship (November 1922) was a short one-act play written by Chambers and entitled *A Play for Puppets*, purportedly by one John Kelly. According to a review of the magazine in the *Columbia Spectator* on the 23rd October 1922, *A Play for Puppets* was 'conceived in the purest profanism and

1. *Witness*, op cit p164.

dedicated to the Antichrist . . . the idea – but that will come out in the reading, when the question also may be decided whether the author was merely blasphemous or merely brilliant.'

The publication of the play caused an uproar on the campus and among the college authorities. As soon as it was known that 'John Kelly' was Chambers, he was removed from the editorship and though he was not expelled from the University, he was asked to leave voluntarily and did so.

At the suggestion of his former supervisor of studies, Mark Van Doren, he approached the Society of Friends and asked to join their famine relief expedition to Russia. News of the *A Play for Puppets* furore, however, had reached the outside world, and the Quakers rejected his request. Instead he sailed for Europe in June with two Columbia friends, Meyer Schapiro and Henry Zolinsky.

The trio travelled through Holland into Germany, to Berlin, where they shared an apartment. After a month in the German capital they made their way through Belgium to France. At the beginning of September his two friends had to leave him to return to their studies at Columbia, and Chambers went on to Paris alone. Late in September, he, too, set out again for America.

On the 28th September 1923 Chambers obtained a post in the Newspaper Division of the New York Public Library. It was a night job and not onerous, and during the slack time he planned to produce a collection of poems. In his off-duty hours he spent much of his time at Columbia visiting friends, and this seems to have engendered in him a desire to return to the University himself. At all events, he approached the Dean, and though he has not recorded the undertakings he must have been asked to give, they must have satisfied the authorities, for he was read-mitted. In a letter to Mark Van Doren giving this news, he said, 'I lied to him quite simply, and told him I wanted to teach history,' a sentence which was to confront him again and again a quarter of a century later. But once back at the University he made no real attempt to study seriously and before the end of the term had stopped attending lectures. During this time he continued to work at the New York Public Library, from 5-10 pm on weekdays and 1-10 pm on Sundays.

On the 17th February 1925 Chambers joined the Communist Party. In *Witness* he has written, 'The dying world of 1925 was without faith, hope, character, understanding of its malady or will to overcome it . . . the dying world had no answer at all to the crisis of the twentieth century . . . only in Communism had I found any practical answer at all to the crisis, and the will to make that answer work. . . . I went to my campus friends who had so long and patiently worked to convert me to Communism and said that at last I was ready; I asked them where the Communist Party could be found. To my great surprise, they did not know.'[1] However, he recalled a young man called Sender Garlin whom he had met briefly at Columbia when Garlin had spent a night there, and Garlin told him that the Communist Party, which had lately emerged into the open, for reasons of expediency, was calling itself the Workers' Party. He did not, he said, know how one contacted the Party, but Chambers did not believe this, and sure enough, a few nights later he received a visit, while on duty at the Public Library, from 'the first American Communist I had ever seen.'

Out of this meeting came an introduction to various members of the Communist Party and eventually Chambers was accepted for membership. Despite the advice of a new Communist friend, he joined under his own name – Whittaker Chambers. Within a short time he had made an impact on the Party, and was soon working for the *Daily Worker*.

1. Op cit pp195 and 196.

On the 9th September 1926, Richard Chambers, Whittaker's younger brother, committed suicide at the age of twenty-two and a half. He had made one or two previous attempts which had been thwarted. As I shall be considering Chambers's relationship with his brother in a later chapter in some detail, I will do nothing more here but record the fact.

In the spring of 1927, Chambers was sacked from his job in the New York Public Library. A number of books had been missed, detectives were called in, and the books were found in Chambers's locker. He was now given a full-time job on the *Daily Worker*, which he has described as acting editor, though it was in fact very much an inferior one. However, while working for the Communist newspaper he met most of the prominent members of the Party.

Here I would refer the interested reader to part four of *Witness* for Chambers's version of his experiences with the American Communist Party in this early period. In 1929 he was removed from the *Daily Worker* as the result of his refusal to submit to some aspect of Party discipline, and for a short period left the Party. At this time the American Communist Party was being purged of its Trotskyite elements, and it was his revulsion to this process which led to the break. However, he was soon back again within the fold and in 1931 he was appointed editor of the *New Masses*.

Among his fellow-workers in the Party was a young woman artist called Esther Shemitz, to whom Chambers became attracted. Esther Shemitz was far more of a dedicated Communist than Chambers ever was throughout his whole Party membership. They married in New York City Hall on the 15th April 1931.

Chambers's work on the *New Masses* was extremely successful and gave him a new rating within the Party. It had given him the first real opportunity he had had for realising his literary bent.

However, he was not to remain long with the journal, for in June 1932 he received a telephone call from Max Bedacht, a member of the Central Committee of the American Communist Party and head of the International Workers Order, a Communist-controlled benefit and insurance society. This telephone call was to bring the greatest change in his life so far.

'It was seven years since Comrade Krieger had appeared at my desk in the Public Library,' he wrote in *Witness*, 'to guide me into the Communist Party. Comrade Bedacht was about to summon me into crypts of Communism I scarcely dreamed existed, into its deep underground, whose door was about to close noiselessly behind me almost as if I had never existed.'[1]

As instructed over the telephone, Chambers met Bedacht in his office, and there received the surprising news that those in authority had decided that he should henceforward work in the clandestine organisation of the Party. If the man or woman so chosen happened to be a member of the open Communist Party, the first step to joining the underground was for the candidate to cut himself or herself off from the open Party. Chambers pointed out to Bedacht that if this happened to a member so well-known as he (Chambers) was, there was sure to be a good deal of gossip. Bedacht replied that they appreciated that, but had nevertheless decided that they needed him in the underground.

Chambers said that he would have to have time to think it over. Now that he was married, his life was not entirely his own. Bedacht gave him until the following morning.

Chambers's comments on his reactions are interesting. 'Just the implication of undefined power lurking behind a figure like Bedacht and suddenly giving him ambiguous meaning, is disturbing. The terms "special institution" and "underground" could only mean secret, possibly dangerous, Party work. They could

1. Op cit p271.

only mean that, somewhere beside the open Communist Party, there existed a concealed Party which functioned so smoothly that in seven years as a Communist I had not suspected it . . . as a Communist, I felt a quiet elation at the knowledge that there was one efficient party organisation and that it had selected me to work with it . . . in the nature of its work, such an organisation could not pick its personnel at random. Therefore, for some time, it must have been watching me. Unknown to me, eyes must have been observing me.'[1]

Chambers and his wife were at this time living on 'a wild lonely farm, six miles from Glen Gardner, in Hunterdon County, in western New Jersey.' He seems to have possessed an inner craving to farm, for after his final break with Communism, he returned to farming in a small way, and was so engaged at the time of his death in 1961. Though Bedacht had warned him that he must not tell his wife about the new proposal, he hurried to the farm and told her. She urged him to refuse, and like a good husband he promised he would.

When Chambers told Bedacht next day of his decision, Bedacht told him that he had no choice. In fact, he was going to take him immediately 'to someone from the "special institution".' This 'someone' turned out to be a man he knew – John Sherman, alias 'Don', who had been a writer on the *Daily Worker* staff, and a victim of the local purge, whereupon he was conscripted as a secret agent by Russian military intelligence in the United States.

Sherman introduced him to a Russian officer, whom Chambers was to know under the cover-names of Otto, Carl or Herbert. Herbert asked if he knew anything about the nature of clandestine organisation, and 'seemed very much amused when I said that I did not.' He instructed Chambers to move in from the country and settle in a New York suburb, where he was to take on the

1. *Witness*, op cit p276.

cover of a respectable bourgeois. He would receive a hundred dollars a month from the *aparat* (Russian term for underground network or organisation) which he would receive from Sherman, who would be his immediate superior. It was also decided to give him the cover-name Bob.

According to Chambers, Sherman gave him a certain amount of instruction in undercover techniques. (I shall be referring to these later.) Chambers then rented an apartment in Greenwich Village. There he seems to have been left high and dry for a time, for both Herbert and then Sherman disappeared. Presently, however, he was introduced to the underground headquarters on Gay Street, Greenwich Village. 'The apartment on Gay Street was one terminal of an international communications system whose other terminal was presumably Moscow, and which had way stations in Hamburg and probably other European cities.'[1] In the apartment, microfilmed messages were enlarged, messages written in invisible ink developed, messages from New York to Moscow photographed. 'A human chain of couriers and contacts stretched across the ocean and the continent of Europe, speeding communications back and forth between Moscow and New York. The last link which tied that chain to the Gay Street workshop was an underground worker known as "Charlie".'[2]

Charlie, says Chambers, was, in fact, a well-known Communist named Leon Minster. Born in Russia, he had been reared in the United States, had American citizenship and was a brother-in-law of the Russian leader Molotov.

In Gay Street, Charlie taught Chambers the skills required to make him useful in the workshop. Chambers then became the liaison between Charlie and the young German Communist courier, known as Henry. This lasted until the Nazis ferreted out

1. *Witness*, op cit p299.
2. *Witness*, op cit p299.

the couriers and this particular communications system collapsed, and the Gay Street workshop, having no *raison d'être* any longer, ceased to exist.

By this time, Mrs Chambers had become pregnant. On the 16th October 1933, their first child, a daughter, Ellen Chambers, was born.

Shortly after the collapse of the courier system, Russian intelligence decided to disband the apparat to which Chambers was attached. Chambers was redeployed, and set to work in the clandestine section of the American Communist Party, whose leader was a mysterious figure known as J Peters, who, says Chambers, 'was delighted to have me.'

Chambers was attached to a group operating in Washington, DC. The group, known as the Ware Group from its leader Harold Ware, consisted of members of the US Administration, who were feeding information to the Russians. So as to be more available Chambers moved from New York to Baltimore, using the name Lloyd Cantwell.

Chambers's role in Washington was that of go-between between the group and Russian intelligence. He claimed that he received the Party dues of the group's members every month, that they handed state documents to him which he had photographed for onward transmission to the Russian Embassy in Washington while returning the originals to their suppliers for replacement in the files from which they had been abstracted.

Chambers joined the Washington apparat in the spring of 1934. In June or July 1934 he claimed he met Alger Hiss, to whom he was introduced merely as Carl.

The stories of the two men now become interwoven, and I will pause here in Chambers's story, since the remainder of it will be revealed in our consideration of subsequent events.

The character that emerges from even this brief outline is of a somewhat strange, rebellious, unconventional man whose moral code did not match up to the accepted moral standards. His lying, his thieving (of books), his constant adoption of names not his own, which was to increase in frequency as his career in the Soviet underground developed – and not always prompted by necessity – present him as a creature psychologically disturbed. The trained psychiatrist would have a field-day analysing him. One American, Dr Meyer Zeligs, of California, recently has, in a study of both Chambers and Hiss in a book called *Friendship and Fratricide*,[1] and has brought down coals of fire on his head from the pro-Chambers faction. Some of their strictures are justified, but a great many are not, for whether one is for or against psychiatric analysis, one cannot say with any truth that Chambers was a normal man. Only in one aspect of his performance can one speak with anything like certainty, and that is in consideration of the man's literary ability, but even that is restricted. He had a felicitous facility with words, and he wrote a nicely balanced, evocative prose; but his actual published writings – his autobiography *Witness*, and *Cold Friday*, a posthumously published collection of fragments edited by one of his close friends, Duncan Norton-Taylor, of Time Inc – display a lush sentimentality and an obvious over-dramatisation of events, situations, relationships, which led him, both, to misrepresentation of facts.

Perhaps one example may illustrate what I mean. In part two of *Witness* ('The Story of a Middle-Class Family'), Chambers has written, 'I was born in the house of my grandfather, James S Chambers. I began to come into the world very early in the morning. Snow was falling and soon turned into a blizzard.' Dr Zeligs checked with the United States Weather Bureau in Philadelphia (where Chambers was born), who reported to

1. Andre Deutsch, London, 1967.

38

him: 'On 1st April 1901, the maximum temperature (in Philadelphia) was 56°; the minimum temperature was 38° and the average temperature was 47°. No precipitation occurred on the above-mentioned date.'[1]

As for the sentimentality, I find many passages of *Witness* painfully nauseating, though this, I have to admit, is probably a very personal reaction. This is particularly true of the prefatory chapter Chambers wrote in the form of a letter to his children, and which contains several passages that cause me acute discomfort to read. For example: 'Dear children, one autumn twilight, when you were much smaller, I slipped away from you in play and stood for a moment alone in the apple orchard near the barn. There I heard your two voices piping together anxiously, calling to me, "Papa! Papa!" from the harvested cornfield. In the years when I was away five days a week in New York, working to pay for the farm, I used to think of you both before I fell asleep at night. And that is how you almost always came to me – voices of beloved children, calling to me from the gathered fields at dusk.'[2]

This sentimentality was to be a trait that remained with Chambers throughout his life. It was what prompted him to add that touching gloss to his alleged scene with Alger Hiss, in which he urged Hiss to break with the Communist Party, and Hiss refused, *weeping* as he did so. Anyone who knows Alger Hiss would suspect this scene immediately; from only a brief personal contact with him, I would be very surprised if I learned that Hiss was at all easily moved to tears.

As for the dramatisation, and the lying – we shall meet them, too, as the story of the Hiss-Chambers Case develops.

1. Op cit pp28 and 29.
2. *Witness*, op cit p20.

ii. *Alger Hiss*

Alger Hiss was born at Baltimore, Maryland, on the 11th November 1904. His father was Charles Alger Hiss, his mother formerly Mary Lavinia Hughes, familiarly known as Minnie.

Charles Hiss after leaving high school began immediately to look for a job and became a salesman for the Traxell Carriage and Harness Company, of Baltimore. Determined to be a success in business, after a year or two he apprenticed himself to a textile firm, and having worked out his indentures became a salesman for a large wholesale store in Baltimore. Minnie Hughes came of a highly respectable Baltimore family, but Charles Hiss's prospects were reckoned such that the Hugheses thoroughly approved of the young people's marriage.

The subsequent family of Charles and Minnie Hiss arrived at very irregular intervals. The first child, a daughter, was not born until they had been married five years (1893). Another daughter appeared two years later (1895) and then there was a gap of five years before Mrs Hiss produced her first son, in 1900. Another four years went by before another child was born – a second son, Alger, while the third son and youngest child, Donald, was born two years later.

Charles Hiss fulfilled his ambition to be a successful businessman. By 1902 he was an executive, a stockholder and a voting member of one of Baltimore's foremost importers, Daniel Miller & Co.

In 1906, Albert Hughes, whom Charles Hiss had brought into Daniel Miller, entered into a financial transaction involving the firm's money. The transaction failed and Hughes defaulted, in consequence of which Charles Hiss, who seems to have underwritten the venture, lost a good deal of money. He was compelled to sell his securities, and he withdrew from Daniel Miller.

The experience apparently affected Charles Hiss's health, and when some months passed without his finding new employment, for which the economic depression of 1906 was responsible, he began to brood. Early in 1907, however, he and his brother George entered into a partnership for the purchase of a large and (allegedly) prosperous cotton mill. Returning to Baltimore, seemingly in good spirits, he began to plan the move of his family to North Carolina, but his wife, however, was firmly against the move and, in fact, he, also, was very worried by it for, having consulted his doctor about his chronic insomnia and melancholia, he had been advised to enter hospital. Then, suddenly it all became too much for him, and on Sunday the 7th April 1907, he killed himself.

Having recovered from the shock of her husband's death, Minnie Hiss, advised by her brother-in-law, George, set about bringing up her widely spaced family, with the practical help of her sister-in-law, Eliza Hiss. Alger was two and a half when his father died, his brother Donald only a few months. The loss of his father at such an early age was not entirely compensated by a sensible, vigorous mother, who welded her diverse family into a cohesive unit, and yet could not quite take the place of 'the man about the house.'

Hiss has described his boyhood to Dr Zeligs as typical. The children were expected to help with the chores about the house, 'to be punctual at meals, come in with hair combed, hands washed, and the boys with their jackets on.'[1] On the other hand the routine found place for a wide variety of activities according to individual dispositions. What probably distinguished the family from the average was the very high intellectual ability of all the children, the girls as well as the boys.

In 1909, at the age of five, Alger Hiss entered the Baltimore

1. *Friendship and Fratricide*, op cit p150.

Public School No 14, and from there, in September 1917, went on to Baltimore City College, a public high school for boys. At the City College he was very popular among his fellow students, the school magazine for his last year describing his career there 'as far more successful than that of the average fellow.'

From the City College, Hiss went on to a private preparatory school at Duxbury in Massachusetts, followed by a term at the Maryland Institute in Baltimore, where he studied art. While at Duxbury he lived with his sister Mary who, now in her middle twenties, was married.

In September 1922 Alger Hiss entered Johns Hopkins University where he quickly made a most favourable impression on both teaching staff and fellow-students. He was an extremely good-looking young man, tall, with a trim figure. (Forty-five years later he has lost neither looks nor figure.) He was a keen and serious student, yet he took part in many activities of the campus in all of which he excelled.

In 1924 he made his first trip to Europe with a party of students. On the voyage from New York he made the acquaintance of and fell in love with Priscilla Fansler. They were to marry five years later.

He had by this time chosen his future career – the American Consular Service. Taking the advice of Professor Hudson, professor of International Law at Harvard, on graduation from Johns Hopkins he applied for entrance to the Harvard Law School.

During the first of his three years at Harvard, a personal tragedy overtook him. His older brother, Bosley, who in character and approach to life was the antithesis of the serious young man fast beginning to acquire strict moral standards, died. Notwithstanding their differences, Alger had been very fond of Bosley, and the impression Bosley made on him during his formative years, are, according to Dr Zeligs, key factors in his own development.

At Harvard he came under the influence of three members of the teaching staff: Francis B Sayre, who later became Assistant Secretary of State and appointed Hiss his assistant; Professor Edward Morgan; and Professor Felix Frankfurter, who was destined to become one of the most distinguished of American judges. These men were to make an impression on him that was to become welded into one aspect of his own character – that of the meticulous, precise, almost over-precise lawyer.

Immersed in his legal studies, it was not long before he decided to give up his intention to enter the Consular Service, and to become a practising lawyer instead. To this end he now devoted all his efforts, and in doing so left a lasting impression on his contemporaries and teachers.

A month before he graduated from Harvard, a second personal tragedy overtook him. His sister, Mary Ann Emerson, committed suicide. He had spent much of his time with Mrs Emerson, both when he was at Duxbury and since coming to Harvard. The tragedy was totally unexpected, and at the time incomprehensible. According to Dr Zeligs, Hiss only recently learned that she had suffered from 'recurrent periods of mental depression and elation, and spent brief periods as a patient in a private sanatorium.'[1]

Hiss graduated from the Harvard Law School *cum laude* in June 1929, and in the autumn he took up the post of secretary to Supreme Court Justice Oliver Wendell Holmes Jr, for which he had been selected by Professor Frankfurter in recognition of his academic achievements. His duties were to study briefs filed in cases which were to come before the Supreme Court, summarise them and give a verbal account of them to the judge. But besides his official duties, he did much more. Mr Justice Holmes, who

1. *Friendship and Fratricide*, op cit p175 fn.

was eighty-nine, had recently lost his wife, and the young man did much to alleviate the old man's loneliness. The relationship between them quickly developed into an ideal father-son relationship, with Hiss becoming a filially devoted companion. For his part, the young man admired the old man without qualification; and Justice Holmes's fondness for him was reflected in his will by the bequest of a large Queen Anne mirror which had been in the Holmes family for several generations. After Holmes died in 1935 and the mirror was passed to Hiss, henceforward it filled the most prominent position in the Hiss home. He still regards it as one of his most prized possessions.

On the 11th December 1929, two months after becoming Holmes's secretary, Alger Hiss married Priscilla Fansler, whom he had met five years before on the trip to Europe. In the meantime, Miss Fansler had married Thayer Hobson, who worked in a New York publishing house, and had given birth to a son, Timothy, on the 19th September 1926. The couple, however, had quickly discovered their incompatibility and after Timothy's birth they separated, Mrs Hobson becoming office manager for Henry Luce, editor of *Time* magazine.

The Hobsons divorced in January 1929, and Hiss, on hearing this, began to court Priscilla. She responded to his advances, and as her family approved of the good-looking, gay and yet serious young man, whose future was bound to be successful unless an extremely unkind fate decreed otherwise, she agreed to marry him.

The secretaryship to Holmes – a much sought after honour – was an annual appointment with no possibility of renewal, so in October 1930 Alger Hiss launched into private practice with the Boston legal firm of Choate, Hall and Stewart. By the end of his first year he had given ample signs of fulfilling his initial promise. But Priscilla Hiss did not find Cambridge, where they lived, nor

Boston, suited to her temperament, and despite the good start he had made in Boston, Hiss agreed to withdraw from Choate, Hall and Stewart and move to New York, so that his wife might carry out the research for which she had been awarded a grant by the Carnegie Corporation.

Because Hiss was engaged on a very protracted law suit in Boston and had agreed to remain with the firm until it was concluded, Priscilla and Timothy Hobson moved to New York without Hiss. Only at weekends, for several months, could they all be together.

The world economic depression of 1931 was now being felt with all its impact in the United States, and its consequences were particularly visible in New York, where unemployment and poverty reached all-time heights. Touched by the queues for free food outside the headquarters of the Uptown-Upper Broadway Section of the Socialist Party, Priscilla offered her services, and during the next few months she helped to make sandwiches and serve coffee. When, however, Hiss did eventually leave Boston and they rented another apartment in the Central Park area, she gave up this voluntary work, but it was to be remembered *against* them sixteen years later.

After a short time with the New York law firm of Cotton and Franklin, Hiss decided to enter Government service, and in May 1933 he became assistant general counsel to the new Agricultural Adjustment Administration (AAA). This entailed yet another move, this time to Washington, and there Priscilla and Timmie Hobson joined him the following month.

Hiss was one of three assistant general counsel to the AAA; the other two were Lee Pressman and Philip Wenchel. Pressman and Hiss had been friends at Harvard, and retained this friendship now. Since Pressman, when accused by Chambers of being a member of the same underground group as Hiss, admitted to having been a Communist, it was later to be argued that Pressman brought Hiss into the group.

The AAA had been set up by President Roosevelt to be one of the agents in the implementation of the New Deal. From the time of its formulation by the President until the present day, Hiss has been an ardent New Dealer and has always proudly announced the fact.[1] This, too, when the Hiss-Chambers case blew up, was counted against him by the anti-New Dealers, prominent among whom was Richard Nixon.

In July 1934, Hiss was seconded from the AAA as legal assistant to the Nye Committee, a small body set up by Congress to investigate the activities of both American and foreign armaments industries. Hiss became very interested in the work of the Committee and in March 1935 he resigned from the AAA. However, when the Committee began to exhibit signs of supporting isolationist policies with which Hiss did not agree, he applied for a post in the office of the Solicitor-General, and this being successful, he joined the staff of the Department of Justice in August 1935.

From this moment on, Hiss's promotion in the Government service was rapid. Six months after joining the Justice Department, he was transferred to the State Department as assistant to Assistant Secretary of State, Francis B Sayre, who had been one of his teachers at Johns Hopkins University. He remained with Sayre for three years, and then became assistant to Mr Stanley Hornbeck, adviser on political relations. From this position he moved on to the State Department Office of Special Political Affairs in the spring of 1944.

By this time such was his reputation that from August to

1. When I was carrying out research in New York in the autumn of 1966, Mr Hiss had to cancel an appointment he had made with me so that he might deliver some lectures on the New Deal, in Washington.

October 1944 Hiss acted as executive secretary of the American delegation to the Dumbarton Oaks Conference. In the latter month he was appointed Deputy Director of the Office of Special Political Affairs and accompanied Secretary of State Stettinius to the Yalta Conference in February 1945. On his return from Yalta Hiss was promoted Director of the OSPA and almost at once was appointed Secretary-General of the United Nations San Francisco Conference (April–June 1945). In January 1946 he attended the first meeting of the UN General Assembly in London as principal adviser to the American delegation. Twelve months later he left the Government service on being elected President of the Carnegie Endowment for International Peace. He was still upholding this position of great trust with dignity when on the 3rd August 1948 Whittaker Chambers denounced him to the House Committee on Un-American Activities as having been a secret Communist from 1935 to 1938.

The career of Alger Hiss from his university days to the 3rd August 1948 is an undeniable success story. That he deserved his success as a reward for his intellectual ability and hard work is equally undeniable. As will be seen it was the absolute antithesis of Whittaker Chambers's career, just as his personal character is the exact opposite of Chambers's.

At one point in the House Committee hearings, Congressman Hébert exclaimed, 'Whichever one of you is lying is the greatest actor that America has produced.' At this time the Committee was unaware of Chambers's record. Within a short time, however, they were to have personal experience of several examples of his lying, and yet they were able to overlook them, probably on the basis of another exclamation from Mr Hébert, 'Mr Hiss ... show me a good police force and I will show you the stool-pigeon who turned them in. Show me a police force with a poor record, and I will show you a police force without a stool-pigeon. We have to have people like Chambers or Miss Bentley to come in and tell us. . . . I don't care who gives the facts to me, whether a confessed liar, thief or murderer, if it is the facts.'

In all of Hiss's public record there was not a single example of dishonesty of any kind – at least if he had committed a dishonest act he had done it so secretly that no public suspicion was roused. In his private life his personal integrity had been a by-word among his friends and acquaintances, close and distant.

Earl Jowitt, who never met Hiss, has written in his fascinating appraisal of the case from the point of view of an English lawyer, 'On reading the evidence, I get the impression of a man some-what conceited, too conscious that he had met on intimate terms the most distinguished of his countrymen, not over ready to be forthcoming with his less distinguished compatriots, and in short not suffering fools gladly and not being a "good mixer". I get the impression, too, of a man so immersed in his official life that he took little or no trouble about the affairs of his private life. *I do not, however, from reading and re-reading his evidence, get the impression of dishonesty*; indeed, if he had been dishonest, I find myself wondering why he did not supply the answers which must have been – to such an intelligent man – an obvious way out of the difficulties which arose in his cross-examination.'[1]

Chambers himself described him as 'a man of great simplicity and great gentleness and sweetness of character,' and again, in *Witness*, 'The outstanding fact about Alger Hiss was an unvarying mildness, a deep consideration and gracious patience that seemed proof against any of the ordinary exasperations of work and fatigue or the annoyances of family or personal relations.'[2]

1. The Strange Case of Alger Hiss, The Earl Jowitt, Doubleday & Co., New York, 1953. p51. The italics are added.

2. Op cit p363.

I cannot agree entirely with Lord Jowitt's assessment of Hiss from my own reaction to reading the record of the House Committee hearings and the two trial transcripts – which I had done before I met him. My major impression was that of the over-meticulous lawyer who was so constitutionally influenced by his legal training that intelligent as he was he did not realise that he was often seriously damaging his case by applying his legal training to his presentation of his evidence. He seemed quite incapable of giving a straightforward unqualified 'yes' or 'no' to questions to which he did not have the fullest knowledge of the direct answer. His replies to the questioning of the Committee Members, and later to lawyers, abound with such phrases as, 'To the best of my recollection', 'I *think* I can definitely say', 'I cannot swear'. Another, untrained as a lawyer, would, I believe, have given answers unqualified in this way, by what, to an ordinary observer, seems to be unnecessary niggling if not a downright attempt to mislead without actually lying. It certainly struck several members of the Committee in this light, who from time to time made exclamations of impatience. At one point, in retort to Hiss's reply, 'I have no present recollection of the disposition of the Ford', Congressman Hébert riposted, 'You are a remarkable and agile young man, Mr Hiss'; and a little later on, 'I repeat you are a very agile young man and a very clever young man and your conduct on all appearances before this Committee has shown that you are very self-possessed and you know what you are doing and you know yourself why you are answering and how you are answering', concluding that he could not understand why a man of Hiss's intelligence had to be so cautious in his responses.

But the contrast between the two men is remarkably demonstrated in this very point. Hiss, with his fastidious mind, could not say definitely what he did not definitely know. Chambers, on the other hand – at least in the Committee hearings – calmly and quietly gave unqualified answers, and in so doing, as was later proved, deliberately lied. Not a single answer given by Hiss was *shown* to be a deliberately dishonest one.

Earl Jowitt's comment that Hiss was 'too conscious that he had met on intimate terms the most distinguished of his compatriots', I do not understand. He showed a definite reluctance to name several prominent men in the early stages of the affair. On the other hand, I did get the impression that Hiss did not suffer fools gladly and that he was not a 'good mixer'; but these two attributes cannot be held against a man to the extent that they should be detrimental to the point of adding to his damnation.

My overall impression from reading the various records was of a rather infuriatingly meticulous man, who foolishly allowed his scrupulousness to work against him; of a proud and perhaps even haughty man, who recognised his own attainments, knew his record to be exceptional and saw no reason why he should pretend that he was not proud of himself. But I found no sign of overbearing, and the fact that he was not ashamed of revealing his self-pride I felt underlined his basic honesty.

To many who heard Hiss in the Old House Office Building and in the New York law courts he seemed too good to be true. Such an impression I also found lurking somewhere in the shadows of my subconsciousness in the early stages of my studies; until, in fact, I had read two interchanges between him and his inquisitors which showed him to be human and possessed of some spirit. The interchanges occurred on the same occasion with only a short time between them. On his way to a hearing Hiss had read in the newspapers the news that Harry Dexter White (also accused by Chambers of having been a Communist) had died of a heart attack a couple of days after a gruelling by the Committee. As soon as the hearing opened, Hiss asked permission to make a statement, and this being granted, he said 'with a good deal of heat', 'I would like the record to show that on my way downtown from my uptown office, I learned from the press of the death of Harry White, which came as a great shock to me, and I am not sure that I feel in the best possible mood for testimony. I do not for a moment want to miss the opportunity of seeing Mr Chambers. I merely wanted the record to show that.'

This incident shows, in my view, first that Hiss was a loyal man. Harry Dexter White had not been a particularly close friend, but Hiss held the Committee responsible for his death and out of loyalty felt that he must make a protest. But it also demonstrates Hiss's courage. This loyalty could have been very dangerous. White had been accused by another defector besides Chambers, and there was no telling what future investigations might have proved. Had they proved that White had definitely been a Communist, Hiss's protest would certainly have been recalled and held against him. But Hiss, though ignorant of the true state of affairs, did not hesitate to show his feelings for a dead colleague without any regard for the possible consequences to himself.

The second interchange occurred an hour or so later. The record runs thus:

MR MCDOWELL : Mr Chambers, is this the man, Alger Hiss, who was also a member of the Communist Party at whose home you stayed?

MR NIXON : According to your testimony?

MR MCDOWELL : You make the identification positive?

MR CHAMBERS : Positive identification.

(At this point, Mr Hiss arose and walked in the direction of Mr Chambers)

MR HISS : May I say for the record at this point, that I would like to invite Mr Whittaker Chambers to make those statements out of the presence of this committee without their being privileged for suit for libel. I challenge you to do it, and I hope you will do it damned quickly.

I am not going to touch him (addressing Mr Russell). You are touching me.

MR RUSSELL : Please sit down, Mr Hiss.

MR HISS : I will sit down when the chairman asks me, Mr Russell, when the chairman asks me to sit down——

MR RUSSELL : I want no disturbance.

MR HISS : I don't——

MR MCDOWELL : Sit down, please.

MR HISS : You know who started this.

MR MCDOWELL : We will suspend testimony here for a minute or two, until I return.

Hiss's jumping up and approaching Chambers in such an attitude that some present believed he was about to strike his accuser; his use of the word 'damned', which was not at all in line with the parliamentary language Hiss habitually used; and his refusal to sit down until directed by the chairman to do so; all show that Hiss's apparent imperturbability had been breached, and that the man was susceptible to human passions.

As I have said, I had completed my study of the records and had reached the conclusion that my theory was a feasible one before I met Mr Hiss. I had also formed in my mind a picture of him from the printed pages.

When we eventually met, we spent six hours together during which I plied questions unceasingly. There were one or two points on which I wanted elucidation, but for the most part I asked questions which went over ground covered by the records. I did this deliberately because I wanted to test for myself, in my own way, Mr Hiss's reactions to questions worded differently but which probed mercilessly the most difficult phases of what may be called the Hiss Defence.

Every single question I asked, Mr Hiss answered without the slightest hesitation and with absolute frankness. The phrase 'To the best of my recollection', or any analogous one, was *not* used once. If one of us was embarrassed, it was me.

The impression I had of Mr Hiss from this long and intimate meeting was of an entirely honest man, still slightly puzzled by the fact that twelve of his peers had chosen to reject his word in favour of the word of a proven liar and perjurer.

The gentleness and the charm noted by so many of his friends before and at the time of the case, and underlined by Chambers himself, is still there. I think what impressed itself on me – as it did on my wife, who was present throughout – was the complete absence of bitterness for a lost brilliant career and the comparative poverty in which he lives as a salesman for a firm of stationers.

The good looks are still discernible under the encroachment of physical maturity. One has no difficulty at all in imagining what a strikingly good-looking young man he must have been. The contrast he must have made with the plump, flabby, carelessly dressed Chambers must have been tremendous.

3

The Confrontation

Hiss had said in his telegram to the Committee, 'I do not know Mr Chambers and insofar as I am aware have never laid eyes on him.' In his prepared statement to the Committee he had declared, 'To the best of my knowledge I never heard of Whittaker Chambers until 1947, when two representatives of the Federal Bureau of Investigation asked me if I knew him and various other people some of whom I knew and some of whom I did not know. I said I did not know Chambers. So far as I know, I have never laid eyes on him, and I should like to have the opportunity to do so.'

Nothing could be less ambiguous than either of these statements, and though both of them include the Hiss qualifying phrases, they have the air of being categorical denials. Nevertheless, though the press photographs of Chambers rang no distinct bell in Hiss's memory, 'there seemed to be a degree of familiarity about some of these. Perhaps I had met him at some large gathering and failed to catch, or now failed to recall, his name. Or, perhaps he resembled someone I actually did know . . . Chambers's identity preoccupied me. I could not be sure, without seeing him, whether I had ever met him.'[1]

Since, in view of these denials by Hiss, a question of mistaken identity on Chambers's part had clearly been injected into the proceedings, or, if not of mistaken identity, downright lying by Chambers, one would have imagined that the Committee would have confronted the two men at the earliest opportunity. Hiss had certainly expected such a confrontation to take place at his

1. *In the Court of Public Opinion*, op cit p9.

first hearing on the 5th August. He said as much to acting chairman Mundt.

The Committee, however, were very conscious that if Hiss could show that he and Chambers had never met, the whole of Chambers's evidence would have to be rejected, and that they would stand the risk of becoming a national laughing-stock. In consequence they decided to go carefully.

Chambers in *Witness* records the Committee's predicament thus: '. . . on 5th August, by flat denials and by drawing the toga of his official career about him, Hiss had made the Committee look like the gullible victim of a vulgar impostor – myself.

'Gladly the Committee turned its back on Alger Hiss and filed into its chambers. It severally stood or sat for a moment in attitudes of mute gloom.[1] Then a member said: "We're ruined." It was one of history's moments of high irony. For a decade, the Committee . . . had been trying to hack off the Gorgon head of Communist conspiracy, which it had never quite succeeded in locating. Now, almost casually, the snaky mass had been set down on the congressmen's collection desk. It was terrifying. It petrified most of them.

'Their terror was justified. It was election year, and the seat of every member of the Committee was at stake. Moreover, the hostile clamour in the press and from public personages, together with other pressures, had battered the Committee into a state bordering on anxiety neurosis. The Committee's instinctive reaction was to get away as fast as possible from the monstrous challenge that had been set down before it. Someone proposed that the Committee drop the Hiss-Chambers controversy at

1. It will occur to the reader to ask how Chambers knew what went on in the Committee's retiring room. In this connection, it is impossible not to mention that Congressman Nixon and Robert Stripling were to come to know Chambers very intimately. They visited him several times at his farm and chatted with him. In the light of this knowledge, it is impossible not to draw the obvious inference.

once and switch to some subject sensational enough to distract public attention from its unnerving blunder. . . .

'That the Committee did not act on its fears is a fact of history that no one can take from it. Its stand was greatly strengthened by one man. Richard Nixon argued quietly but firmly against a switch from the Hiss investigation to any other subject.'[1]

According to Chambers, it was Benjamin Mandel, the director of research, who suggested the solution. A sub-committee would be appointed to question Chambers exhaustively in secret session about all the details of Hiss's life which Chambers must know if his claim to have been on intimate terms with Hiss were true. Hiss would then be summoned to a secret session and the same questions put to him. The two sets of answers would then be compared.

So it was that on the 7th August, Chambers appeared before the sub-committee appointed – Richard Nixon, chairman, Congressmen Hébert and McDowell, members – in the United States Courthouse in New York.

Nixon opened the questioning.

NIXON : Mr Hiss in his testimony was asked on several occasions whether or not he had ever known, or knew, a man by the name of Whittaker Chambers. In each instance he categorically said 'No.' At what period did you know Mr Hiss? What time?

CHAMBERS : I knew Mr Hiss, roughly, between the years 1935 and 1937.

NIXON : Did you know him as Mr Alger Hiss?

CHAMBERS : Yes.

NIXON : Did you happen to see Mr Hiss's pictures in the news-papers as a result of these recent hearings?

CHAMBERS : Yes, I did.

1. Op cit pp557 and 558.

NIXON : Was that the man you knew as Alger Hiss?

CHAMBERS : Yes, that is the man.

NIXON : You are certain of that?

CHAMBERS : I am completely certain.

NIXON : During the time that you knew Mr Hiss, did he know you as Whittaker Chambers?

CHAMBERS : No, he did not.

(One can imagine the surprise this answer must have caused the sub-committee, though no one asked why Chambers had not given this information before. The record carries straight on . . .)

NIXON : By what name did he know you?

CHAMBERS : He knew me by the Party name of Carl.

NIXON : Did he ever question the fact that he did not know your last name?

CHAMBERS : Not to me.

NIXON : Why not?

CHAMBERS : Because in the underground Communist Party the principle of organisation is that functionaries, and heads of the group in other words, shall not be known by their right names, but by pseudonyms or Party names.

NIXON : Were you a Party functionary?

CHAMBERS : I was a functionary.

NIXON : This entire group with which you worked in Washington did not know you by your real name?

CHAMBERS : No member of that group knew me by my real name.

NIXON : All knew you as Carl?

CHAMBERS : That is right.

NIXON : No member of that group ever inquired of you as to your real name?

CHAMBERS : To have questioned me would have been a breach of Party discipline, Communist Party discipline.

NIXON : I understood you to say that Mr Hiss was a member of the Party.

CHAMBERS : Mr Hiss was a member of the Communist Party.

NIXON : Is there any other circumstance which would substantiate your allegation that he was a member of the Party?

CHAMBERS : I must also interpolate here that all Communists in the group in which I originally knew him accepted him as a member of the Communist Party.

NIXON : Referred to him as a member of the Party?

CHAMBERS : That doesn't come up in conversation, but this was a Communist group.

NIXON : Could this have possibly been an intellectual study group?

CHAMBERS : It was in no wise an intellectual study group . . . its primary function was to infiltrate the Government in the interest of the Communist Party.

NIXON : At that time, incidentally, Mr Hiss and the other members of this group who were Government employees did not have Party cards?

CHAMBERS : No member of that group to my knowledge ever had Party cards, nor do I think members of any such group have Party cards.

NIXON : The reason is——?

CHAMBERS : The reason is security, concealment.

NIXON : In other words, people who are in the Communist underground are in fact instructed to deny the fact that they are members of the Communist Party.

CHAMBERS : I was told by Peters (J Peters, said by Chambers to be the chief of the American Communist underground) that Party registration was kept in Moscow and in some secret file in the United States.

With his next question, Nixon launched into the real test. Did Mr Hiss have any children? he asked.

CHAMBERS : Mr Hiss had no children of his own.

(Anthony Hiss, Hiss's only child, was not born until 1941.)

NIXON : Were there any children living in the house?

CHAMBERS : Mrs Hiss had a son.

NIXON : Do you know his name?

CHAMBERS : Timothy Hobson.

NIXON : Approximately how old was he at the time you knew him?

CHAMBERS : It seems to me that he was about ten years old.

(Timothy Hobson had been born on the 19th September 1926.)

NIXON : What did you call him?

CHAMBERS : Timmie.

NIXON : Did Mr Hiss call him Timmie also?

CHAMBERS : I think so.

NIXON : Did he have any other nickname?

CHAMBERS : Not that I recall. He is the son, to the best of my knowledge, of Thayer Hobson, who I think is a member of the publishing house of William Morrow, here in New York.

NIXON : What name did Mrs Hiss use in addressing Hiss?

CHAMBERS : Usually 'Hilly'.

NIXON : 'Hilly'?

CHAMBERS : Yes.

NIXON : Quite often?

CHAMBERS : Yes.

NIXON : In your presence?

CHAMBERS : Yes.

NIXON : Not Alger?

CHAMBERS : Not Alger.

('My wife at times addresses me as "Hill", though more often than not she calls me simply by my given (Christian) name. Rarely she adds a "y" to the occasional "Hill".')[1]

1. *In the Court of Public Opinion*, op cit p45.

NIXON : What nickname, if any, did Mr Hiss use in addressing his wife?

CHAMBERS : More often 'Dilly' and sometimes 'Pross'. Her name was Priscilla. They were commonly referred to as 'Hilly' and 'Dilly'.

NIXON : They were commonly referred to as 'Hilly' and 'Dilly'?

CHAMBERS : By other members of the group.

('I have never called my wife "Dilly" or anything remotely like it. We have never been known by anyone, whatever his politics, as Hilly and Dilly. No friend has ever used Hill or Hilly in addressing me.')[1]

Following with this kind of questioning, Nixon and the sub-committee extracted from Chambers the following information : that he had stayed in the Hisses' house for several days : that the Hisses had a maid and a cook who came in daily, and that at one of their houses they had a rather elderly Negro maid 'whom Mr Hiss used to drive home every evening'; that he did not recall the names of any of these servants; that they had a cocker-spaniel which they used to leave in kennels on Wisconsin Avenue when they went on holiday on the Eastern Shore of Maryland.

NIXON : You state the Hisses had several different houses when you knew them? Could you describe any one of those houses to us?

CHAMBERS : I think so. It seems to me that when I first knew him he was living on 28th Street in an apartment house. There were two almost identical apartment houses. It seems to me that is a dead-end street and this was right at the dead-end and certainly it is on the right-hand side as you go up.

It also seems to me that the apartment was on the top floor. Now, what was it like inside, the furniture? I can't remember.

MANDEL : What was Mr Hiss's library devoted to?

1. Op cit p45.

CHAMBERS : Very nondescript, as I recall.

.　　.　　.　　.　　.

NIXON : Was there any special dish they served?

CHAMBERS : No. I think you get here into something else. Hiss is a man of great simplicity and a great gentleness and sweetness of character, and they lived with extreme simplicity. I had the impression that the furniture in that house was kind of pulled together from here or there, maybe got it from their mother, or something like that, nothing lavish about it whatsoever, quite simple.

Their food was in the same pattern and they cared nothing about food. It was not a primary interest in their lives.

MANDEL : Did Mr Hiss have any hobbies?

CHAMBERS : Yes, he did. They both had the same hobby, amateur ornithologists, bird observers. They used to get up early in the morning and go to Glen Echo, out to the canal, to observe birds.

I recall once they saw, to their great excitement, a prothonotary warbler.

(This was to become an important issue in the subsequent attempt by the Committee to prove Hiss 'guilty by association'.)

MCDOWELL : A very rare specimen?

CHAMBERS : I never saw one. I am also fond of birds.

Nixon then asked if the Hisses had a car, and Chambers replied that, as he recalled, when he first knew them, they had had a Ford roadster, colour black and very dilapidated. 'I remember very clearly that it had hand windshield wipers. I remember that because I drove it one rainy day and had to work these windshield wipers by hand.' In 1936 they changed to a new Plymouth sedan, giving the Communist Party the old Ford for use by a 'poor organiser in the West or somewhere.'

Chambers added: 'Much against my better judgment and much against Peters's better judgment, he finally got us to permit him to do this thing. Peters knew where this lot[1] was and he either took Hiss there, or he gave Hiss the address and Hiss went there, and to the best of my recollection of his description of that happening, he left the car there and simply went away, and the man in charge of the station took care of the rest of it for him. I should think the records of that transfer would be traceable.' Hiss still had the Plymouth when he, Chambers, broke with Communism. (This was to become a major point against Hiss.)

Chambers could not recall if the Hisses had a piano, but he did remember a small red leather-covered cigarette-box with gold tooling. He could not recall if their cutlery was silver, nor what the china was like.

NIXON: What kind of cocktail glasses did they have?

CHAMBERS: We never drank cocktails.

NIXON: Did they drink?

CHAMBERS: They did not drink. They did not drink with me. For one thing I was strictly forbidden by the Communist Party to taste liquor at any time.

NIXON: And you didn't drink?

CHAMBERS: I never drank.

Asked to describe Hiss's physical appearance Chambers said he was five feet eight or nine, slender; his eyes were wide apart and bluish-grey; if you watched him from behind, you could observe a slight mince as he walked. He described Mrs Hiss as 'a short, highly nervous, little woman. I don't, as a matter of fact, recall the colour of her eyes, but she has a habit of blushing red when she is excited or angry, fiery red.'

1. According to Chambers the Communist Party had in Washington a service station. 'That is, the man in charge or owner of this station was a Communist – or it may have been a car lot.'

Told by Mandel that in one of his photographs Hiss had his hand cupped to his ear, Chambers answered promptly that Hiss was deaf in one ear, though he could not remember which. He did not recall if Hiss had ever told him how he became deaf. 'The only thing I remember he told me was as a small boy he used to take a little wagon – he was a Baltimore boy – and walk up to Druid Hell Park, which was at that time way beyond the civilised centre of the city, and fill up bottles with spring-water and bring them back and sell it.'

Timmie Hobson he described as 'a puny little boy, also rather nervous.' He could not remember the name of the school Timmie attended, 'they told me Thayer Hobson was paying for his son's education, but they were diverting a large part of that money to the Communist Party.'

HÉBERT : Hobson was paying for the boy's education?

CHAMBERS : Yes; and they took him out of a more expensive school and put him in a less expensive school expressly for that purpose. That is my recollection.

Asked if he recalled anything about Hiss's hands, Chambers said he did not remember anything special.

MANDEL : How is it he never wrote anything publicly?

CHAMBERS : Well, he came into the underground like so many Communists did – this was a new stage in the history of American Communists.

MANDEL : He was never in the open Communist Party?

CHAMBERS : He was never in the open Communist Party, came in as an underground Communist.

·   ·   ·   ·   ·

STRIPLING : Did he go to church?

CHAMBERS : He was forbidden to go to church (presumably by the Party).

63

STRIPLING : Do you know whether he was a member of a church?

CHAMBERS : I don't know.

STRIPLING : Do you know if his wife was a member of a church?

CHAMBERS : She came of a Quaker family. Her maiden name was Priscilla Fansler before she married. She came from the Great Valley, near Paoli, Pennsylvania.

NIXON : Did she tell you anything about her family?

CHAMBERS : No; but she once showed me while we were driving beyond Paoli the road down which their farm lay.

NIXON : You drove with them?

CHAMBERS : Yes.

NIXON : Did you ever go on a trip with them other than by automobile?

CHAMBERS : No.

NIXON : Did you stay overnight on any of these trips?

CHAMBERS : No.

So the questioning went on. Chambers's answers, and his volunteered information, unless disproved at every point, seemed to show overwhelmingly that he must have known Hiss quite intimately, and that, therefore, Hiss must be lying about never having met him and *ergo* was very probably lying when he claimed never to have been a Communist. Presently Nixon came to the end of his questions and Mr Hébert took up the interrogation. After asking Chambers for more detailed information about the houses in which the Hisses had lived, the hearing was closed.

One would have imagined that the Committee would have been so eager to know the answer to their major question – 'Which of these two men is lying?' – that they would have summoned Hiss before them as soon as possible after dismissing Chambers. For some reason they waited nine days, and it was not until the 16th August that they questioned him in secret session.

In the meantime, Hiss had been trying to discover whether he might have known Chambers under another name. After much searching of memory he began to recall that he had met in 1935 a man calling himself George Crosley to whom he had rented his apartment for a short time and to whom he had given his ancient Ford roadster when he had bought a new Plymouth in 1935. But this was only brought back to memory by his seeing an item in the press on the 15th August to the effect that Chambers in his secret evidence had said that he had stayed at Hiss's house and had driven his car. 'I recognised then the possibility that he might have some connection with the mystery of the unknown Chambers. But I couldn't even then bring myself to believe that Crosley would have made up these charges against me. I had treated him well. He had no reason to bear a grudge against me. Chambers on the 3rd August hadn't said that he had been a freelance writer, as Crosley had been when I knew him. He hadn't said that he had subleased my apartment or that I had given him my 1929 roadster. Surely if he were Crosley, he would have mentioned some of these facts at his first appearance.'[1]

When Hiss appeared before the sub-committee in secret session. Parnell Thomas took the chair. This was his first appearance. It was Nixon, however, who did most of the questioning. Having explained to Hiss the Committee's bewilderment, he asked him to be patient if some of the questions he was now going to put had been asked before. The atmosphere was friendly, and Hiss reciprocated.

Asked when he had first heard the name 'Whittaker Chambers', he repeated his answer of the 5th August: When the FBI had called on him in 1947 and asked him about a number of names, one of which was Whittaker Chambers. Had he ever

1. *In the Court of Public Opinion*, op cit p12.

known anyone called Carl between 1934 and 1937? Yes, Hiss said, but this was not the Carl.

Now, on the 7th August, Chambers had included in his testimony a long description of Hiss's membership of the Communist Party. The interchange between him and Mr Nixon had run thus:

NIXON: I understood you to say that Mr Hiss was a member of the Party.

CHAMBERS: Mr Hiss was a member of the Communist Party.

NIXON: How do you know that?

CHAMBERS: I was told by Mr Peters.

NIXON: You were told that by Mr Peters?

CHAMBERS: Yes.

NIXON: On what facts did Mr Peters give you?

(The grammar of eminent Congressmen frequently goes awry. In some cases it goes so awry that it is difficult to comprehend what the inquisitor wishes to say.)

CHAMBERS: Mr Peters was the head of the entire underground, so far as I know.

NIXON: The entire underground of the Communist Party?

CHAMBERS: Of the Communist Party of the United States.

NIXON: Do you have any other evidence, any factual evidence to bear out your claim that Mr Hiss was a member of the Communist Party?

CHAMBERS: Nothing beyond the fact that he submitted himself for the two or three years that I knew him as a dedicated and disciplined Communist.

NIXON: Did you obtain his Party dues from him?

CHAMBERS: Yes, I did.

NIXON: Over what period of time?

CHAMBERS: Two or three years, as long as I knew him.

NIXON: Party dues from him and his wife?

CHAMBERS : I assume that his wife's dues were there; I understood it to be.

NIXON : You understood it to be?

CHAMBERS : Mr Hiss would simply give me an envelope containing Party dues which I transferred to Peters. I didn't handle the money.

NIXON : How often?

CHAMBERS : Once a month.

NIXON : What did he say?

CHAMBERS : That was one point it wasn't necessary to say anything. At first he said, 'Here are my dues.'

NIXON : And once a month over a period of two years approximately, he gave you an envelope which contained his dues?

CHAMBERS : That is right.

NIXON : What did you do with the envelope?

CHAMBERS : I gave it to Peters.

NIXON : In New York?

CHAMBERS : Or Washington.

NIXON : This envelope contained dues of Hiss and other members of the group?

CHAMBERS : Only Hiss.

NIXON : You collected dues from the other members of the group individually?

CHAMBERS : All dues were collected individually.

But this directly conflicted with evidence he had given on the 3rd August, when Stripling had asked :

STRIPLING : Mr Chambers, when you met with these people (of whom he named Hiss as one) at Mr Collins's apartment, did you collect Communist Party dues from them?

CHAMBERS : I did not, but the Communist Party dues were handed over to me by Collins, who was treasurer of the group.

Nixon, however, did not ask him to explain this discrepancy on the 7th August, though he did now ask Hiss if he had ever paid any money to Collins at his apartment. Hiss replied that though he had visited Collins's apartment, his visits had been purely social occasions. He had certainly not given Collins or any other of the group named by Chambers any money.

Having cleared these important accusations out of the way, Nixon began to check Chambers's knowledge of the intimate details of the Hisses way of life. The first subject was Timmie Hobson's education.

NIXON: What schools do you recall your son attended in 1934 to 1937?

HISS: Tim was in the Friends School briefly here.

NIXON: Where did he go before that?

HISS: It is going to be hard to be sure. He went to a small school called the Cobb School, I think, in Chevvy Chase.

NIXON: Is that called the Chevvy Chase School also?

HISS: I don't think so. I think it was just called the Cobb School, Mr Cobb ran it. After Friends School he went to boarding school to George School, in Pennsylvania, near Doylestown, right near Newtown, Pennsylvania.

NIXON: Is the Friends School a rather expensive school, would you say, or moderate-priced school?

HISS: I would say moderate.

NIXON: And Cobb School the same?

HISS: Yes. I might say that Timmie's educational expenses were paid by his own father as part of the arrangement.

NIXON: Was Cobb School, do you recall, more expensive than the Friends School?

HISS: I would guess that it was probably less because it didn't carry through the grades thoroughly. It was a pre-school and early primary grades.

NIXON: And you can't recall that there was a school in between that and Friends School?

HISS: I don't recall it, Mr. Nixon. He went to the Landon School here for a while.

NIXON: That is after Friends School?

HISS: That is after he had been at Friends and before he went to George School but not between Cobb and Friends. He went to Landon School, which is off Connecticut Avenue when you get to Bradley Lane.

NIXON: Is that more expensive than the others?

HISS: That was a rather expensive school.

NIXON: More so than Friends School?

HISS: I think so.

NIXON: You don't recall the school he went to immediately before Friends?

HISS: No, I don't.

NIXON: But you would say the Friends School was a moderate-priced school?

HISS: Yes.

HÉBERT: Then you put him in a more expensive school?

HISS: Landon was more expensive than Friends. He hadn't been getting along very well at Friends and we consulted friends and thought that Landon was better.

HÉBERT: You put him in a more expensive school?

HISS: That is correct.

Chambers, it will be remembered, had described Timmie Hobson as 'a puny little boy, also rather nervous.' On this point Hiss comments: 'Had he known us at all in 1937, he would certainly have known that in February Timothy was nearly killed by an automobile while riding his bicycle. For weeks he was bedridden and then castbound for months in the small house to which we had moved in July 1936.'[1] Later, Hiss was to declare

1. *In the Court of Public Opinion*, op cit p44.

in an open hearing to the Committee, apropos Chambers's accusation that he had sent Timmie Hobson to a cheaper school and given the saving in fees to the Communist Party, 'The facts are, the personal facts are, that my stepson's educational expenses were paid by his own father. I could not possibly have saved any money by sending him to any cheaper school. At no time did I transfer him from one school to another for any purpose except to benefit his education.

'As a matter of fact, while he was in Washington, he went, after only one year at the Friends School, to another more expensive school and, when I concluded that he should go to a boarding school, his own father was not then in a position to meet the full expenses and I paid part of the expenses.'

As I have indicated, Hiss categorically denied ever calling his wife 'Dilly' or anything like it. He had constantly called her 'Prossy'. For her part, she had at one time called him 'Hill' or 'Hilly'. He also said that Mrs Hiss is of medium height (Chambers had said she was short) and far from being 'highly nervous' and blushing 'fiery red when excited or angry' she was 'not given to hatred, excitement or anger'.

He also pointed out that Chambers had erred when he had described Mrs Hiss's childhood home as being at 'Great Valley, near Paoli, Pennsylvania.' For the greater part of her childhood Mrs Hiss had lived at St David's, and Frazer, Pennsylvania. Nor was she a Quaker. Her family were Presbyterians, though Mrs Hiss, in adult life, had shown an interest in the Quakers and their activities.

There were several other points, too, on which Chambers had been wrong. Hiss is six feet tall; not five feet eight, as Chambers had said. He has thin fingers, but his eyes are true blue, not bluish-grey. He is not, and never has been, deaf in one ear, though he has a habit of cupping a hand to an ear but 'only when

I wanted to be sure I was hearing.' Chambers was right, however, when he had said that Hiss had collected spring-water and sold it as a boy.

On the other hand, he erred when he said Hiss did not go to church ('he was forbidden to'). 'In fact when we moved to P Street (in April 1935) we attended nearby Christ Church, an Episcopal church whose rector was a college mate of mine. Timothy was a choirboy there at the time of his accident in 1937. I have been a lifelong member of the Episcopal Church.'[1]

Chambers had described Hiss's library as 'very nondescript'. In fact, it contained at least one volume of which Hiss was very proud and showed to all his friends and many visitors to the house. It was a facsimile copy of Justice Oliver Wendell Holmes's notebook, listing all the books Holmes had ever read. The fact that Chambers could describe the library as nondescript implied that he had examined the books; but even a most cursory inspection could not have overlooked the Holmes notebook. Nor did Chambers mention the large gilt-framed Queen Anne mirror which always had the central position in the Hiss home after its acquisition in 1936.

Asked by Nixon, 'Was there any special dish they served?' Chambers had replied, 'No . . . Hiss is a man of great simplicity. . . .' In this latter assessment he was right, but Hiss is very fond of rice in all its forms, and Mrs Hiss constantly pandered to this taste; so much so that anyone claiming the degree of intimacy Chambers claimed, must have noted it.

Chambers could not recall whether the Hisses had a piano. After April 1935 they bought a new one, which though a small model, took up a great deal of space in the tiny sitting-room of the P Street house. On the question of drinking, while not heavy drinkers, the Hisses did take an occasional drink. (When

1. *In the Court of Public Opinion*, op cit p52.

he visited me in New York, Mr Hiss consumed two or three dry Martinis with obvious relish; but this was in the space of six hours. At dinner later, he also enjoyed sharing a bottle of wine with us.) Chambers had told the sub-committee that the Hisses had had a maid and a cook; they had never had more than one servant at a time. The servant they had had at the period in issue had been a 'very, very plump, large cheerful woman', a Negress certainly, but by no means elderly. Hiss had taken her home occasionally, but she had lived too far away for him to make a regular habit of it.

On the question of holidays and pets, Hiss told Nixon, 'My son went to a camp over on the Eastern Shore of Maryland. I am partly an Eastern Shore man myself. . . . When he was at camp we spent two summers, I think, during this period, in Chestertown, Maryland.' This confirmed Chambers's assertion. The Hisses also had a brown cocker-spaniel and in the winter of 1936 acquired a second, livelier cocker. The brown cocker used to spend the holidays in camp with Timmie, not in kennels.

The prothonotary warbler incident was later to be made much of by press and prosecution. On this point the interchange between Hiss and Nixon ran:

NIXON : Have you any hobbies?

HISS : Tennis and amateur ornithology.

NIXON : Is your wife interested in ornithology?

HISS : I also like to swim and also like to sail. My wife is interested in ornithology, as I am, through my interest. Maybe I am using too big a word to say an ornithologist because I am pretty amateur, but I have been interested in it since I was in Boston. I think anybody who knows me would know that.[1]

MCDOWELL : Did you ever see a prothonotary warbler?

1. *Current Biography* of 1947 listed Hiss's hobbies as amateur ornithology and tennis.

HISS : I have right here on the Potomac. Do you know that place?

CHAIRMAN : What is that?

NIXON : Have you ever seen one?

HISS : Did you see it in the same place?

MCDOWELL : I saw one in Arlington.

HISS : They come back and nest in those swamps. Beautiful yellow head, a gorgeous bird. Mr Collins is an ornithologist. Henry Collins – he's a really good ornithologist, calling them by their Latin names.

In *In the Court of Public Opinion* Hiss comments : 'McDowell was a better ornithologist than Chambers. Arlington is in Virginia across from Washington, and the prothonotary nests in swamps along the Potomac River as far *south* of Arlington as Glen Echo is north of Washington.'[1]

On one other major point Chambers had been wrong, as the subsequent production of records was to show, though the Committee was to try to make great capital out of it. Referring to Hiss's old Ford roadster, Chambers, somewhat labouring the point, had told the sub-committee that on buying the new Plymouth Hiss had insisted – against the advice of Chambers and the great man, J Peters – on giving the Ford to the Party for use by 'a poor Communist organiser'. When Peters and Chambers had eventually let Hiss have his way, so Chambers declared, Hiss had delivered it to a car-lot owned by a member of the Party, who had disposed of it for him according to his wishes.

Now, in the United States, when a motor car changes hands, either as a cash sale or a trade-in, the formal owner of the car has to make a legal assignment of it to the new owner. The certificate of title and the last owner's signature have to be notarised by a notary public. The later production of records was

1. Op cit p50. Chambers had said Hiss had told him of seeing the bird at Glen Echo.

to show that in July 1936 Hiss signed the car over to the Cherner Motor Company, one of the largest Ford agencies in Washington.

The final point to which I will refer is that of Chambers stating categorically that Hiss paid his Party dues regularly every month. On this Hiss comments: 'In his book (*Witness*), written after the trials, Chambers employs the stock phrase "dues-paying members of the Communist Party", and says it is his recollection that dues were fixed at ten per cent of salary, added to which were special assessments. He writes: "Alger Hiss continued devoutly to pay exorbitant dues to the Party." My monthly salary check was deposited regularly. A large regular monthly payment to Chambers would have been reflected in my withdrawals, which prior to the trials were carefully scrutinised – as is shown by the later emphasis upon a single withdrawal of mine that bore a mere time relation to a financial transaction by Mrs Chambers.'[1]

I have no cause to doubt Hiss's word on this point – I mean, I do not believe he paid dues – but this explanation cannot be termed proof. An intelligent secret Communist who had any appreciation for security would not draw his Party dues from the bank in one lump sum when they fell due monthly. He would either, in collusion with his wife, include them in the weekly or monthly housekeeping cheque, or save them by instalments from cheques drawn for his own personal use. Supposing Hiss had adopted one of these two methods or any other equally untraceable, it would have been the only illustration of his appreciation of and compliance with espionage or clandestine service techniques. It would have been absolutely at variance with too many of his actions, as will presently emerge.

To summarise what the Committee had gleaned from these two secret hearings: Chambers had been right about –

1. *In the Court of Public Opinion*, op cit p72.

1 Hiss's various addresses.
2 Mrs Hiss calling Hiss 'Hilly'.
3 Hiss seeing a prothonotary warbler.
4 Where Hiss's mother lived.
5 Hiss owning an old Ford roadster and a new Plymouth.
6 The cocker-spaniel.
7 Hiss selling spring-water as a boy.
8 Timmie Hobson's age.
9 The Hisses taking holidays on the Eastern Shore of Maryland.
10 The Hisses having single beds.

Chambers had been wrong about:

1 Timmie Hobson's schools.
2 Hiss's height and the colour of his eyes.
3 Hiss being deaf in one ear (though right about Hiss's habit of cupping one ear).
4 Hiss not going to or being a member of a church.
5 Mrs Hiss being a Quaker.[1]
6 Where Mrs Hiss lived as a child.
7 Hiss's taste in food.
8 Hiss's drinking habits.
9 His description of the Negro maid.
10 Hiss's sister living with her mother in Baltimore.
11 Hiss's sister when he said she did not work.
12 The Hisses sending the dog to kennels when they went on holiday.
13 The disposal of the Ford.
14 The maiden-name of Mrs Donald Hiss.
15 Hiss calling Mrs Hiss 'Dilly'.

He had also missed:

1 The piano.

1. Mrs Hiss never was a Quaker, although she was influenced throughout her life by her girlhood contact with Quakers.

2 The Audubon prints of birds.

3 The Queen Anne mirror.

4 The Holmes notebook.

Now, although the errors and omissions far outnumber the points on which Chambers was correct, this list of correct points is certainly *prima facie* impressive.[2] They impressed Nixon sufficiently for him to suggest to the other members of the sub-committee that the two men should confront each other, as soon as possible. Hiss had no preference for either a private or a public confrontation, though after there had been some discussion on the point, in which Nixon and Stripling had favoured a private meeting, he came down on the side of a public encounter. After listening to Stripling and Nixon say 'If you have a public meeting it will be ballyhooed into a circus,' Hiss commented that if they were considering his feelings they need not, 'for after what has been done to my feelings and my reputation, I think it would be like sinking the Swiss Navy.' It was eventually agreed that Chambers should be asked which he preferred. The date, however, was fixed – the 25th August, nine days from the present sitting.

Though Chambers had been summoned before the sub-committee in New York, Hiss had been required to fly up to Washington for his interrogation. In the aircraft back to New York, Hiss had read the full account of the bullying of Harry Dexter White three days earlier – despite the fact that they had been aware that White was suffering from a heart disease – and had been somewhat sickened by it.

The following morning, while in his office at the Carnegie Foundation, Hiss received a telephone call to the effect that Congressman McDowell was going to be in New York in the

1. One point which particularly interests me is that Chambers knew correctly that the Hisses had single beds, but did not recall their piano. Yet, after the piano was purchased he had twice stayed overnight in the house. I have a theory about how Chambers could have acquired his knowledge to which I will refer later.

late afternoon and would like to see him for ten or fifteen minutes. Hiss had known McDowell before they had met at the Committee hearings, and he asked if it was on Committee or private business that McDowell wished to see him. The caller did not know, he said. Hiss said he would make himself available. Later he received a telegram from McDowell saying that he would telephone at 5 30 pm.

During the afternoon, Hiss learned of Harry Dexter White's sudden death.

A little before 5 30 McDowell telephoned and instead of saying that he would shortly be with Hiss, he asked Hiss to meet him at the Commodore Hotel, a short distance away, adding that Nixon and 'one other' would also be there. On hearing this last piece of news Hiss realised that it was not to be a private meeting with McDowell, and as by this time Hiss doubted the good faith of some members of the Committee, he asked a friend and colleague, Charles Dollard, to go with him.

Hiss relates in *In the Court of Public Opinion*: 'We went to McDowell's hotel room and, as we entered, found that it was still in the process of being hastily converted into an improvised hearing room. McDowell and Nixon were there; Thomas arrived a good deal later . . . suddenly the connection between White's death and the hastily summoned hearing struck me. The impact of the press accounts of White's fatal heart attack was hardly favourable to the Committee . . . my experience with the Committee up to this point led me to conclude that they had decided to meet the crisis of a bad press by a sudden and sensational move.'[1]

Meanwhile the Committee had been looking for Chambers. He recounts in *Witness*: 'One morning I forced myself to leave the farm to go to New York. But, by the time I reached Balti-

1. Op cit p81.

more, I felt a curious need to go and see the Committee, as if its members were the only people left in the world with whom I could communicate . . . but the impulse was so strong that, after buying a ticket for New York, I took the train for Washington. It was about noon when I started up the steps of the Old House Office Building . . . out of the door, as I climbed the steps, crowded Ben Mandel, the Committee's chief researcher, Donald Appell, an investigator and other members of the Committee's staff. They were astonished to see me and greeted me with wild relief. They had been frantically trying to reach me at home, in New York and Washington . . . no one would tell me why I was wanted. Instead, the sub-committee bundled me into a car crammed with its staff. As we rolled to the Union Station, Appell wrestled a newspaper out of his pocket and pointed to a headline: Harry Dexter White had died of a heart attack . . . the Committee swept me through the station, out to the platforms and on to a Pullman. By then, I had learned that we were going to New York. I still did not know why . . . (arrived in New York) we loitered around the streets before taking a taxi that let us out at the ramp entrance of the Hotel Commodore in midtown Manhattan.'[1]

The suite taken by the Committee at the Commodore had two rooms. Since Hiss could recognise the people in the sitting-room, Chambers must have been concealed in the bedroom.

As soon as the room was ready Nixon told Hiss that the reason for the hastily arranged meeting was to give him the opportunity of confronting Chambers in person. He gave no reason for the sudden change of date from the 25th August to the 17th August.

Hiss was taken aback. He was beginning to feel annoyed at the way McDowell had got him there. He told the Committee that McDowell had said he would be needed for ten or fifteen minutes;

1. Op cit pp600 and 601.

obviously the proceedings would take much longer. He asked permission to send a message cancelling a six o'clock engagement he had made. He then requested to be allowed to make a brief statement, and made his somewhat heated remarks about Harry White's death, to which I have referred on page 51.

Nor was this all. He went on: 'I would like to make one further comment. Yesterday, I think I witnessed – in any event, I was told that those in the room were going to take an oath of secrecy.' Yet, he said, the press now carried the news that Mrs Hiss was going to be asked to testify in secret session. He continued: 'There were other statements in the press which I read coming down which referred to other bits of my testimony which could only have come from the Committee. They did not come from me.' It was because of this that he had asked Mr Dollard to accompany him today.

McDowell, who was taking the chair, said, 'Obviously, there was a leak, because the story that appeared in the various papers I read was part of the activities of yesterday afternoon. As a Member of Congress, there is nothing I can do about that. It is a regrettable thing, and I join you in feeling rather rotten about the whole thing.'

No other member made a comment. Nixon asked an aide to fetch Chambers. When Chambers appeared –

NIXON: Sit over here, Mr Chambers. Mr Chambers, will you please stand?

And will you please stand, Mr Hiss?

Mr Hiss, the man standing here is Mr Whittaker Chambers. I ask you now if you have ever known that man before.

* * * * *

Now, at the secret hearing on the previous afternoon, Hiss had been shown photographs of Chambers, and the following interchanges had taken place. As I have previously hinted, Hiss had felt that though he could not specifically say that he recognised Chambers, there seemed to be something familiar about the photographs.

NIXON: I am now showing you two pictures of Mr Whittaker Chambers, also known as Carl, who testified that he knew you between the years 1934–37, and that he saw you in 1938.

I ask you now, after looking at those pictures, if you can remember that person either as Whittaker Chambers or as Carl or as any other individual you have met.

HISS: May I recall to the committee the testimony I gave in the public session when I was shown another photograph of Mr Whittaker Chambers, and I had prior to taking the stand tried to get as many newspapers that had photographs of Mr Chambers as I could. I testified then that I could not swear that I had never seen the man whose picture was shown me. Actually the face has a certain familiarity. I think I also testified to that.

It is not according to the photograph a very distinctive or unusual face. I would like very much to see the individual face to face. I had hoped that would happen before. I still hope it will happen today.

I am not prepared to say that I have never seen the man whose pictures are now shown me. I said that when I was on the stand when a different picture was shown me. I cannot recall any person with distinctness and definiteness whose picture this is, but it is not completely unfamiliar.

Whether I am imagining that or not I don't know, but I certainly wouldn't want to testify without seeing the man, hearing him talk, getting some much more tangible basis for judging the person and the personality.

NIXON: Would your answer be any different if this individual were described to you as one who had stayed overnight in your house on several occasions?

HISS : I think, Mr Nixon, let me say this : In the course of my service in Government from 1933 to 1947 and the previous year 1929–30, and as a lawyer I have had a great many people who have visited in my house.

I have tried to recall in the last week or so anyone who would know my house whom I wouldn't know very well. There are many people that have come to my house on social occasions or on semi-business occasions whom I probably wouldn't recall at all.

As far as staying overnight in my house is concerned——

NIXON : On several occasions.

HISS : On several occasions?

NIXON : On several occasions.

HISS : I can't believe, Mr Nixon, that anyone could have stayed in my house when I was there——

NIXON : When you were there.

HISS : Overnight on several occasions without my being able to recall the individual; and if this is a picture of anyone, I would find it very difficult to believe that that individual could have stayed in my house when I was there on several occasions overnight and his face not be more familiar than it is.

NIXON : Yes.

HISS : I don't want to suggest any innovations in your procedure, but I do want to say specifically that I do hope I will have an opportunity actually to see the individual.

NIXON : It is going to be arranged. I might say that before arranging the meeting, we want to be certain that there is no question of mistaken identity, as well as possible, and also that we had a clear conflict on certain pieces of testimony that had been given by both sides, and that we are getting now.

HISS : Yes, sir.

NIXON : I might say this, too : That Mr Chambers, as you may be aware of newspaper accounts, appeared in executive session before us on Saturday.

HISS : Saturday a week ago, I think.

NIXON : Just two days after you appeared.

HISS : I saw newspaper accounts of that.

NIXON : At that time we went into the situation with him, showed him pictures of you, and he declared without question you were the man. . . .

Now, you have never paid any money to Peters?

HISS : No.

NIXON : Never paid any money to Carl?

HISS : Never paid any money to Carl.

NIXON : Never paid any money to Henry Collins that you can recall?

HISS : I can't recall it even on a personal basis.

NIXON : Never paid dues to the Communist Party?

HISS : No.

NIXON : Your testimony now is that you are not a member of the Communist Party?

HISS : That is correct.

NIXON : Never been a member of the Communist Party?

HISS : Never been a member of the Communist Party.

NIXON : Or of any underground organisation connected with the Communist Party?

HISS : I have been angered and hurt by one thing in the course of this Committee testimony, and that was by the attitude which I think Mr Mundt took when I was testifying publicly and which, it seems to me, you have been taking today, that you have a conflict of testimony between two witnesses – I restrained myself with some difficulty from commenting on this at the public hearing, and I would like to say it on this occasion, which isn't a public hearing.

NIXON : Say anything you like.

HISS : It seems there is no impropriety in saying it. You today and the acting chairman publicly have taken the attitude when you have two witnesses, one of whom is a confessed former Communist, the other is me, that you simply have two witnesses saying contradictory things as between whom you find it most difficult to decide on credibility.

Mr Nixon, I do not know what Mr Whittaker Chambers testified to your Committee last Saturday. It is necessarily my opinion of him from what he has already said that I do know that he is not capable of telling the truth or does not desire to, and I honestly have the feeling that details of my personal life which I give honestly can be used to my disadvantage by Chambers then ex post facto knowing those facts.

I would request that I hear Mr Chambers's story of his alleged knowledge of me. I have seen newspaper accounts, Mr Nixon, that you spent the weekend – whether correct or not, I do not know – at Mr Chambers's farm in New Jersey.

NIXON : That is quite incorrect.

HISS : It is incorrect.

NIXON : Yes, sir. I can say, as you did a moment ago, that I have never spent the night with Mr Chambers.

HISS : Now, I have been cudgelling my brains, particularly on the train coming down this morning, and I had three or four hours on the train between New York and Washington, as to who could have various details about my family. Many people could.

Mr Nixon, I do not wish to make it easier for anyone who, for whatever motive I cannot understand, is apparently endeavouring to destroy me, to make that man's endeavours any easier. I think in common fairness to my own self-protection and that of my family and my family's good name and my own, I should not be asked to give details which somehow he may hear and then may be able to use as if he knew them before. I would like him to say all he knows about me now. What I have done is public record, where I have lived is public record. Let him tell you all he knows, let that be made public, and then let my record be checked against those facts instead of my being asked, Mr Nixon, to tell you personal facts about myself which, if they come to his ears, could sound very persuasive to other people that he had known me at some prior time. . . .

STRIPLING: Here is a larger picture. Let the record show this larger picture taken by the Associated Press photo on August 3, 1948, of Mr Mundt and Mr Whittaker Chambers, and as the record previously stated, Mr Chambers is much heavier now than he was in 1937 or 1938. Does this picture refresh your memory in any way, Mr Hiss?

HISS: It looks like the very same man I had seen in the other pictures, and I see Mundt and him in the same picture. The face is definitely not an unfamiliar face. Whether I am imagining it, whether it is because he looks like a lot of other people, I don't know, but I have never known anyone who had the relationship with me that this man testified to and that, I think, is the important thing here, gentlemen. This man may have known me, he may have been in my house. I have had literally hundreds of people in my house in the course of the time I lived in Washington.

The issue is not whether this man knew me and I don't remember him. The issue is whether he had a particular conversation that he has said he had with me and which I have denied and whether I am a member of the Communist Party or ever was, which he has said and which I have denied. . . .

THE CHAIRMAN : Mr Hiss, would you be able to recall a person if that person positively had been in your house three or four times, we will say, in the last ten years?

HISS : I would say that if he had spent the night——

STRIPLING : Ten years?

NIXON : Fifteen years.

THE CHAIRMAN : All right.

HISS : I would say if he had spent the night – how many times did you say?

STRIPLING : He spent a week there.

HISS : A whole week at a time continuously?

STRIPLING : Yes.

HISS : Mr Chairman, I could not fail to recall such a man if he were now in my presence.

THE CHAIRMAN : Wait a minute. You are positive then that if Mr X spent a week in your house in the past fifteen years you would recognise him today, assuming that Mr X looks today something like what he looked then?

HISS : Exactly, if he hadn't had a face lifting.

THE CHAIRMAN : No doubt in your mind?

HISS : I have no doubt whatsoever.

THE CHAIRMAN : Now, here is a man who says he spent a week in your house in the last fifteen years. Do you recognise him?

HISS : I do not recognise him from that picture.

NIXON : Did that man spend a week in your house in the last fifteen years?

HISS : I cannot say that man did, but I would like to see him.

THE CHAIRMAN : You say you cannot believe, but I would like to have a little more definite answer if you could make it more definite. Would you say he did or did not spend a week in your house?

HISS : Mr Chairman, I hope you will not think I am being

unreasonable when I say I am not prepared to testify on the basis of a photograph. On the train coming down this morning, I searched my recollection of any possible person that this man could be confused with or could have got information from about me.

THE CHAIRMAN: Then you are not prepared to testify on this subject from a photograph?

HISS: I am not prepared to testify on the basis of a photograph. I would want to hear the man's voice. . . .

I have written a name on this pad in front of me of a person whom I knew in 1933 and 1934 who not only spent some time in my house but sublet my apartment. That man certainly spent more than a week, not while I was in the same apartment. I do not recognise the photographs as possibly being this man. If I hadn't seen the morning's papers with an account of statements that he knew the inside of my house, I don't think I would even have thought of this name. I want to see Chambers face to face and see if he can be this individual. I do not want and I don't think I ought to be asked to testify now that man's name and everything I can remember about him. I have written the name on this piece of paper. I have given the name to two friends of mine before I came to this hearing. I can only repeat, and perhaps I am being over anxious about the possibility of unauthorised disclosure of testimony, that I don't think in my present frame of mind that it is fair to my position, my own protection, that I be asked to put down here on record personal facts about myself which, if they came to the ears of someone who had for no reason I can understand a desire to injure me, would assist him in that endeavour.

NIXON: This man who spent the time in 1933 and 1934 is still a man with whom you are acquainted?

HISS : He is not.

NIXON : And where were you living at that time?

HISS : He was not named Carl and not Whittaker Chambers.

NIXON :·Where were you living at that time?

HISS : I have again written down here to the best of my recollection because I have not checked down with leases – this is something I did on the train coming down and the leases are in my house in New York – where I believed I lived from June of 1933 until September 1943.

Again, Mr Nixon, if I give the details of where I was, it is going to be very easy if this information gets out for someone to say then ex post facto, 'I saw Hiss in such and such a house.' Actually, all he has to do is look it up in the telephone directory and find where it is.

THE CHAIRMAN : The chairman wants to say this : Questions will be asked and the Committee will expect to get very detailed answers to the questions. Let's not ramble all around the lot here. You go ahead and ask questions and I want the witness to answer.

NIXON : Your testimony is that this man you knew in 1933 and 1934 was in one of the houses you lived in?

HISS : I sublet my apartment to the man whose name I have written down.

NIXON : But you were not there at the same time?

HISS : I didn't spend a week in the same apartment with him. He did spend a day or two in my house when he moved in.

NIXON : This was the apartment you lived in between 1933 and 1934?

HISS : It is exactly that apartment – 1934 and 1935.

NIXON : Between 1934 and 1935?

HISS : That is right.

NIXON : When you sublet your apartment? There was no other

these questions and, frankly, I must insist . . .

HISS : I can testify to the best of my recollection. If this Committee feels, in spite of what I have said——

THE CHAIRMAN : Never mind feelings. You let Mr Nixon ask the questions and you go ahead and answer it.

HISS : I want to be sure Mr Nixon definitely wants me to answer responsively in spite of my plea that I don't think he should ask me. But if he does – Mr Nixon also asked me some questions in the public hearing that I didn't want to answer, and I took the same position that if Mr Nixon insisted on an answer after he knew my position, I will answer. I will give every fact of where I lived.

STRIPLING : Let the record show, Mr Hiss, you brought up this ex post facto business. Your testimony comes as ex post facto testimony to the testimony of Mr Chambers. He is already on record, and I am not inferring that you might know what he testified to, but certainly the United States attorney's office has several copies.

HISS : I do not and made no attempt to find out.

NIXON : Not only does the United States attorney's office have copies of Mr Chambers's testimony before us on the subject – and you can confirm that by calling Mr Morris Fay of that office, because he has two copies; he requested and received, and he will receive this testimony today. He will receive this testimony today, because I will tell you that he asked for it just thirty minutes before you walked into this room, and he will get it just as soon as we have completed this case.

Now, quite obviously, I think that you can see we are not attempting at this time to have you testify to facts with which we are going to brief Mr Chambers. What we are trying to do is test the credibility of Mr Chambers, and you are the man who can do it, and you can help us out by answering apartment and you can't testify as to what apartment that was?

HISS : If you insist, I will, of course, answer . . .

HÉBERT : Mr Hiss, let me say this to you now – and this is removed of all technicalities, it is just a man-to-man impression of the whole situation. I think it is pertinent. I don't surrender my place on this Committee to any individual who has an open mind, particularly regarding you and Mr Chambers. I am not interested in who is lying except to the extent that it will only give us an insight to further the case and that we are about to find out whether espionage was in effect in this country to the detriment of the security of this country.

I do not take the stand and never have taken the stand in this Committee that anything involved other than to get to the facts. I have tried just as hard in the public hearings to impeach those witnesses who are assumed to be so-called Committee witnesses as I have tried to impeach the other witnesses. I think the record will speak for that.

We did not know anything Mr Chambers was going to say. I did not hear your name mentioned until it was mentioned in open hearing.

HISS : I didn't know that.

HÉBERT : As I say, I am not trying to be cagey or anything, but trying to put it on the line as certainly one member of this Committee who has an open mind and up to this point don't know which one of the two is lying, but I will tell you right now and I will tell you exactly what I told Mr Chambers so that will be a matter of record, too : Either you or Mr Chambers is lying.

HISS : That is certainly true.

HÉBERT : And whichever one of you is lying is the greatest actor that America has ever produced. Now, I have not come to the conclusion yet which one of you is lying and I am trying to find the facts. Up to a few moments ago you have been very open, very co-operative. Now, you have hedged. You may be standing on what you consider your right and I am not objecting to that. I am not pressing you to identify a picture when you should be faced with the man. That is your right.

Now, as to this inquiry which you make much over, and not without cause, perhaps, we met Mr Chambers forty-eight hours after you testified in open session. Mr Chambers did not know or have any inclination of any indication as to the questions that we were going to ask him, and we probed him, as Mr Stripling says, for hours and the committee, the three of us – Mr Nixon, Mr Stripling and myself – and we literally ran out of questions. There wasn't a thing that came to our minds that we didn't ask him about, these little details, to probe his own testimony or rather to test his own credibility.

There couldn't have been a possible inkling as to what we were going to say about minor details, and he could not have possibly by the farthest stretch of the imagination prepared himself to answer because he didn't know where the questions were coming from and neither did we because we questioned him progressively; so how he could have prepared himself to answer these details which we now, and Mr Nixon has indicated, we are now checking and for the sake of corroboration – for my own part I can well appreciate the position you are in, but if I were in your position, I would do everything I humanly could to prove that Chambers is a liar instead of me.

HISS : I intend to.

HÉBERT : And that is all we are trying to do here. Further than that, I recognise the fact that this is not an inquisitorial body to the extent of determining where the crime lies. We are not setting forth to determine ourselves as to which one of you two has perjured yourself. That is the duty of the United States attorney for the District of Columbia. He is confronted with the fact that perjury has been committed before this congressional committee, which is a crime. It is up to the United States district attorney and the Department of Justice to prosecute that crime and that is all we are trying to do.

Now, if we can get the help from you and, as I say, if I were in your position I certainly would give all the help I could because it is the most fantastic story of unfounded – what motive would Chambers have or what motive you would have – one of you has to have a motive. You say you are in a bad position, but don't you think that Chambers himself destroys himself if he is proven a liar? What motive would he have to pitch a twenty-five thousand dollar position as the respected senior editor of *Time* magazine out of the window?

HISS : Apparently for Chambers to be a confessed former Communist and traitor to his country did not seem to him to be a blot on his record. He got his present job after he had told various agencies exactly that. I am sorry but I cannot but feel to such an extent that it is difficult for me to control myself that you can sit there, Mr Hébert, and say to me casually that you have heard that man and you have heard me, and you just have no basis for judging which one is telling the truth. I don't think a judge determines the credibility of witnesses on that basis.

HÉBERT : I am trying to tell you that I absolutely have an open mind and am trying to give you as fair a hearing as I could possibly give Mr Chambers or yourself. The fact that Mr Chambers is a self-confessed traitor – and I admit he is – the fact that he is a self-confessed former member of the Communist Party – which I admit he is – has no bearing at all on whether the facts that he told – or, rather, the alleged facts that he told——

HISS : Has no bearing on his credibility?

HÉBERT : No; because, Mr Hiss, I recognise the fact that maybe my background is a little different from yours, but I do know police methods and I know crime a great deal, and you show me a good police force and I will show you the stool-pigeon who turned them in. Show me a police force with a poor record, and I will show you a police force without a stool-pigeon. We have to have people like Chambers or Miss Bentley to come in and tell us. I am not giving Mr Chambers any great credit for his previous life. I am trying to find out if he has reformed. Some of the greatest saints in history were pretty bad before they were saints. Are you going to take away their sainthood because of their previous lives? Are you not going to believe them after they have reformed?

I don't care who gives the facts to me, whether a confessed liar, thief, or murderer, if it is facts. That is all I am interested in.

HISS : You have made your position clear. I would like to raise a separate point. Today as I came down on the train I read a statement – I think it was in the *New York Times* – that a member of this Committee, an unidentified member of this Committee had told the press man who wrote the article that this Committee believed or had reason to believe from talking to Chambers that Chambers had personally known Hiss, not that Chambers had had the conversation which is the issue here, that Chambers had been in Hiss's house. That is not the issue before this Committee. You are asking me to tell you all the facts that I know of people who have been in my house or who had known me whom I would not feel absolutely confident are people I know all about, personal friends, people I feel I know through and through. I am not prepared to say on the basis of the photograph——

HÉBERT : We understand.

HISS : That the man, that he is not the man whose name I have written down here. Were I to testify to that, what assurance have I that some member of this Committee wouldn't say to the press that Hiss confessed knowing Chambers?

In the first place, I have testified and repeated that I have never known anybody by the name of Whittaker Chambers. I am not prepared to testify I have never seen that man.

HÉBERT : You have said that.

STRIPLING : Have you ever seen that one (indicating picture)?

CHAIRMAN : What is the question?

STRIPLING : Have you ever seen the individual whose photograph appears there?

HISS : So far as I know; no.

STRIPLING : You have never seen that person?

HISS : No.

.   .   .   .   .

After a brief recess the interchanges began again.

HISS : The name of the man I brought in – and he may have no relation to this whole nightmare – is a man named George Crosley. I met him when I was working for the Nye committee. He was a writer. He hoped to sell articles to magazines about the munitions industry.

I saw him, as I say, in my office over in the Senate Office Building, dozens of representatives of the press, students, people writing books, research people. It was our job to give them appropriate information out of the record, show them what had been put in the record. This fellow was writing a series of articles, according to my best recollection, freelancing, which he hoped to sell to one of the magazines.

He was pretty obviously not successful, in financial terms, but as far as I know, wasn't actually hard up.

STRIPLING : What colour was his hair?

HISS : Rather blondish, blonder than any of us here.

STRIPLING : Was he married?

HISS : Yes, sir.

STRIPLING : Any children?

HISS : One little baby, as I remember it, and the way I know that was the sub-leasing point. After we had taken the house on P Street and had the apartment on our hands, he one day in the course of casual conversation said he was going to specialise all summer in getting his articles done here in Washington, didn't know what he was going to do, and was thinking of bringing his family.

I said, 'You can have my apartment. It is not terribly cool, but it is up in the air near the Wardman Park.' He said he had a wife and little baby. The apartment wasn't very expensive, and I think I let him have it at exact cost. My recollection is that he spent several nights in my house because his furniture van was delayed. We left several pieces of furniture behind.

The P Street house belonged to a naval officer overseas and was partly furnished, so we didn't need all our furniture, particularly during the summer months, and my recollection is that definitely, as one does with a tenant trying to make him agreeable and comfortable, we left several pieces of furniture behind until the fall, his van was delayed, wasn't going to bring all the furniture because he was going to be there just during the summer, and we put them up two or three nights in a row, his wife and little baby.

NIXON : His wife and he and little baby did spend several nights in the house with you?

HISS : This man Crosley; yes.

NIXON : Can you describe his wife?

HISS : Yes; she was a rather strikingly dark person, very strikingly dark. I don't know whether I would recognise her again because I didn't see very much of her.

NIXON : How tall was this man, approximately?

HISS : Shortish.

NIXON : Heavy?

HISS : Not noticeably. That is why I don't believe it has any direct, but it could have an indirect bearing.

NIXON : How about his teeth?

HISS : Very bad teeth. That is one of the things I particularly want to see Chambers about. This man had very bad teeth, did not take care of his teeth.

STRIPLING : Did he have most of his teeth or just weren't well cared for?

HISS : I don't think he had gapped teeth, but they were badly taken care of. They were stained and I would say obviously not attended to.

NIXON : Can you state again just when he first rented the apartment?

HISS : I think it was about June of 1935. My recollection is – and again I have not checked the records – that is, I went with the Nye Munitions Committee in the early winter of 1934. I don't even remember now when the resolution was passed. In any event, I am confident I was living on Twenty-ninth Street from December 1934 to June 1935 and that coincided with my service with the Nye Committee. I say that because one reason we took the apartment was to reduce our living costs, because after I had been on loan from the Department of Agriculture for some months, I thought it would only be a two-month assignment or so, it became evident that I was to stay on longer if I should complete the job, and my deputy in the Department of Agriculture was doing all my work and not getting my salary and I did not feel it fair, so I resigned from the Department of Agriculture to go on with the Nye Committee work at the Nye Committee salary and contemplated that and talked it over with my deputy in the Department of Agriculture for some time before I did it. So I am sure, from my recollection, that the Twenty-ninth Street apartment is definitely linked in time with my service on the Nye Committee.

STRIPLING: What kind of automobile did that fellow have?

HISS: No kind of automobile. I sold him an automobile. I had an old Ford that I threw in with the apartment and had been trying to trade it in and get rid of it. I had an old, old Ford we had kept for sentimental reasons. We got it just before we were married in 1929.

STRIPLING: Was it a model A or model T?

HISS: Early A model with a trunk on the back, a slightly collegiate model.

STRIPLING: What colour?

HISS: Dark blue. It wasn't very fancy but it had a sassy little trunk on the back.

NIXON: You sold that car?

HISS: I threw it in. He wanted a way to get around, and I said, 'Fine, I want to get rid of it. I have another car, and we kept it for sentimental reasons, not worth a damn.' I let him have it along with the rent.

NIXON: Where did you move from there?

HISS: Again my best recollection is that we stayed on P Street only one year because the whole heating plant broke down in the middle of the winter when I was quite ill, and I think that we moved from 2905 P Street to 1241 Thirtieth Street about September 1936. I recall that quite specifically though we can check it from the records, because I remember Mr Sayre, who was my chief in the State Department, who had been my professor at law school, saying he wanted to drive by and see where I was living. I remember the little house on Thirtieth Street which we had just got, a new development, was the little house I drove him by, and it must have been September or October 1936, just after starting to work in the State Department.

NIXON: Going back to this man, do you know how many days approximately he stayed with you?

HISS: I don't think more than a couple of times. He may have come back. I can't remember when it was I finally decided it wasn't any use expecting to collect from him, that I had been a sucker and he was sort of deadbeat; not a bad character, but I think he just was using me for a soft touch.

NIXON: You said, before he moved into your apartment he stayed in your house with you and your wife, about how many days?

HISS: I would say a couple of nights. I don't think it was longer than that.

NIXON: A couple of nights?

HISS: During the delay of the van arriving.

NIXON: Wouldn't that be longer than two nights?

HISS: I don't think so. I wouldn't swear that he didn't come back again some later time after the lease and say, 'I can't find a hotel. Put me up overnight', or something of that sort. I wouldn't swear Crosley wasn't in my house maybe a total of three or four nights altogether.

NIXON: You don't recall any subjects of conversation during that period?

HISS: We talked backwards and forwards about the Munitions

Committee work. He told various stories that I recall of his escapades. He purported to be a cross between Jim Tully, the author, and Jack London. He had been everywhere. I remember he told me he had personally participated in laying down the tracks of the streetcars in Washington, DC. He had done that for local colour, or something. He had worked right with the road gang laying tracks in Washington, DC.

STRIPLING: Was his middle initial 'L'?

HISS: That I wouldn't know . . .

NIXON: You gave this Ford car to Crosley?

HISS: Threw it in along with the apartment and charged the rent and threw the car in at the same time.

NIXON: In other words, added a little to the rent to cover the car?

HISS: No; I think I charged him exactly what I was paying for the rent and threw the car in in addition. I don't think I got any compensation.

STRIPLING: You just gave him the car?

HISS: I think the car just went right in with it. I don't remember whether we had settled on the terms of the rent before the car question came up, or whether it came up and then on the basis of the car and the apartment I said, 'Well, you ought to pay the full rent . . .'

. . . . .

STRIPLING: What kind of a bill of sale did you give Crosley?

HISS: I think I just turned it over – in the District you get a certificate of title, I think it is. I think I just simply turned it over to him.

STRIPLING: Handed it to him?

HISS: Yes.

STRIPLING: No evidence of any transfer. Did he record the title?

HISS : That I haven't any idea. This is a car which had been sitting on the streets in snows for a year or two. I once got a parking fine because I forgot where it was parked. We were using the other car.

STRIPLING : Do those model Fords have windshield wipers?

HISS : You had to work them yourself.

STRIPLING : Hand operated?

HISS : I think that is the best I can recall.

.   .   .   .   .

STRIPLING : On this man, George Crosley, you say you gave him this car?

HISS : Yes, sir.

STRIPLING : Did you ever go riding with Crosley in this automobile?

HISS : I might very well have.

STRIPLING : I mean did you go around with him quite a bit, take rides?

HISS : You mean after I gave it to him did he ever give me a ride?

STRIPLING : Before or after.

HISS : I think I drove him from the Hill to the apartment.

STRIPLING : Did you ever take any trips out of town with George Crosley?

HISS : No; I don't think so.

STRIPLING : Did you ever take him to Pennsylvania?

HISS : No. I think I once drove him to New York City when I was going to make a trip to New York City, anyway.

NIXON : Was Mrs Hiss along?

HISS : That I wouldn't recall. She may have been. I think I may have given him a lift when I went to New York.

STRIPLING : Did you go to Paoli?

HISS : If Mrs Hiss was along; yes.

THE CHAIRMAN : Route No 202?

HISS : Route 202 goes through that part of Pennsylvania, and that is the route we would take.

NIXON : Did you ever drive to Baltimore with Crosley?

HISS : I don't recall it. I think he moved to Baltimore from here, as a matter of fact, but I don't recall that I ever drove him.

NIXON : How did you know that?

HISS : I think he told me when he was pulling out. He was in my apartment until the lease expired in September.

NIXON : What year?

HISS : I think it was September 1935 and I think I saw him several times after that, and I think he had told me he moved from here to Baltimore.

NIXON : Even though he didn't pay his rent you saw him several times?

HISS : He was about to pay it and was going to sell his articles. He gave me a payment on account once. He brought a rug over which he said some wealthy patron gave him. I have still got the damned thing.

NIXON : Did you ever give him anything?

HISS : Never anything but a couple of loans; never got paid back.

NIXON : Never gave him anything else?

HISS : Not to my recollection.

NIXON : Where is he now?

HISS : I have no idea. I don't think I have seen him since 1935.

NIXON : Have you ever heard of him since 1935?

HISS : No; never thought of him again until this morning on the train.

STRIPLING : You wouldn't say positively George Crosley and this person are the same?

HISS : Not positively.

STRIPLING : You would not say positively?

HISS: I think they are not. That would be my best impression from the photographs.

Hiss, on seeing the short, plump Chambers, found a certain familiarity in his appearance – 'I thought I saw Crosley in the added pounds and rumpled suit . . . I wanted to hear his voice and to see if he had Crosley's bad teeth before expressing my feeling that this was George Crosley.'

Hiss's critics have made a great deal of his caution in this matter of recognising Crosley, and on the face of it, he does seem to have carried this caution rather further than was necessary. But it was as essential to him that he should be certain of Chambers's identity as Crosley, as it was to the Committee, for on it would hang the future. The charges made by Chambers were as serious as a charge of murder normally is. Hiss knew that unless he could *prove* them false, his whole career would come tumbling about his ears. Before he could begin to refute the charges, he had to *prove* that Chambers was the man he had known as George Crosley, for only then could he file factual answers to the accusations.

In the scene that followed, we again see the cautious lawyer's mind working. The man before him only vaguely resembled the Crosley he had known, but there were two definite points about Crosley which could go a very long way towards helping him in the identification – the voice and the teeth. Crosley had had extremely bad teeth.

So he asked Nixon to ask Chambers to say something, and Nixon asked him to state his name and business. Chambers replied that his name was Whittaker Chambers. 'At this point,' says the Committee record, 'Mr Hiss walked in the direction of Mr Chambers.' He said to Chambers, 'Would you mind opening your mouth wider.' To Nixon he said, 'You know what I am referring to, Mr Nixon.' He asked Chambers to go on talking.

Hiss's recollection was that Crosley's voice had 'a deepness, a lowness of tone,' while Chambers's voice was light. Hiss asked Nixon to request Chambers to read some more, and Nixon handed him a copy of *Newsweek*. But before he could begin to read, Hiss said, 'I think he is George Crosley, but I would like him to talk a little longer.' Then turning to Chambers he asked, 'Are you George Crosley?'

'Not to my knowledge,' Chambers replied, and began to read.

Nixon almost at once interrupted him and suggested he should be sworn. Hiss, with a good deal of sarcasm, remarked that that was a good idea. The remark and the tone in which it was delivered riled Nixon, and he said angrily, 'Mr Hiss, may I say something? I suggested that he be sworn, and when I say something like that, I want no interruptions from you.' Hiss, with Harry White's death in mind, retorted with equal heat, 'Mr Nixon, in view of what happened yesterday (White's death) I think there is no occasion for you to use that tone of voice to me, and I hope the record will show what I have just said.'

At Nixon's request, Chambers began to read again. Hiss was now sure in his mind that Chambers was Crosley, but he was puzzled by Chambers's denial that he was. 'The voice sounds a little less resonant than the voice of the man I knew as George Crosley,' he said. 'The teeth look to me as though either they have been improved upon or that there has been considerable dental work done since I knew George Crosley, which was some years ago. I believe, I am not prepared without further checking to take an absolute oath, that he must be George Crosley.'

Nixon put a series of questions to Chambers which elicited the information that he had had considerable renovations made to his teeth since 1934. Again the cautious lawyer asked for the name of the dentist who had carried out the work, and once more said that he had a feeling that Chambers was the man who had called himself George Crosley, a freelance writer.

Nixon would not allow Hiss to ask Chambers why he had denied he had called himself Crosley, and instead took him over again the account Hiss had given on the previous day about how he had first met Crosley. Stripling intervened towards the end of this phase with a question which showed which way his mind was working to ask whether Hiss was still relying on the teeth to identify a man whom he had known 'so well that he was a guest in your house.' In a lengthy reply Hiss said that he was not 'given on important occasions to snap judgments or simple, easy statements.' He was certain that Crosley had had 'notably bad teeth'. 'I would not call George Crosley a guest in my house. I have explained the circumstances. If you choose to call him a guest, that is your affair.'

Stripling[1] had the good grace to withdraw the word 'guest', and Hiss went on to say that 'if this man had said he was George Crosley, I would have no difficulty in identification. He denied it right here.' He thought he should be asked to explain his denial. Stripling suggested that Hiss should be allowed to question Chambers on this point, and the other members agreeing, Hiss asked point-blank: 'Did you ever go under the name of George Crosley?'

And Chambers repeated his previous reply: 'Not to my knowledge.'

(Not until several months later was Chambers to admit that he *may* have used the name George Crosley.)

More questioning followed, going over ground already well trodden. By this time Parnell Thomas, chairman of the full Committee, had arrived and taken over the chair from McDowell.

---

1. Stripling, by the way, was not a trained lawyer. From being an assistant doorkeeper in the Capitol he had become a clerk to the Committee, and was now its chief investigator.

It was he who presently announced that 'as a result of this testimony the Committee has decided to bring about a meeting of the full Committee in public session Wednesday August 25 at 10 30 in the caucus room of the Old House Office Building, at which time both Mr Hiss and Mr Chambers, whom Mr Hiss identified as the person he knew as Mr Crosley, will appear as witnesses.' He instructed Stripling to serve subpoenas on both men. Hiss tried to intervene to say that it was quite unnecessary to issue a subpoena for him; he would be there without compulsion.

Throughout the hearing there had been undertones of animosity between the Committee and Hiss which had flared to a climax when the two men had been asked to make positive identification of one another, and the scene had followed which I have described on page 52, when Hiss went towards Chambers and the Committee thought he intended to strike him. Hiss had then issued his challenge to Chambers to repeat his charges outside the protection of the immunity afforded by the Committee.

The hearing ended, the animosity by no means dissolved. After Parnell Thomas had made his announcement Hiss asked about Mrs Hiss's appearance before the sub-committee, which he had been asked to arrange as quickly as possible. Nixon suggested she might be able to reach New York the following day, and McDowell said that Hiss might accompany her.

HISS : Thank you. Am I dismissed? Is the proceeding over?

THE CHAIRMAN : Any more questions to ask of Mr Hiss?

NIXON : I have nothing.

THE CHAIRMAN : That is all. Thank you very much.

HISS : I don't reciprocate.

THE CHAIRMAN : Italicise that in the record.

HISS : I wish you would.

4

25th August 1948

Between the first Chambers hearing (3rd August) and the last hearing on the 25th August, the seven members of the Ware Group, as the group was called to which Hiss was alleged to belong, were subpoenaed, and appeared before the Committee in open sessions. With one exception, Donald Hiss, Alger Hiss's brother, all claimed the protection of the Fifth Amendment, and refused to answer any questions if their answers might tend to incriminate them.

The effect of this is well illustrated by the testimony given by Henry Collins, alleged by Chambers to be the treasurer of the group, in whose apartment the members, including Hiss, were said by Chambers to have met. Collins appeared on the 11th August, and he answered the preliminary questions thus:

COLLINS: My Federal employment started late in 1933 with the National Recovery Administration. In 1935 I went with the Soil Conservation Service; in 1938, I think, I went with the Department of Labour in the Wage and Hour Division. From there, I was loaned to the House Committee on the Interstate Migration of Destitute Citizens, and later to the Senate Committee on Small Business, and subsequently to the Kilgore Committee, a sub-committee of the Military Affairs Committee on War Mobilisation. From there, I received a commission and went into the School of Military Government at Charlotteville and was shortly sent overseas and spent two years in the European theatre, in England, France and Germany. The relevant period of Chambers's charges are 1934 or 1935 to

1937 or early 1938. It is difficult to see what information interesting to Russia that Collins could have supplied from his official posts between these dates.

STRIPLING : Are you a member of the Communist Party?

COLLINS : I decline to answer that question on the grounds that my answer might tend to incriminate me.

He was shown a press photograph of Chambers and asked if he could recognise him. He said that he could not, though later he said that he did recall having a man called George Crosley in for cocktails.

STRIPLING : You cannot recognise this man? Did you ever know anybody by the name of Whittaker Chambers?

COLLINS : I never knew a man by the name of Whittaker Chambers.

STRIPLING : Do you know an individual known to you as Carl in 1935?

COLLINS : I refuse to answer that question on the grounds of possible self-incrimination . . .

STRIPLING : Mr Collins, did you ever live at St Matthews Court in Washington?

COLLINS : I did.

STRIPLING : Did you ever meet John Abt at that apartment?

COLLINS : I decline to answer that question on the grounds of possible self-incrimination.

STRIPLING : Did you ever meet Alger Hiss at that apartment?

COLLINS : I decline to answer that question for the same reason.

STRIPLING : Did you ever meet in the apartment of Alger Hiss on P Street in Georgetown in 1935?

COLLINS : I decline to answer that question on the grounds of possible self-incrimination . . .

HÉBERT : Mr Collins, were you ever investigated by the FBI for loyalty?

COLLINS : I do not know, sir. I was called down and interviewed by them about six years ago, I think.

HÉBERT : You know what that interview was. What was it?

COLLINS : Well, it is in the record.

HÉBERT : I am not asking for the record. I am asking you.

COLLINS : Sir, I do not think I understand that question.

. . . . .

HÉBERT : Did they ask you about your connection with certain organisations in Government – I mean outside of Government but certain organisations in the country?

COLLINS : Yes, that is the kind of questions that they asked.

HÉBERT : Did they ask you about any communistic activity?

COLLINS : I do not remember, sir.

. . . . .

HÉBERT : Why won't you say whether you know Carl or not? That is in the record.

COLLINS : For the same reason, sir, that I refuse to answer any questions about knowing any individuals at this time in connection with these accusations.

HÉBERT : But you just said you did not know Whittaker Chambers. You are blowing hot and cold. Which way do you want to blow, hot or cold? We have had a lot of talking out of both sides of the mouth on this, so we may as well give you the chance to do it. It is a great acrobatic feat. How do you justify, then, saying you do not know Whittaker Chambers? You did answer that question.

COLLINS : I just go back to my previous statements, sir, in connection with that.

HÉBERT : Why do you refuse to say whether you know Alger Hiss or not? He has made no accusations against you.

COLLINS : I refuse to answer that question, sir, on the grounds that my answer might tend to incriminate me.

Collins, here, was clearly being much more cautious even than Hiss. Hiss had readily accepted that Collins was not guilty of Chambers's accusation, had admitted acquaintanceship with him and that he had visited Collins's apartment. Collins would admit to none of these things, possibly fearing that Hiss might be a secret Communist.

So it went on. John Abt, Nathan Witt, Lee Pressman, Victor Perlo and Charles Kramer (alias Krivitsky) all responded in the same vein to the Committee's probings. It must have been very frustrating to the Committee to have their questioning met by such a blank wall; and especially refreshing to have Donald Hiss appear and answer every single question frankly and straight-forwardly, without calling upon the Fifth Amendment once.

Chambers had been as definite about Donald Hiss being a member of the group as he had been about Alger Hiss. If his evidence against Donald were to prove false, his evidence against Alger would have to be very suspect indeed.

Chambers had not merely mentioned Donald Hiss along with the other members of the group on the 3rd August 1948. He had included Donald with Alger in his interview with Assistant Secretary of State Adolf Berle in 1939 (I shall come to this presently); again on the 20th March 1945 to the FBI; at the first hearing by the Committee on the 3rd August 1948; and at the secret hearing on the 7th August. On this occasion what he had said was especially interesting.

Asked when he first met Donald Hiss, he replied, 'Probably within the same week in which I met Alger Hiss.' He said that his relationship with Donald was always a formal one, and he went on that Donald knew him as Carl, and had once met Donald's wife. He declared that he had collected Donald's Party dues: 'Probably in Alger's home. He frequently came there.'

Donald Hiss had heard of Whittaker Chambers, he was later

to declare, at a party in February or March 1948, when someone had told him that Chambers was accusing him of being a Communist. He had not mentioned this to his brother until Alger had come to him later, having also heard the story.

As soon as he had read Chambers's testimony of the 3rd August, Donald Hiss had written to the chairman asking to be called before the Committee when he would give evidence under oath and would answer any questions put to him. Except for the facts noted by Chambers about his brother and his own employment 'I flatly deny every statement made by Mr Chambers with respect to me.' He concluded: 'I have no recollection of ever having met any person by the name of D Whittaker Chambers, nor do I recognise his photograph which I have seen in the public press. I am not and never have been in sympathy with the principles of the Communist Party. Any interested person could easily have discovered these facts by inquiry of any of the distinguished, respected and unquestionably loyal Americans with whom I have been intimately associated.'

On the 13th August he fulfilled his promises in minute detail. The Committee were impressed, and Nixon was undoubtedly voicing the majority of members' reactions to the whole affair when he said, 'As the chairman is aware, I have been making a particular study of that phase of the case regarding the conflict in testimony between that submitted by Whittaker Chambers and that submitted by Alger Hiss. It is of course clear that perjury has been commited in this case. It is, of course, the duty of the Committee *not* to reach a conclusion in this matter. That is a matter which will have to be decided in a court. But I think the statement should be made that not only do we have on the one side the very forthright statement of Mr (Donald) Hiss today and of his brother Alger Hiss the other day, denying the charges of Mr Chambers factually or otherwise, but we also have the charges which Mr Chambers made originally and which were made by him in the knowledge of the fact that he was making those charges subject to the laws of perjury, which would bring a ten thousand dollar fine and ten years in jail in the District of Columbia. It is not a situation where we have the charges made by an individual who has no standing whatever in the community, but it is a case in which charges have been made by an individual who, if these charges are false, has undoubtedly had a motive which in effect would result in destroying his own career if it is proved that these charges were false.'

It was all very puzzling. But neither now nor later did Nixon or anyone else speculate on Chambers's motive. Later, it was essential that his only motive should be pure patriotism.

However, about Donald Hiss's appearance on the 13th August, two points have a particular significance for me. In the passages in *Witness* in which Chambers refers to the hearings concerned with the Ware Group, while he quotes verbatim extracts from the Committee records relating to Collins and Abt, and refers to the performances of other members, *he makes no mention whatsoever* of Donald Hiss's appearance. Similarly he makes no mention of Donald Hiss's testimony at the trials.

The second point is this. Though the charges against Donald Hiss were never formally withdrawn, he was never the subject of investigation by the Committee or of trial in the courts. The prosecutor at neither of the trials made any attempt in his cross-examination of Donald Hiss to question him even, about the substance of Chambers's charges against him. Yet, as Lord Jowitt writes in *The Strange Case of Alger Hiss*,[1] 'This at any rate seems to be clear, and must leave a most damaging impression of the truth of Chambers's evidence as a whole : that the allegations were demonstrated, so far as human testimony can demonstrate,

1. Op cit p179.

to be entirely without foundation. There was, as it seems to me, no scope for explaining away the discrepancies as mere differences of recollection.

'The categorical statement that Chambers had met Donald Hiss at Alger's house and had collected Communist dues from him is either true or false, and Mr Murphy (the prosecutor) made no attempt to prove that it was true. I think anyone acquainted with this evidence must feel grave doubts about the reliability of the testimony of Chambers when it is not corroborated from other sources.'

(A third point of interest, which I quote out of chronological order, but mention it here because it has areas of similarity, is this. In his description of the hearings involving the group, in *Witness* (p624), Chambers says, 'Lee Pressman came next. It may be borne in mind that three years later, Pressman was to testify before the House Committee on Un-American Activities that he had been a member of the Communist Party and of the Ware Group. . . .' Chambers completely omits to say that at this hearing *Pressman categorically denied that Alger Hiss had ever been a member of the group*.)

Before the 25th August, Hiss had drawn up a statement in the form of a letter to the chairman of the Committee, certain passages of which it is necessary to quote verbatim. Hiss's motive in writing this letter was 'to bring into the open the political motivations which, I was now convinced, had led some members of the Committee to seek to attack the New Deal, Yalta and the United Nations (with all of which I could be associated) by unwarranted and sensational attacks on me.'

The letter, then – which during the hearing he was able to read into the record – contained these passages.

'Tomorrow will mark my fourth appearance before your Committee. I urge, in advance of that hearing, that your Committee delay no longer in penetrating to the bedrock of the facts relevant to the charge which you have publicised – that I am or have been a Communist.

'This charge goes beyond the personal. Attempts will be made to use it, and the resulting publicity, to discredit recent great achievements of this country in which I was privileged to participate.

'Certain members of your Committee have already demonstrated that the use of your hearings and the ensuing publicity is not a mere possibility. It is a reality. Your acting chairman, Mr Mundt, himself, was trigger-quick to cast such discredit.'

Here Hiss interpolated: 'Although he now says that he was very favourably impressed with my testimony.' He went on:

'Before I had a chance to testify, even before the press had a chance to reach me for comment, before you had sought one single fact to support the charge made by a self-confessed liar, spy and traitor, your acting chairman pronounced judgment that I am guilty as charged, by saying that the country should be aware of the peace work with which I have been connected.

'I urge that these Committee members abandon such verdict-first-and-testimony-later tactics, along with dramatic confrontations in secret sessions, and get down to business.

'First, my record should be explored. It is inconceivable that there could have been on my part, during fifteen years or more in public office, serving all three branches of the Government, judicial, legislative, and executive, any departure from the highest rectitude without its being known. It is inconceivable that the men with whom I was intimately associated during those fifteen years should not know my true character far better than this accuser. It is inconceivable that if I had not been of the highest character, this would not have manifested itself at some time or other, in at least one of the innumerable actions I took as a high official, actions publicly recorded in the greatest detail.

'During the period cited by this accuser, I was chief counsel to the Senate Committee Investigating the Munitions Industry, at a great many public hearings, fully reported in volumes to be found in libraries in every major American city. During my term of service under the Solicitor General of the United States, I participated in the preparation of briefs on a great many of the largest issues affecting the United States. Those briefs are on public file in the United States Supreme Court, in the Department of Justice, and in law libraries in various American cities.

'As an official of the Department of State, I was appointed secretary-general, the top administrative officer, of the peace-building international assembly that created the United Nations. My actions in that post are a matter of detailed public record. The same is true of my actions at other peace-building and peace-strengthening international meetings in which I participated – at Dumbarton Oaks and elsewhere in this country, at Yalta, at London, and in other foreign cities. All my actions in the executive branch of the Government, including my work in the Agricultural Adjustment Administration on farm problems are fully recorded in the public records.

'In all this work I was frequently, and for extensive periods, under the eye of the American press and of the statesmen under whom or in association with whom I worked. They saw my every gesture, my every movement, my every facial expression. They heard the tones in which I spoke, the words I uttered, the words spoken by others in my presence. They knew my every act relating to official business, both in public and in executive conference.

'Here is a list of the living personages of recognised stature under whom or in association with whom I worked in the Government (there may be omissions which I should like to supply in a supplemental list) :

[There followed a scintillating array of names, among which were Senator Arthur Vandenberg, Senator Tom Conally, Cordell Hull, Edward Stettinius, James Byrnes (the last three had all been Secretaries of State), Senator Nye, Dean Acheson, James Pope, director of the TVA, John Foster Dulles, Mrs Eleanor Roosevelt, Harold Stassen and Chester Davis. In all, he listed thirty-four men prominent in American political affairs.]

'These men I have listed are the men with whom and under whom I worked intimately during my fifteen years in Government service – the men best able to testify concerning the loyalty with which I performed the duties assigned me. All are persons of unimpeachable character, in a position to know my work from day to day and hour to hour through many years. Ask them if they ever found in me anything except the highest adherence to duty and honour.

'Then the Committee can judge, and the public can judge, whether to believe a self-discredited accuser whose names and aliases are as numerous and as casual as his accusations.

'The other side of this question is the reliability of the allegations before this Committee, the undocumented statements of the man who now calls himself Whittaker Chambers.

'Is he a man of consistent reliability, truthfulness, and honour? Clearly not. He admits it, and the Committee knows it. Indeed, is he a man of sanity?

'Getting the facts about Whittaker Chambers, if that is his name, will not be easy. My own counsel have made inquiries in the past few days and have learned that his career is not, like those of normal men, an open book. His operations have been furtive and concealed. Why? What does he have to hide?

'I am glad to help get the facts.

'At this point I should like to repeat suggestions made by me at preceding hearings with respect to the most effective method of getting facts so far as I can supply them. The suggestions I made, beginning with the very first time I appeared before your Committee, were not then accepted, and the result has only been confusion and delay. Let me illustrate by recalling to your minds what I said when you asked me to identify the accuser, not by producing him under your subpoena power but by producing only a newspaper photograph taken many years after the time when, by his own statements, I had last seen him. I said to you on the occasion of my first appearance :

' "I would much rather see the individual – I would not want to take oath that I have never seen that man. I would like to see him, and I would be better able to tell whether I had ever seen him. Is he here today – I hoped he would be."

'Let me add one further example of how the procedures followed have caused confusion and delay. In your secret sessions you asked me housekeeping and minor details of years ago that few, if any, busy men would possibly retain in their memories with accuracy. I told you, and one of your own members acknowledged, that you or I should consult the records. I warned you that I had not checked them and that I doubted if I could be helpful under those circumstances.

'I am having a check made of the records, and will furnish the results to you.

'One personal word. My action in being kind to Crosley years ago was one of humaneness, with results which surely some members of the Committee have experienced. You do a favour for a man, he comes for another, he gets a third favour from you. When you finally realise he is an inveterate repeater, you get rid of him. If your loss is only a loss of time and money, you are lucky. You may find yourself calumniated in a degree depending on whether the man is unbalanced or worse.'

Hiss's assessment of the Committee's attitude towards him –

'The open hostility of the Committee members present at the Commodore made it obvious to me that my next encounter with the Committee was to be what lawyers call an adversary proceeding'[1] – was correct. He was refused the aid of counsel, whom he had brought with him, and had to meet alone the onslaught of the Committee.

The questions put to Hiss were all based on his previous testimony. Many were asked with the obvious intention of testing his veracity, others with the purpose of eliciting additional information on certain points. But, as Alastair Cooke has put it,[2] 'There were two items that formed the core of the Committee's new suspicion. . . . One was Hiss's urgent obligation to find somebody else who knew George Crosley. The other was his account of the 1929 Ford he had "thrown in" with the sublease of the apartment – a topic on which the Committee had already procured disturbing documentary evidence.'

On the 17th August, Hiss had been challenged to name three people who would support his contention that Chambers had called himself Crosley, and he had given three names. Inquiries had shown that one was dead, the other could not be traced, While the third said he could not remember anything that would help. The Library of Congress – where American copyright is registered – had also reported that they could trace no writings by a George Crosley that could possibly have been written by Chambers in the period at issue.

With the testimony to his detriment, Hiss was grilled about the Ford. The questioning on this point took up the greater part of the hearing. Hiss was at his most cautious. Alastair Cooke says that by the Committee's count Hiss qualified his replies no fewer than 198 times by some such phrase as 'According to my best

1. *In the Court of Public Opinion*, op cit p101.

2. *A Generation on Trial*, op cit p86.

recollection'. The effect of his caution was to damn him, and it surprises me that trained lawyer as he was, he did not appreciate what he was doing to himself and desist.

Hiss had said that he had given Crosley the old car. Chambers had said that against his advice Hiss had given it to the Party for use by 'a poor organiser in the West.' Hiss still maintained that he had given the car to Crosley, though he did qualify his previous assertion by saying he had given Crosley 'the use of the car'.

Having got as positive a statement from Hiss as seemed possible on this point, the Committee then introduced its trump card. This was to be the first important point on which the Committee had been able to *prove* Hiss wrong, and it was this which gave the date of the signing over of the car its "trump-card" quality. It is clear that the Committee's incredulity was greatly enhanced by this revelation, and from this moment there is no doubt about its partisanship. The trump card was this.

One of the Committee's investigators had subpoenaed the records of the Cherner Motor Company – which proved Hiss right on the part of his contention that he had not, as Chambers had asserted, delivered the Ford to a car lot owned by a Communist—but had discovered that on the 23rd July 1936 a (year later than Hiss maintained he had given the car to Crosley) Hiss had signed over the car to the company, and that the same day a William Rosen had either bought it, or had had it transferred to him. The certificate of title signed by Hiss was produced, and the notary who had notarised it was called to prove his own signature.

Hébert at this point asked Hiss if, now that his memory had been refreshed, he could remember the transaction over the Ford. 'No,' Hiss had told him, 'I have no present recollection of the disposition of the Ford.' It was then that Hébert remarked, 'You are a remarkable and agile young man, Mr Hiss.'

From this moment, and for the rest of the hearing they pummelled Hiss with questions so far-ranging that he was asked in effect to relive his life of fourteen years before. They pressed him about the dates of Crosley's tenancy of the apartment on 28th Street; they showed him snapshots of Chambers and his family taken in 1934; they asked him about the people of the alleged Ware Group; they left, so it seemed, nothing untouched.

Hiss answered all with his customary caution and eventually requested the Committee to put a series of questions to Chambers.

Hiss requested the Committee:

'Ask him to give his complete employment record during his membership in the Communist Party, since his resignation from the Communist Party, stating the name of each employer, stating his occupation, and his compensation, also the name by which he was employed in each instance.

'I would like him to give a complete bibliography of all his writings. He says that he was a writer. Give the writings under any and every name he has used.

'I would like him to be asked whether he has ever been charged or convicted of any crime.

'I would like him to give the full particulars, if so, as to where, when, and for what.

'I would like him to be asked whether he has ever been treated for a mental illness.

'Ask him about his marriage and how many children he had and where his wife now lives.

'Ask him the circumstances under which he came into contact with this Committee and to make public all written memoranda which he may have handed to any representative of the Committee.'

Alastair Cooke, who was present, says, 'They asked Chambers all this, and much more. . . . Chambers was a very different witness. Placidly, directly, he ran through names and places, nodded assent, recited the whole charge, with the air of a man sportingly reiterating a list of vital statistics before an insurance company that was sorry it had misplaced them. Only once did the inventory turn into confession, when his voice faltered and through tears he said he was testifying against his former friend "with remorse and pity, but in a moment of history in which this Nation now stands, so help me God, I could not do otherwise".[1]

One question the Committee did not ask Chambers: 'Would he be prepared to repeat the charges he had made against Hiss outside the protection of the Committee?'

This challenge Hiss had thrown down once more.

Two nights later, on a radio programme called *Meet the Press*, Chambers replied to the challenge. During the interview in which a number of journalists of national standing took part, among the exchanges was the following –

Asked by Edward Folliard of the *Washington Post* whether, having said publicly that Hiss had at all events been a member of the Communist Party – he had done so in response to the very first question asked him – he was now prepared to answer a suit for slander or libel, Chambers replied: 'I do not think Mr Hiss will sue me for slander or libel.'

'Would you charge Alger Hiss with an overt act as a Communist, as you said he was?' asked Tom Reynolds of the *Chicago Sun-Times*. 'Did Alger Hiss at any time, to your knowledge, do anything that was treasonable or beyond the law of the United States? That, I believe, brings you the opportunity to accept the Hiss challenge.'

'Whether or not it brings me the opportunity to accept the Hiss challenge, I am quite unprepared to say whether he did or not,' Chambers replied, adding, 'I am not familiar with the laws of treason.'

And a little later, being pressed by Reynolds, who asked, 'Are

1. *A Generation on Trial*, op cit p90.

you prepared at this time to say that Alger Hiss was anything more than, in your opinion, a Communist? Did he do anything wrong? Did he commit any overt act? Has he been loyal to the country?' Chambers replied : 'I am only prepared at this time to say he was a Communist.'

'It seems to me, then, sir,' Reynolds retorted, 'if I may say so, that in some respects this may be a tempest in a teapot. You say that he was a Communist, but you will not accuse him of any act that is disloyal to the United States.'

'I am not prepared legally to make that charge,' Chambers told Reynolds. 'My whole interest in this business has been to show that Mr Hiss was a Communist.'

'Would you be prepared, for instance,' Reynolds urged him, 'to put on the record the testimony that you gave during the three or four or five interrogations by the FBI?'

'The gist of that testimony is already on the record in the Un-American Committee,' Chambers evaded.

'I am not interested in the gist,' Reynolds told him. 'But I presume that there were assertions that overt acts were committed. Are you willing to put on the record, so that it can be tested in the courts under the laws of evidence, that this man did something wrong?'

'I think,' Chambers replied, 'that what needs clarification is the purpose for which that group was set up to which Mr Hiss belonged. That was a group, *not, as I think is in the back of your mind, for the purpose of espionage*, but for the purpose of infiltrating the Government and influencing Government policy by getting Communists in key places.'

On the basis of the broadcast, Hiss instructed his lawyers to file a civil action for libel, claiming fifty thousand dollars, which was later increased to seventy-five thousand dollars. The lawyers advised that Chambers should be sued in Maryland, where he lived, and Hiss asked an old friend, a Baltimore lawyer, William Marbury, to represent him. Marbury happened to be in Europe, and did not return until the end of September, which explains the delay in filing the suit, which was done on the 27th September.

5

Espionage After All

'I think what needs clarification,' Chambers had told Tom Reynolds in the radio interview, 'is the purpose for which the group was set up to which Mr Hiss belonged. That was a group, not, as I think is in the back of your mind, for the purpose of espionage, but for the purpose of infiltrating the Government and influencing Government policy by getting Communists in key places.'

That declaration he made in a nation-wide broadcast on the 27th August. Before 1948 was out, he had completely gone back on it, and had directly charged Hiss with espionage.

It happened like this.

In American legal procedure covering certain types of civil actions, in which libel and slander actions qualify, is a process known as a pre-trial. At a pre-trial only the principals, their lawyers and the official stenographers are present. The press is excluded. But perhaps the most important feature of the process is that the ordinary rules of examination and cross-examination which would apply in court are not applied in the pre-trial. The questioning by the lawyers on both sides is absolutely unrestricted. The object is to clear out of the way a mass of evidence which would clog the trial procedure.

The pre-trial is an optional procedure at the decision of the plaintiff. Hiss decided to invoke his right to call for it, and to summon Chambers and Mrs Chambers to attend. It began in Baltimore on the 4th November.

The onus of proof in the libel suit lay on Chambers. He had to convince the court that Hiss had been a member of the Communist Party. If he failed to do that, he must lose.

Hiss's lawyers, therefore, from the very outset of the pre-trial directed their questioning to the discovery of whether Chambers could produce such evidence or not. 'It became clear in the second day of Chambers's examination that he had no evidence that I had been a Communist,' Hiss says.[1] Failing this, he had to rely entirely on what has since become known as 'guilt by association', which the Committee may be said to have invented. That is to say, having confessed himself to be a Communist, he could cast doubts on Hiss's denials if he were to show that he and Hiss had been very intimate friends. The assumption is that if he could prove that Hiss was lying when he denied knowing Chambers intimately, the inference could be legitimately drawn that Hiss was lying when he denied having been a Communist.

This was the line Chambers took, and in doing so he found himself under tremendous pressure from Hiss's lawyers in the relentless probing of every aspect of his former life, of his claims to have known Hiss, of his descriptions of the Hiss home and so on.

Commenting on this aspect of the pre-trial in *Witness*,[2] Chambers has said : 'I had reasoned that, once Alger Hiss made the gesture of suing me, there was an outside possibility that he would postpone the action, on one pretext or another, until people lost interest. Instead, Hiss's lawyers summoned me almost at once to a pre-trial examination in Baltimore. I had no further doubt that . . . the purpose of the libel suit was to destroy me . . . I did not know, I could scarcely have guessed, the intent behind many of the questions, or the dark thoughts that were living in the minds of the men who were my legal seconds. I could not avoid knowing that I was being treated, with a blistering condes-

1. *In the Court of Public Opinion*, op cit p158.

2. Op cit pp730 and 733.

cension, as a kind of human filth.' He does not admit that, exaggerated though his reaction was – if it was his true reaction – he had brought it on himself.

On the very first day of the hearing Chambers had been requested by Hiss's lawyers to produce any letters and papers from Hiss and the members of his family on the following day. At the beginning of the next morning's session he was asked if he had brought any such papers, and replied that he had not. His counsel interposed to say that Chambers had told them that he had not 'explored all the sources where some conceivable data might be'. Chambers says in *Witness*:[1] 'This time Cleveland warned me that if I did have anything of Hiss's I had better get it.'

Note the date – 5th November 1948.

In many places in *Witness*, which was published in 1952, Chambers has demonstrably juggled with the order of events, and with the benefit of hindsight has been able to produce reasons for why he did this and that in such a way as to bolster his case. The passage dealing with the request for papers is just such an example of this.

Hiss's lawyers made their request on the first day of the hearings – 4th November – and repeated it at the opening of the hearing the very next day – 5th November. Chambers describes this as follows: 'Then one afternoon, Marbury (Hiss's counsel) asked me his precipitating question – did I have in my possession any letters or communications from Alger Hiss? If so, would I turn them over to him? A recess occurred in the pre-trial examination at this point; perhaps only a weekend, perhaps several days. In any case, when the examination was resumed and Marbury reminded me of his request, I said that I had not looked yet. . . . He repeated his demand. I had not gone to look for the Hiss memos for two simple reasons. I did not believe that they were

1. Op cit p735.

of much importance, and I was overcome with a deep inhibiting lethargy. I had realised from the tone and the manœuvres of the pre-trial examination, how successfully the Hiss forces had turned the tables in the libel suit. . . . The whole strategy of the Hiss defence consisted in making Chambers a defendant in a trial of his past, real or imaginary. . . . It was at that moment that there occurred the incident which I have described in the Foreword to this book and which I have called "the death of the will". I saw I might well lose the libel suit, though it was not in my nature to lose it without a fight. . . . My lethargy made every effort seem futile. The idea of making the long trip to New York City, to reclaim some scraps of paper that I had left there ten years before, seemed an unendurable effort. I wanted only to be with my family and not to leave the sanctuary of the farm. And so Marbury had to ask me a second time. This time Cleveland told me that if I did have anything of Hiss's I had better get it. . . . I communicated with my wife's nephew, Nathan Levine, merely telling him that I was going to New York, and asking him if he would have "my things" ready for me.'[1]

Now the actual sequence of events was this:

1 The pre-trial examination begins on 4th November. Chambers is asked to produce any Hiss papers he may have.

2 On 5th November, Chambers is asked if he has any Hiss papers with him, and replies that he has not.
   Cleveland tells him that if he does possess any such papers he had better produce them.
   The examination is adjourned until 16th November.

3 On Sunday 14th November (ie nine days later) Chambers goes to New York, to the house of his nephew Nathan Levine. In the afternoon Levine drives him to his parents' home, 260 Rochester Avenue. There Levine goes up to the bathroom and

1. *Witness*, op cit pp734 and 735.

from a recess near a dumb-waiter he takes a large dust-covered envelope which he hands to Chambers. Chambers carries it into the kitchen, and while Levine is clearing up the mess caused by retrieving the envelope from its hiding-place in the bathroom, Chambers, alone in the kitchen, opens the envelope and later declares that he found in it a mass of documents and some film of documents.

4 On that evening, 14th November, Chambers returns with the envelope and contents by train to Baltimore.

5 On the morning of 15th November Chambers tells his lawyers of the documents he has found (but says nothing of the film). He does not show the documents to his lawyers, but says he wants time to think whether to introduce the documents or not. The lawyers inform Hiss's lawyers that Chambers will not be available for examination next day but that Mrs Chambers will be. The lawyers drive to his farm and he shows them the documents.

6 On 16th November Mrs Chambers is examined and because of the nature of her evidence is closely questioned by Hiss's lawyers.

7 During 16th November Chambers contemplates suicide.

8 On 17th November Chambers is examined and during the hearing produces the documents (but not the film) he says found in the envelope. The documents are photostated by Chambers's lawyers.[1]

---

1. Chambers's account of this in *Witness* is another example of his deliberate attempts to mislead. It gives the impression that they saw the papers when they returned with him to his farm. He has the dates wrong saying that Mrs Chambers testified on Wednesday 17th November, when she actually testified on Tuesday 16th November. The documents, according to later evidence, were photographed after they had been produced on the 17th November, and Chambers specifically says '[Photostats] were made a day or two later', and since he has not mentioned the actual date specifically, gives the impression that he discovered the papers far earlier than he did.

9 On 18th November, Hiss's lawyers take photographs of the documents to New York to show Hiss, who had not been present at the hearing on the previous day. Hiss immediately insists that the United States Attorney General shall be informed of what has happened and that the documents shall be placed at his disposal.

The production of the documents was sufficient to put an entirely new complexion on the whole case, for they purported to be:

(a) Four memoranda in Hiss's handwriting, brief notes commenting on incoming State Department cables received on 28th January, 2nd, 3rd, and 11th March 1938.

(b) Sixty-five typewritten pages, either copies or summaries of State Department documents (all typed, according to Chambers, by Mrs Hiss on her personal typewriter).

(c) A document (typed on a different typewriter) later to become known as Exhibit 10.

The pre-trial hearings were, naturally, suspended to await the Attorney General's decision. They were to be renewed but only for one or two sessions, for in a short time other events had taken place which were to turn Hiss into the defendant and eventually to send him to prison.

Now, the production of the documents by Chambers meant a reversal of all his previous contentions that the Ware Group had not been an espionage group; and it meant that instead of accusing Hiss of being a Communist he was accusing him of active espionage and treachery.

Never had the House Committee on Un-American Activities had such a plum fall into their laps. Towards the close of their examinations of Hiss and Chambers before and during the 25th August final hearing, they had given very clear indications that they were at least wishing to give the impression that they were investigating espionage activities. In fact, during the 25th August session, Stripling – from the transcript, it seems, deliberately – read out the mandate under which the Committee had been brought into being, and had then gone on: 'Pursuant to this mandate the Committee has been conducting an investigation in the past several months into alleged Communist infiltration by Communist agents in the Federal Government and the operation within the Government of certain persons who were collecting information to be turned over to a foreign government. *The hearing this morning is for the purpose of pursuing this investigation*' (my italics), thus implying that the Committee had formed the opinion that Hiss had been more than just a member of the Communist Party and of the Ware Group.

When the hearing was over Nixon had apparently, according to Chambers – who must have been a great disappointment to the Committee in this respect – pressed him to say now if he was quite certain he had not omitted to tell them something. He had denied it.

Yet another indication of the Committee's desires was given in the heading of the Interim Report it issued on the 28th August. It read, 'Interim Report on Hearings Regarding Communist Espionage in the United States Government'.

(There were reasons for these implications of espionage, political reasons, into which I shall be going later.)

For some time the Grand Jury of the South-West District of New York had been investigating charges of espionage. For months it had been inactive, but as a result of the Committee hearings it was re-convened. It summoned Chambers to appear before it on the 14th October at the instance of the Department of Justice. At one point in the proceedings a juror asked him if he had any direct knowledge of Soviet espionage. 'If I answered yes,' he says in *Witness*, 'there would be no choice but to tell the whole story, implicating all the others. I asked to be permitted to think about the question overnight. . . . That second day the grand juror repeated his question about espionage. I knew that there was no other way than by answering no that I could possibly jeopardise myself before the law. I answered: no.'[1]

I refer to these appearances before the Grand Jury for two reasons. They occurred *after* Hiss had issued his libel suit; secondly, he was, by his answer, patently guilty of perjury – if all his later testimony was true.

Now the typewritten documents found in the envelope were not the only alleged evidence that Hiss was guilty of espionage. There were, it will be remembered, some rolls of film about which Chambers had said nothing to his lawyers. These rolls of microfilm were undeveloped, and were so light-struck, it was later discovered, that they were useless. Two strips of film, however, had been developed, and these consisted of fifty-eight pages of documents, the bulk of which dealt with negotiations for a trade agreement with Germany.

According to Chambers, he had not mentioned the films to his lawyers because he did not know what they contained, and so 'I did not know whether or not they had any bearing on the Hiss case'. When he did know the contents he considered for a time destroying both the films and himself. He decided against neither, and for the safekeeping of the film he chose the melodramatic safety of a hollowed-out pumpkin in his pumpkin-patch.

Since the handing over of the documents, both sides had gone extraordinarily quiet. However, according to Robert Stripling, in his book *The Red Plot Against America*,[2] one of Chambers's lawyers, Nicholas Vazzana, let drop a hint to the Committee that something had happened in which documents were involved.

1. Op cit pp725 and 726.

2. Edited by Bob Considine of the (Hearst) International News Service.

Then on the 1st December a comment appeared in the *Washington Post* to the effect that something 'new and sensational' had happened in the Hiss libel case.

On reading this, Stripling found himself badly wanting to see Chambers once more. He did not want to see him alone, and asked Nixon to go with him. But Nixon was due to sail on a cruise within a few hours. However, he agreed to drive with Stripling to Chambers's Maryland farm.

According to Stripling, as soon as Chambers saw them he said, 'I know why you're here. You were right, Mr Stripling, I was withholding information.' He could say nothing more lest he should be held guilty of contempt, but he admitted that he had 'dropped a bombshell in Baltimore recently. But the first one was nothing compared to the second.'

Because of Nixon's sailing-time the two men dashed back to New York, and Nixon embarked on his cruise. On the 2nd December, Stripling served a subpoena on Chambers requiring him to hand over to the Committee any other material he might have. That night Chambers led the Committee representative and accompanying newsmen to the pumpkin-patch and handed over the films.

As soon as Stripling read the developed film, he radioed Nixon, 'Second bombshell obtained. Contents amazing. Can you get off the boat?' Nixon could and did, and on arriving took charge.

The new evidence was very opportune. The Committee had heard that the Grand Jury, on the basis of Chambers's answers about espionage on the 15th October and his production of the documents on the 17th November, had decided to indict him for perjury. If this happened, Nixon was later to say, their whole case against Hiss would collapse, for their star witness would have his credibility utterly destroyed if he were to be found guilty of perjury, as he must be. A night sitting of the Committee was held with the sole purpose of preventing this, and succeeded.

On the 7th December the Committee sat again in public, under the chairmanship of Mundt. (Parnell Thomas had by this time been indicted for padding his payroll and removed from his offices. He was later convicted, dismissed from his seat in Congress, and jailed.) At this hearing and at subsequent hearings Chambers was questioned about his espionage role while he was a Communist and purported to give full details. The microfilm documents were printed and enlarged and distributed to the press. A number of witnesses were called who allegedly corroborated parts of Chambers's evidence. Others were called who testified that the documents were, in fact, State Department documents.

He was summoned to appear before the Grand Jury and for eight days was questioned by it. On the 11th December Nixon released more copies to the press of the documents Chambers had produced, and announced that he was flying personally to New York to hand the films to the Grand Jury. On the 13th December Nixon appeared before the Grand Jury.

On the 14th December Hiss again appeared before the Grand Jury. Throughout the whole case from The Confrontation on the 17th August until this date Hiss had maintained that he had known Crosley (Chambers) only to the end of 1936; and since the 17th November that he had never passed any documents to Chambers.

On the 15th December, by a majority of two, the Grand Jury indicted Hiss for perjury on two counts. (Note that all the documents produced by Chambers were dated on various days in the first three months of 1938.)

Part of the indictment read as follows:

4. That, at the time and place aforesaid, the defendant Alger Hiss, duly appearing as a witness before the said Grand Jurors,

and then and there being under oath as aforesaid . . . testified falsely before said Grand Jurors with respect to the aforesaid material matters as follows :

Q : Mr Hiss, you have probably been asked this question before, but I should like to ask the question again. At any time did you, or Mrs Hiss in your presence, turn any documents of the State Department or any other Government organisation, or copies of any other Government documents, over to Whittaker Chambers?

A : Never. Excepting, I assume, the title certificate to the Ford.

Q : In order to clarify it, would that be the only exception?

A : The only exception.

JUROR : To nobody else did you turn over any documents, to any other person?

THE WITNESS : And to no other unauthorised person. I certainly could have to officials.

COUNT TWO

2. That at the time and place aforesaid, the defendant, Alger Hiss, duly appearing as a witness before said Grand Jurors, and there and then being under oath aforesaid . . . testified falsely before said Grand Jurors with respect to the aforesaid material matters, as follows :

Q : Now, Mr Hiss, Mr Chambers says that he obtained typewritten copies of official State documents from you.

A : I know he has.

Q : Did you ever see Mr Chambers after you entered into the State Department?

A : I do not believe I did. I cannot swear that I did see him some time, say in the fall of '36. And I entered the State Department September 1, 1936.

Q : Now, you say possibly in the fall of '36?

A : That would be possible.

Q : Can you say definitely with reference to the winter of '36, I mean, say, December '36?

A : Yes, I think I can say definitely I did not see him.

Q : Can you say definitely that you did not see him after January 1, 1937?

A : Yes, I think I can definitely say that.

MR WHEARTY : Understanding, of course, exclusive of the House hearings and exclusive of the Grand Jury.

THE WITNESS : Oh, yes.

That the aforesaid testimony of the defendant, as he then and there well knew and believed, was untrue in that the defendant did, in fact, see and converse with the said Mr Chambers in or about the months of February and March 1938, in violation of Title 18, US Code, Section 1621.

On Tuesday the 31st May 1949, Alger Hiss appeared before the Hon Samuel H Kaufman, District Judge, and a Jury, in the United States District Court, Southern District of New York, to answer these charges.

6

The Revised Chambers Story

The revised story told by Chambers after the production of the documents had necessarily to include descriptions of how Hiss came into the Communist underground and how he handed documents to Chambers for passing on to the Russians. In sustaining his allegations against Hiss, he had necessarily to reveal his own role in the Communist underground. This also necessitated that he should revise some of his previous statements, but in order that the reader may be clear of the complete story which emerged from Chambers's testimony, at the risk of being slightly repetitious, I will recount the revised version from the beginning.

When he first came to Washington it was as a 'functionary' in the Communist underground. Never very good on dates – I suspect deliberately – he said that he could have arrived there in May or June 1934.

In Washington he had met Harold Ware, whom he had already met in New York. At this time Ware was the leader of a fairly large Communist group in Washington, and through Ware he met Hiss, who was a member of Ware's group.

This meeting took place in a restaurant in Washington – which he could not now identify. Also present had been J Peters, head of the American Communist underground. Chambers maintained that he was introduced to Hiss by his underground cover-name Carl. (Questioned on this, he explained that it was the customary practice of Communist intelligence that clandestine leaders should be known only by a single pre-name.)

The reason for the meeting was a proposal that Hiss should

leave Ware's group and transfer to a group which Chambers was to form. This proposal was discussed between the four over a meal, and in the outcome it was decided that Hiss should join Chambers.

A fortnight later Chambers, still known to Hiss only as Carl, called at Hiss's apartment on 28th Street by appointment. He met Mrs Hiss as well as Hiss. Asked to give an account of the conversation on this occasion, he said that it was in general terms since the meeting had been designed purely that he might become better acquainted with Hiss.

At an unspecified date some time later Chambers again called at the 28th Street apartment. This time he could remember at least a part of the conversation. Hiss had told him, he said, that through his position on the Nye Committee, he could obtain State Department documents, and asked whether or not he should do so, and bring them out for copying. He told Hiss that he would have to consult J Peters before making a decision. Peters thought it would be a good idea, and shortly afterwards he instructed Hiss to produce such documents as he could.

Hiss complied. By this time the Hisses had moved to a house on P Street, Washington, and it was there that Chambers photographed the documents, which, according to Chambers, deal with 'some phase of the munitions traffic'.

(It should be noted that the Hisses lived in the 28th Street apartment from the 9th June 1934 to the 19th April 1935, and in the P Street house from April 1935 to June 1936.)

Chambers then explained how he came to occupy the Hisses' 28th Street apartment. He said that when the Hisses took over the P Street house there was still some months of the 28th Street lease to run. The house in P Street was furnished, so they could leave some of their own furniture in the 28th Street apartment and the Chamberses could live there until the lease expired. Since

Hiss had already paid for the lease, Chambers might live there rent free. Chambers accepted this offer.

Describing the move from Baltimore to Washington, Chambers said that Hiss drove to Baltimore in the old Ford roadster, and brought back to Washington in it the Chamberses' baby's collapsible bath, high-chair and one or two odds and ends.

The Chamberses stayed in the 28th Street apartment some two or three months, and then moved back to New York where they lived in the house of Professor Meyer Schapiro on 4th Street. The family went to New York by train and Mrs Hiss drove down with the baby's accoutrements.

They were not comfortable in the Schapiro house, and on telling Hiss he showed them an advertisement for a house at Long Eddy on the Delaware River. Hiss drove them over to see this house one Sunday, but as soon as they saw it they realised that it would not do.

Presently, however, the Chamberses moved to a cottage at Smithton, six miles south of Frenchtown, New Jersey. The owner of the cottage was a Mr Boucot who lived in Smithton. They were accompanied by a friend, a fellow Communist called Maxim Lieber (who incidentally was for a time Trotsky's literary agent though he was himself a Stalinist. At the request of the Party, Lieber, John Sherman, and Chambers formed the American Feature Writers' Syndicate. The plan was to set up a branch office of the Syndicate in Tokyo, under Sherman's personal direction, to act as "cover" for Soviet military intelligence in Japan.") They stayed at Smithton two or three months, and then went to stay with the Hisses in the P Street house.

By this time it had been mooted that Chambers should go to England to work with an operator there. While staying with the Hisses, Chambers said, he broached with Hiss the subject of Mrs Chambers and the baby staying with the Hisses if he were transferred to England. He also testified that it was in anticipation of this trip to England – which did not, in fact, materialise – that he obtained a false passport in the name of David Breen. Asked if he told Hiss about this passport, he said that he had not.

In August 1935 Hiss joined the Department of Justice. Before accepting the invitation to do so, Chambers said, Hiss sought the advice of J Peters, who approved. After further months in the Justice Department Hiss was transferred to the State Department, joining on the 1st September 1936, again with the Communist Party's approval.

Next, Chambers said, he discussed Hiss and the potential he represented, with Colonel Boris Bykov, a member of the Soviet Military espionage, attached to the Russian Embassy in Washington, who was his contact with the Russians. (Chambers said that Bykov's cover-name was Peter, but as this might confuse the reader with J Peters, head of the American Communist underground, I shall refer to him as Bykov.) Bykov found Hiss interesting and asked Chambers to arrange for him to meet Hiss.

The meeting was arranged, and took place some time in January 1937 in New York. This is one of the few occasions on which Chambers declared himself sure of the date, and he explained that he had, a short time before on Bykov's instructions, given Hiss an oriental rug, as a token of Russian gratitude for what he had already done for them.

The meeting with Bykov was, according to Chambers, one of the major developments in Hiss's involvement. I shall be referring to this meeting later in some detail because of the various points of espionage techniques which it raises. For the time being, I will say that Bykov, whose English was poor, and who, therefore, spoke in German which was translated by Chambers, told Hiss that the Soviet Union stood in great peril from the Nazis and Fascists, and that he could be of tremendous assistance if he would pass to the Russians all the State Department documents on which he could lay hands and in particular those relating to Germany, Italy and Japan.

Hiss showed no hesitation whatsoever, so Chambers declared, in agreeing to do what he could. Bykov also asked if Donald Hiss, who was currently with the Department of Labour, and was not to transfer to the State Department until February 1938, could get hold of documents, too. Hiss replied that he did not think that Donald was 'yet sufficiently developed for such work', to which Bykov replied, 'Perhaps you can persuade him'.

Following upon this meeting, Chambers called at Hiss's house once a week or once every ten days to pick up the documents that Hiss had managed to 'borrow' from the State Department. These documents Chambers took to Baltimore – he was, by the way, now living in Baltimore – where they were photographed by Felix Inslerman in Baltimore. When the documents had been photographed he would return them to Hiss at his house, somewhere around one o'clock in the morning.

In this connection, Chambers declared that he believed Hiss had given him a key to the P Street house. On the other hand he could not remember whether he had a key to the house in 30th Street, where the Hisses lived from July 1936 to December 1937, or to their house in Volta Place, where they lived from December 1937 until October 1943.

However, if he could not let himself in, he rang the bell, and either Hiss or Mrs Hiss opened the door and let him in and took back the documents.

(I shall be referring to this in greater detail later.)

All went well until about the middle of 1937 when Bykov told Chambers that the volume of documents being delivered by Hiss was insufficient and must be increased. Chambers told Hiss 'we wished to have the papers brought out every night or approximately every night', and it was further suggested that to help meet the demand some of them 'should be typed as nearly verbatim as possible and some of them paraphrased'. Hiss agreed.

Then there remained the question of who should do the typing. Hiss, said Chambers, told him that Mrs Hiss had always been unhappy at the small contribution she was able to make to the work of the Communist underground, and if she did the typing they could be sure of absolute discretion and make her happy. Chambers agreed.

This new arrangement made no difference to Chambers's established practice with regard to the collection, photographing and returning of the documents. Either he or Felix Inslerman took the documents to Baltimore (after Chambers had collected them from Hiss); they were photographed in Baltimore, and returned, always by Chambers, the same night. The typed documents were photographed and then burnt.

From time to time, Chambers declared, Hiss gave him short handwritten notes referring to documents he had seen, which he considered important, but which he was not able to bring out of the State Department. Sometimes he handed these handwritten over to Bykov just as they were.

On his own admission, after the suicide of his brother Richard in 1926, Chambers had become 'a fanatical Communist'. By the middle 'thirties, however, much of the gilt had begun to wear off the gingerbread, and just as the new arrangement got into full swing he decided to break with Communism. In the autumn of 1937 he talked it over with his wife and began to make certain preparations to meet what then looked like an uncertain and perhaps risky future.

These preparations included his applying for a post in the National Research Project, a Government agency. With the backing of George Silverman and Irving Kaplan, two fellow-

Communists in the US Government, he quickly obtained the job. His application form, on which he gave a number of personal details about himself and particulars of his past work, was dated the 18th October 1937. He entered the Project at once, having taken the oath of loyalty and sworn to defend the Constitution of the United States against all its enemies, but since he had not yet made the break with the Party he continued to collect the documents from Hiss as before, and did not stop doing so until the 15th April 1938.

Also among his preparations for his break with the Party was the purchase of a motor car. In this connection, in November 1937 he borrowed four hundred dollars from Hiss, telling him that he needed the car to help him in his Party work.

The Chamberses were living at this time in Mount Royal Terrace in Baltimore. There, Chambers declared, at Christmas 1937 they were visited by Hiss and Mrs Hiss.

He finally made his break with Communism on the 15th April 1938. His method of doing so was to fail to turn up at his next scheduled meeting with Bykov. Naturally, he stopped collecting documents from Hiss after this date.

Since defectors from the Party were often liquidated by SMERSH, Chambers said that he went in fear of his life during the first months of his break. To throw off pursuit he moved from Mount Royal Terrace to a house in the Old Court Road, Baltimore, the latter being more conveniently placed for observing anyone who approached. He declared that for a year he had slept with a gun always ready to hand. For a few months he had disappeared with his family down into Florida. His sole means of support was some translation work, among which was Dr Martin Gumpert's book *Dunant – Founder of the Red Cross* for the Oxford University Press (New York) and the Bambi story. (He had, by the way, been furloughed from his job with the

National Research Project on the 21st January 1938.)

His final preparation for the break with the Party was to keep back some of the documents he had received from Hiss, which he intended to keep as a kind of 'life-preserver' should he be attacked for leaving the Party. (In a way these documents could be regarded as a "life-preserver" for the Party might hesitate to attack him if they knew he could prove the extent of the Party's infiltration of the US Administration, as he undoubtedly could have by producing such documents, always supposing he had them in his possession. I regard this point as a weak one in Chambers's argument. To have made the "life-preserver" really effective, he should have kept specimens of documents he had received from other sources.) He put these documents, including one he had received from Harry Dexter White, a prominent official in the US Treasury, into an envelope and in May or June 1938 he gave the envelope to his wife's nephew, Nathan Levine, asking him to hold it for him. (The envelope had remained hidden where Levine had put it until he had claimed it in November 1948.)

In June 1938, using the name of David Chambers, he bought 2610 St Paul Street, Baltimore. In December 1938 he called on Hiss and pleaded with him to break with the Party, as he had done. Hiss refused ('with tears in his eyes'). He also went down to Harry White's house – he was driven there by Mr and Mrs Hiss – to persuade him to do the same.

The last time he had seen Hiss was a day or two before Christmas 1938. He called at the Hiss house in Volta Place. The Hisses were out, but a coloured maid opened the door to him. At this moment Mrs Hiss drove up in her car, and he went into the house with her. She left him to telephone to someone, and he believed she was telling whoever it was that he was there. He had a sudden apprehension that the Hisses or their friends were planning to kill him, but before he could leave Hiss came home, and as they talked his fears left him and he accepted an invitation to stay to supper. The visit lasted two hours, and as he was leaving Hiss asked him what kind of a Christmas he expected to have. He replied that he feared it would be a poor Christmas, whereupon Hiss went away and presently returned with a toy rolling-pin for Chambers's little girl.

He next met Hiss at The Confrontation in the Commodore Hotel on the 17th August 1948.

In September 1939, a fortnight or so after the signing of the Molotov-Ribbentrop Pact, Chambers called on his friend Isaac Don Levine (no relation of Nathan Levine), an eminent journalist and anti-Soviet writer. Levine knew of his Communist past, because Chambers had already approached Levine for help in placing some anti-Communist articles (which did not happen because Chambers would not be explicit enough). The Nazi-Soviet Pact had sickened him, he said, and he felt that the time had come when he must do something positive. Levine suggested that he should go and tell Adolf Berle, whom Levine knew, and who was Assistant Secretary of State with responsibility for security.

Berle agreed to see them, and together they went to Berle's house, arriving shortly after Berle had finished dinner. In Berle's garden, while the assistant secretary took notes with mounting excitement, Chambers 'talked'. Ten years later a typed copy of Berle's notes was read into the record.

LONDON   Underground Espionage Agent

(1) *Dr Philip Rosenbliett* – Formerly of 41st B'way, NE

     Dr Grunberg – MD (West 70th, NY)

     Brother-in-law.

     American leader of British Underground C.

     Head in America Mack Moren (alias Philipovich) – allegedly Yugoslav – real name –?

Rosenbliett – in US

connected with Dr Isador Miller – Chemists' Club – 41st Street. Chemist, Explosive Arsenal, Picatinny NJ war 'front' behind Mack Moren existed – in Miller's employ.

Knew Pressman – his alias was 'Cole Philipo' – Introduced him to Mack Moren, buying arms for Spanish (Loyalist) Gov't. –

Pressman – as counsel – helped Moren – made a flight to Mexico with him, forced down at Brownsville, Tex. in late '36, or early '37 – probably fall of '36.

Pressman

Underground organised by the late Harold Ware[1]; Pressman was in his group – (1932–33??). Pressman then in AAA –

Nathan Witt – Secretary of NLRB head of underground group after Harold Ware –

John Abt – followed Witt in that group – Tax Div'n – Dep't of Justice &c now in CIO (M Warr's widow – Jessica Smith Ed Soviet Russia).

Mr Abt – sister : Marion Bacharach – Secretary – Communists from Minnesota.

(Jessica Smith : With Reuters in 1926 – friend of Louis Fischer)

Meeting place : John Abt's house – 15th St.

Charles Krivitsky – alias Charles Kramer – (CIO) worked in La Follette Committee – Physicist.

Vincent Reno – Now at Aberdeen Proving Grounds – Computer – Math. Assist. to Col Zornig (Aerial bombsight Detectors) – Formerly CP organiser under

---

1. Ware, who almost always drove recklessly fast, was killed in a motor accident in 1935.

alias 'Lance Clark'

Philip Reno – in Social Security (??) – was head of Underground Trade Union Group Political Leader

Elinor Nelson, treasurer of Fed Employees' Union – (Fed Workers' Union, CIO – headed by Jane Baker)

Reno – connected with Baltimore Party

organiser – Benjamin (Bundey) Friedman alias Field – then California – then Russia – now organiser for Baltimore & Washington of Above-ground Party – Underground connections –

STATE

Post – Editorship, *Foreign Service Journal*. Was in Alexandria Unit of CP – in 'Underground Apparatus' – Duggan – Laurence – (Member CP??)

(Wadleigh?) Wadley – Trade Agreement Section

Lovell – Trade Agreement Section

Communist Shop Group

Elinor Nelson – Laurence Duggan – Julian Wadleigh – West European Div'n – *Field* – still in –

(Levine says he is out west into IEO)

Then in committee for Repatriation

His leader was Hedda Gompertz

Laughlin Currie: Was a 'Fellow Traveller' – helped various Communists – never went the whole way.

SEC

Philip Reno – used to be

TREASURY

Schlomer *Adler* (Sol Adler?)

Counsel's Office

Sends weekly reports to CP (Gen Counsel's office)

Frank Coe – now teacher at McGill.

  There are two: brothers – One of them in CP's 'Foreign Bureau' – Bob Coe

Known from Peters – formerly in Bela Kun Govt.

  Agricultural Commissariat – called Gandorz (?)

  Then to Russia – then here, in Business Office of Communist paper 'Uj Elori' – then, after 1929 – head of CP Underground, lived in Hamilton Apts., Woodside, LI – under alias 'Silver' – & lectured in Communist camps –

  Friend: 'Blake' of 'Freiheit' – real name – *Weiner*

  American: Polish, Jew –

  Peters was responsible for Washington Sector

  Went to Moscow – where is he now?

  Wife – A Comintern courier –

West Coast – Head: 'The Old Man' – Volkov is his real name – daughter a Comintern courier. He knows the West Coast underground – Residence: San Francisco or Oakland –

Alexander Trachtenberg – Politburo –

  member of the Execu. Committee

  Head of the GPU in US

  Works with Peters –

  Plans for two Super-battleships –

  secured in 1937 – who gave –

  Karp – brother-in-law of Molotov – working with Scott Ferris – got this released –

  Now: Naval Architect working on it, why??

  Field was original contact

  He introduced Duggan to Gompertz (Hedda)

Duggan's relationship was casual –

Shall excuse? – Where is Hedda Gompertz? –

Duggan & Field supposed to have been both members of the party.

Donald Hiss

(Philippine Adviser)

Member of CP with Pressman & Witt –

Labour Dep't – Ass't to Francis Perkins –

Party wanted him there – to send him as arbitrator in Bridges trial –

Brought along by brother –

Alger Hiss

Ass't to Sayre – CP – 1937

Member of the Underground Comm. – Action

Baltimore Boys –

Wife – Priscilla Hiss – Socialist –

Early days of New Deal

NOTE – When Loy Henderson interviewed Mrs Reubens his report immediately went back to Moscow. Who sent it? Such came from Washington.[1]

Berle took the information to Roosevelt, who, apparently, laughed and shrugged the whole thing off. In other words, the President didn't believe the story and was disinclined to waste anyone's time on Chambers's allegations.

Two years later, however, an FBI agent telephoned Chambers

1. On page 469 of *Witness*, Chambers, referring to these notes, says: 'These notes are obviously rambling and garbled. Even I can no longer remember what some of the references mean or how I came to know of them. . . . But if the notes are studied carefully, it will be seen that the essential framework of the conspiracy is here, even down to such details as the fact that Reno was working as Colonel Zornig's assistant at the Aberdeen Proving Grounds. It is equally clear that I am describing not a Marxist Study Group, but a Communist conspiracy.'

at *Time* – he had already joined *Time* before his interview with Berle – and asked to have a talk with him. When the man and a colleague arrived, Chambers said he could not answer any of their questions without first getting Berle's permission, and telephoned Berle who gave it.

Neither the FBI, nor anyone else in Government, had yet heard of the Berle notes. The two had asked to see him because he had been denounced as a Communist by a former friend, Ludwig Lore. He did not know this at the time, concluded that the visit sprang from his interview with Berle, and in speaking to them he went over the same ground, telling them that in 1939 he had forgotten to name George Silverman and Harry Dexter White.

(The authority for this visit is *Witness*, p492, and Chambers's reference to it, though he displaces it by a year, in his testimony before the Committee.)

It was not until 1945 that he was contacted again, this time by a State Department security officer, Mr Ray Murphy, who visited Chambers on his Maryland farm. He repeated to Murphy what he had told Berle, and Murphy made a memorandum of the conversation which was later produced, and accepted by Chambers as a true record of the conversation.

According to this memorandum, he named Harold Ware, Lee Pressman and Alger Hiss as the top leaders of the underground 'in that order'. He also mentioned Harry Dexter White, whom he had omitted to name to Berle. 'Harry White of the Treasury was described as a member at large but rather timid. He put in as assistant in the Treasury Glaser, a member of the underground group, and an Adler or Odler, another Party member.' But he did not mention George Silverman as he claims to have done to the FBI agents who called on him in 1941.

That meeting was on the 20th March 1945. On the 28th August

1946 Mr Murphy saw Chambers again, and went over the same ground, receiving the same answers with one or two additions. 'Harry White was reported to be a member of one of the cells, not a leader, and his brother-in-law, a dentist in New York, is said to be a fanatical Communist.' There was also the following interesting passage: 'The heads of the various underground groups in Washington who met with Peters were the Hisses, Kramer (Krivitsky), Henry Collins, who was either Secretary or Treasurer of the group, John Abt, Lee Pressman, Nat Perlow and Nat Witt. These men met regularly at special meetings. With the exception of Donald Hiss, who did not have an organisation, they headed parallel organisations. But they did not know the personnel of the different organisations.'

But there was no mention again of George Silverman.

There was also one other significant omission in the two accounts Chambers gave to Murphy.

Under the section headed STATE in his notes, Berle has –

(Wadleigh?) Wadley – Trade Agreement Section.

In the two memoranda of his conversations with Chambers in March 1945 and August 1946, Murphy makes no mention of Wadleigh. Indeed, Chambers did not refer to Wadleigh again until *after* he had made his first appearance before the Committee. In *Witness* he has written '. . . when I was testifying before the House Committee on Un-American Activities in 1948, and I foresaw that I might have no choice but to go into the espionage story, I was disturbed by the fact that I could not remember the name of one of the sources in the State Department. I telephoned Levine.[1] The name I had forgotten, he was able to inform me by glancing at the jottings he had made in 1939, was Julian Wadleigh.'[2]

1. Isaac Don Levine, who had accompanied Chambers to Berle and had taken independent notes of what Chambers told Berle, and preserved them.

2. Op cit p470.

Chambers's appearance before the Committee did not take him unawares. 'From 1946 through 1948, special agents of the FBI, too, were frequent visitors. Usually they were seeking information about specific individuals. . . . At that time I had no way of knowing that they were checking a story much more tricky than mine – that of Elizabeth Bentley.'[3]

3. *Witness*, op cit p510.

7

The Hiss Story

Alger Hiss's story was maintained by him throughout. Except for one or two small corrections of errors in memory, which any man might commit after twelve or fourteen years, it never varied from the statements he made to FBI special agents Daniel F X Callahan and Frank G Johnstone, on the 4th December 1948; that is, before he appeared before the Grand Jury. The statement was introduced in evidence at his trials, and I reproduce it here since it contains everything pertinent and has the great value of being in Hiss's own words. His attorney, William L Marbury, was with him, and the FBI agents told the court that throughout the four-hour interview Hiss had been wholly co-operative and forthcoming. After the introductory paragraph the statement read as follows:

'At the request of my attorneys, MR WHITTAKER CHAMBERS, defendant in a libel suit filed by me in the United States District Court for Maryland at Baltimore, was called for an examination before trial. This examination took place in MR MARBURY's office, 1000 Maryland Trust Building, Baltimore, Maryland, on November 4, 5, 16, and 17, 1948, but a portion of the time stated was consumed in taking depositions from MRS WHITTAKER CHAMBERS.

'On the afternoon of November 17, 1948, in the course of the pre-trial examination, Mr Chambers introduced sixty-five letter-sized pages of typewritten material and four small sheets of paper bearing handwritten material. For simplification, hereafter in this statement the sixty-five pages will be referred to as the large documents and the four smaller pages as the small documents.

'In introducing these documents, Mr Chambers stated that they had been received by him from me for transmittal to a Russian named Colonel Bykov. Photostatic copies of the documents introduced by Mr Chambers at the pre-trial examination were first exhibited to me by Mr Marbury in New York City on November 18, 1948. The agents have exhibited to me similar photostatic copies of these documents, which I am satisfied are photostatic copies of the same documents introduced by Mr Chambers under the above circumstances. I had read portions of the court reporter's transcription of the deposition of Mr Chambers and I know from the portion of that transcription which I have read that on November 5, 1948, Mr Chambers was asked whether he had ever obtained any documents from me for transmittal to the Communist Party and he replied that he had not.

'With reference to the large documents, I would say from a cursory examination of them that they appear to be authentic copies of United States State Department documents or summaries of such documents. From the date standpoint, these documents appear to be restricted to a period extending from about January to March 1938. At that time I was Assistant to the Assistant Secretary of State, the Honourable Francis B Sayre. Documents similar to these normally passed over my desk for perusal prior to being referred to Mr Sayre. I do not have any independent recollection of having seen any of these documents or the documents summarised while I was in the employ of the State Department. By and large, these do not appear to be documents of a very highly confidential nature, and would not have been treated in the State Department with any special precautions at that time, according to security regulations in effect then.

'With reference to the smaller documents, three of the four

pages appear to be in my handwriting. The fourth page, consisting of five handwritten lines, may or may not be in my handwriting, but it does not look to me as if it were.

'I have learned from talking with Mr Marbury and from reading the abovementioned deposition that Mr Chambers claimed these documents and others like them were obtained by me from the State Department, and that I took them to my home, where typewritten copies of the larger documents were made on a typewriter in my home by either my wife or me. Chambers claimed that I then returned the documents to the State Department files. The agents have told me that Mr Chambers claims that on some occasions I turned over the actual State Department documents to him, upon which he would have photographic copies made in a manner unknown to me, and then would return the original documents to me for replacement in the files of the State Department.

'I deny that any of the above claims of Mr Chambers is true. I also deny that I ever gave the originals of the small documents to Mr Chambers at any time for any purpose whatsoever.

'From Mr Marbury and the deposition, I have also learned that Chambers claims he introduced me to a Russian named PETER, whom he claims later to have discovered was Colonel Bykov. Chambers claims that this meeting took place on the mezzanine floor of a movie theatre in Brooklyn, New York. Chambers claims that after the meeting, the three of us took a long walk and that during the conversation while walking, Colonel Bykov asked me if I could obtain documents for him from the files of the State Department. Chambers claims that I agreed to co-operate in this regard with this Colonel Bykov and that as a result of this oral agreement, I later produced the documents mentioned above. I deny that any of these claims of Chambers is true. I have never met and had never heard of any Russian named Peter or Colonel

Bykov until I was told of the testimony given by Mr Chambers.

'During the period from about June 1, 1936, to about January 1938, I resided with my family at 1245 30th Street, NW, and subsequent thereto, until sometime in 1943, at 3415 Volta Place, NW, both Washington, DC. During the period from 1936 to sometime after 1938, we had a typewriter in our home in Washington. This was an old-fashioned machine, possibly an Underwood, but I am not at all certain regarding the make. Mrs Hiss, who is not a typist, used this machine somewhat as an amateur typist, but I never recall having used it. Possibly samples of Mrs Hiss's typing on this machine are in existence, but I have not located any to date, but will endeavour to do so. Mrs Hiss disposed of this typewriter to either a second-hand typewriter concern or a second-hand dealer in Washington, DC, sometime subsequent to 1938, exact date or place unknown. Prior to this typewriter coming into the possession of my immediate family, it was the property of Mr Thomas Fansler, Mrs Hiss's father, who was in the insurance business in Philadelphia. Mr Fansler lived the later years of his life on Walnut Street in Philadelphia, but is now deceased, having died in the early 1940s.

'Until I met Mr Chambers face to face at a hearing of a sub-Committee of the House Committee on Un-American Activities on August 17, 1948, in the Hotel Commodore, New York City, I did not know whether I had ever previously met Chambers although I thought that newspaper pictures of him looked somewhat familiar. At that time it had not occurred to me that he might be George Crosley. On August 16, 1948, before a sub-committee of the House Committee on Un-American Activities in Washington, DC, I stated that Chambers might be a person previously known to me as George Crosley. Upon confrontation on August 17, I realised that Chambers is identical with a man

I had previously known as George Crosley. I first met Chambers as George Crosley when I was employed as Legal Assistant to the United States Senate Munitions Committee, commonly known as the Nye Committee, about December 1934, or January 1935. Chambers came to me in my office in the Senate Office Building in Washington, DC, and stated that he was a freelance magazine writer and desired information for a series of articles on the munitions investigations. At that time I was on loan to the United States Senate Munitions Committee by the Agricultural Adjustment Administration of the United States Department of Agriculture, where I was regularly employed as Assistant General Counsel. At that time Chambers gave me the impression that he was making periodic trips to Washington from New York City, where, I assumed, he lived.

'Between the turn of the year 1934–5 and the spring or summer 1936, Chambers contacted me perhaps six or eight times, always for the purpose of obtaining information for his magazine articles or discussing the problems of the munitions investigation. Chambers was merely one of the number of newspaper men, writers, and students, who came to see the employees of the Munitions Committee about the Committee's activities. I deny that I ever saw or heard from Chambers from the spring or summer of 1936 until we confronted one another at the above-mentioned hearing in the Commodore Hotel in New York City.

'During the period when Chambers periodically contacted me in Washington, he occasionally borrowed small sums of money from me, totalling twenty to thirty dollars, four or five dollars at a time. He appeared to be hard-pressed financially. Also during this period, under an oral agreement, I sub-let my apartment at 2831 28th Street, NW, Washington, DC, to Mr and Mrs Chambers and child. Prior to sub-letting this apartment to Chambers, at sixty dollars a month, I and my family moved into a three-storey house at 2905 P Street, NW, Washington, DC. Before taking occupancy of the abovementioned apartment, Chambers and his family spent two or three days on the third floor of my home on P Street. My recollection is that Mr Chambers informed me that some of his furniture or other possessions had not arrived on time; that his family and he could not, therefore, move into the 28th Street apartment immediately.

'We put them up as a favour to sub-tenants. As far as I know, Chambers and his family lived in the apartment on 28th Street until the expiration of my lease on July 1, 1935. During subtenancy of my apartment on 28th Street by Chambers, I continued to pay the rent and Chambers has never reimbursed me nor has he repaid the small loans. He did on one occasion give me a rug which he said he had received from some patron of his and while they were staying at my house on P Street, his wife painted a portrait of my young stepson, Timothy Hobson, who was then eight years old. I have no clear recollection of the date of my last contact with Chambers, which probably occurred in the spring or summer of 1936, while I was employed as an attorney by the Department of Justice in Washington, DC. However, I do recall the contact quite well and on this occasion I told Mr Chambers that I did not think he would ever repay the loans he had made, and that I thought we should discontinue any further contacts. I also want to state that Chambers never paid me any funds for any purpose. During the period mentioned above when Chambers was contacting me, most of the contacts were made by him at my office or for lunch, with the possible exceptions that he may have contacted me on several occasions at my residence.

'In connection with the sublease of the apartment, I occasionally lent Mr Chambers the use of my 1929 model Ford roadster. This Ford was dark blue in colour, had a rumble seat and a small trunk (boot) in the rear, and bore District of Columbia plates. Sometime in the summer of 1935, I acquired a 1935 Plymouth, two-door sedan, a demonstration model. Sometime after acquiring the Plymouth I told Mr Chambers he could have the Ford roadster which I had been told had a trade-in value of twenty-five dollars when I bought the Plymouth. If Mr Chambers used the Ford in the fall of 1935 or the winter of 1935-6, it must have been only occasionally because I recall it sitting on the streets of Georgetown during a number of months of that winter. Sometime before I left P Street, about May or June 1936, Chambers took permanent possession of the car under circumstances I do not now exactly recall. At that time or earlier I had turned over to him the certificate of title, I did not have the Ford after that date and have never seen it since. I have no recollections of the occasion on which I signed the certificate of title. The certificate of title for the Ford bears what appeared to be my signature witnessed under the date of July 23, 1936, by Marvin Smith, a notary public, who was also employed in the same office where I was in the Department of Justice. I can only assume that the certificate was brought to me in my office in the Department of Justice by someone who said that I had disposed of the car without completing the legal technicalities and that I signed under those circumstances and asked Marvin Smith to witness my signature.

'As far as I can remember, the above represents a history of all my contacts and dealings with Mr Chambers to date which appear to me to be pertinent.

'I have made an effort personally, through counsel and private investigators, to locate other persons who knew Chambers as George Crosley during the period from the turn of the year 1934-5 to the spring or summer of 1936, but without success.[1]

1. Hiss, asked to produce people on the Nye Committee who might have known Chambers as Crosley, named a Mr Steve Raushenbush, a Mr Robert Wohlford, and a Miss Elsie Gullender.

I have discovered one person who claims that Chambers at one time submitted for publication under the name George Crosley, but that was during a much earlier period, approximately 1926. Both Mr and Mrs Chambers state that during this time they were living in Baltimore under the name of Lloyd Cantwell, as I have learned from the deposition. This search, of course, excepts Mrs Hiss and Timothy Hobson, my stepson, who was only eight years old during the abovementioned period. This search included inquiry among known fellow employees of the United States Senate Munitions Committee, and persons that either my wife or I introduced Chambers or his wife to under the name of Crosley. This search to confirm my statement that Chambers was going under the name of George Crosley during the above-mentioned period will continue and if successful, the Government will be advised.

'I deny that I am now or ever have been a member of the Communist Party or that I have ever attended any Communist Party meetings. Likewise, I deny that I have ever been a member of a Communist Party espionage apparatus or underground group in Washington, DC, or anywhere else, at any time.

'I never saw Mr Chambers at any time in the State Department. I know of no opportunity had by Mr Chambers, either in my office in the State Department or in my residence or any other place, to obtain any documents pertaining to State Department business, during the period 1937–8 or any other time. I do not know whether Chambers personally obtained these documents from the State Department or whether he had some confederate who co-operated with him in obtaining the documents.

'I assert that Mr Chambers's entire story, with respect to the matters covered above that relate to me, is a complete fabrication except as otherwise indicated in this statement by me.

'I do not know what motive Mr Chambers could have for

making these accusations against me, but I think that a thorough examination of Mr Chambers's life and personal background might throw some light on this problem.'

8

The Trials of Alger Hiss

When Alger Hiss was brought to trial in the Southern District Court of New York on the 31st May 1949, though charged with perjury, the real issues were espionage and treason. The perjury charges were merely a device; even if he had admitted espionage on the basis of Chambers's accusations, he could not have been tried on a charge of espionage and its inevitable co-charge of treason, for in American law the Statute of Limitations covers both these crimes. The offences alleged by Chambers were, on his evidence, committed eleven years previously, well outside the operation of the Statute.

The prosecution was led by John F X McGohey, United States Attorney, but the burden fell on Thomas F Murphy, Assistant United States Attorney, now Judge Murphy. The defence was led by Lloyd Paul Stryker, assisted by Edward C McLean, Harold Rosenwald and Harold Shapero.

Murphy and Stryker dominated the whole proceedings, each in his own individual way. Stryker was in the tradition of an F E Smith, though lacking much of that great advocate's dignity. Murphy was a man of spirit, who realising that Stryker might attempt to act him off the scene, was equally determined not so to be dominated. Within a few minutes of Chambers, the first witness, being called to the stand they were hard at it. Alastair Cooke, in *A Generation on Trial*, describes the scene thus:

Mr Murphy leaned forward very slightly.
'As a result of that trip and what you saw, did it leave any impression with you?'

Mr Stryker jumped to his feet.

'I object to that. Suppose it did?'

'Sustained,' said the judge.

Chambers quietly replied : 'It left a profound impression.'

Mr Stryker was on his feet again striding towards the witness. He thrust a red face at Chambers. 'Just a moment, you heard the judge rule.'

'Just a moment, Mr Stryker,' the judge protested.

Mr Murphy was not to be left out. 'Wait a minute,' he shouted, 'I object to Mr Stryker arguing with the witness.'

'Mr Stryker,' the judge admonished, looking hard at him, 'please address your remarks to the Court.'

'I am sorry,' said Mr Stryker with his head up.

Mr Murphy stretched himself.

'And you, too, Mr Murphy?' said the judge.[1]

In closing his opening speech to the jury, Murphy made what I believe all lawyers would stigmatise as a colossal blunder, for that is how it appeared to me, a layman.

Begging the jury to be patient when he put Chambers on the stand, for unless they listened to him with the greatest attention, they would not be able to test his credibility, he told them, 'I want you to examine Chambers. I want you to listen attentively; watch his conduct on the stand; watch the colours of his face; watch the way his features move, because *if you don't believe Chambers then we have no case under the Federal perjury rule.*'

He was, of course, stating the law to them. To sustain a charge of perjury you must have one witness plus corroboration. If either fails, then the charge fails. Here the witness was Chambers and the corroboration, the documents and films. Unfortunately, if Chambers failed to impress the jury with his credibility,

1. p122.

then the corroboration material was worthless; for the whole value of the material, whatever its nature might be ultimately proved to be, depended on whether Chambers was speaking the truth when he said that Hiss had given him the documents. There was no other living witness who could support this contention; therefore the only course for the prosecution to take was to show Chambers to be a wholly truthful witness, thereby proving automatically that Hiss was a liar. And so, this being the only course open to the prosecution, all the previous testimony of all concerned – the testimony before the House Committee, the Grand Jury, the Baltimore pre-trial examination of Chambers, his subsequent testimony before the House Committee once more – all this would have to be gone into again.

Since this was the line the prosecution must take, the defence would naturally set out to prove Chambers a liar, for Hiss could not *prove* that he had not given the documents to Chambers. As it turned out, Mr Murphy was faced with a considerable task, for it was on record already that Chambers had lied several times over. To take just one point:

(1) To Berle he had not mentioned espionage.
(2) To the FBI agents in the alleged interview he had not mentioned espionage.
(3) To Mr Ray Murphy he had not mentioned espionage at either the March 1945 interview or at the August 1946 interview.
(4) He had denied espionage at the House Committee hearings.
(5) He had denied espionage, and so perjured himself, to the Grand Jury on the 14th October 1948.
(6) On neither the 4th November nor the 5th November 1948 had he mentioned espionage.

There were other points, too, on which the records showed that he had lied, and not only in this case, but throughout his life, and to such an extent that it might be possible for the defence to show medically that he was a pathological liar, or as nearly so as made no difference (this was, in fact, attempted).

So, both the prosecution and the defence went over all the testimony which had been given before in various places – Chambers's knowledge of the intimate details of the Hisses' private lives, their houses, their possessions, their activities, the Chamberses' private lives, Chambers's Communist activities, his claimed espionage relationship with Hiss and much more besides.

It is not my intention here to go through the whole of the evidence. (To the reader who would like to acquaint himself with the course and nature of the trials, I can do no better than to recommend to him Alastair Cooke's *A Generation on Trial*,[1] and, for a more exhaustive study than I find necessary for my purposes, Earl Jowitt's *The Strange Case of Alger Hiss*.[2]) For my purposes a consideration of certain cardinal points only is necessary, and to those I shall refer under specific headings. But to round off Hiss's experiences here: the trial which opened on the 31st May 1949 closed on the 7th July 1949 with the jury unable to agree on a verdict.

A new trial was ordered, and opened at the same venue on the 17th November 1949. Judge Kaufman – who was later to come under the lash of Richard Nixon's criticism for having shown himself too well disposed towards the defendant, which a reading of the trial transcript disproves—was replaced by the Hon Henry W Goddard, who apparently, again from the transcript, favoured Chambers. Mr Thomas Murphy once more bore the burden of the prosecution, but Hiss had shed the flamboyant Lloyd Stryker and was this time defended by the quiet, phlegmatic Claud B Cross.

1. Alfred A. Knopf, New York, 1952.
2. Doubleday, New York, 1953.

Once again all the familiar ground was traversed. Again Chambers's past lies were brought up; once again Hiss refuted all the charges Chambers made against him. The same witnesses took the stand, answered their questions and stood down. But there were some variations – Mr Cross brought up several points unraised by Mr Stryker, such as the length of time Chambers had spent with the FBI before the trials, and the questions of the keys to the various Hiss houses, among others.

The trial closed on the 21st January 1950. The jury consisting of seven women, of whom one was the forewoman, and five professional men, were able to reach a verdict. They found Hiss guilty, as charged.

Four days later, Judge Goddard imposed the maximum sentence of five years' imprisonment. Hiss asserted his innocence to the last. He still does.

9

The Meaning of the Verdict

The verdict against Hiss meant two things. First, that the jury accepted Chambers's account of what had happened, and rejected Hiss's; second, that the jury, and all those who agreed with it, had made Hiss the victim of one of the greatest frame-ups perpetrated by an intelligence service, worthy to rank with the outstanding cases of history, to which I shall be referring shortly.

As I have said earlier, I came to my study of the source-material with an open mind. I had probably read a quarter of the fifteen hundred-odd pages of the First Trial transcript – having previously read the transcript of all the proceedings before the House Committee – when I began to realise that I was moving in Hiss's direction, and this was not on account of an emotional motivation, but because the unadorned words on the pages – the transcripts record only the spoken words, there are no 'stage directions', no indication of the emotional responses of any of the participants – revealed to my way of thinking the utter falseness of Chambers's story.

Nor did this conclusion of mine spring from those passages in the evidence which proved Chambers to have lied again and again, though I would not be completely truthful if I maintained that I was not partially influenced by them. But, maintaining my determination to be swayed only by what emerged from the transcripts, I nevertheless found myself sensing that there was something basically wrong with Chambers's confessions.

During my reading of the House Committee transcripts I had

been surprised by the ignorance displayed by the Committee members of classic espionage techniques and practices. (Over and over again, Chambers, when relating his activities in the Communist underground – a clandestine organisation even if not engaged in espionage follows certain basic techniques that are common to the operations of an espionage network – told of actions and events that ran absolutely counter to the accepted techniques.) My first reaction to this apparent Committee ignorance, however, was that I was expecting too much from Parnell Thomas, McDowell, Rankin, Hébert and Mundt. With the possible exception of Mundt, it was clear from the record that these members of the Committee were for the most part completely out of their depth, no matter what subject they might have been investigating, except, maybe, the ramifications of political manœuvring. On the other hand, I did expect Richard Nixon, who revealed himself to be far and away the most intelligent member of the Committee, to have a general – if only a very general – idea of how the practical side of a clandestine organisation is operated. Yet he showed no sign of sensing that there was something odd about several points in Chambers's story. The same is true of Robert Stripling, the Committee's chief investigator.

I gained the same impression of this lack of appreciation of clandestine techniques from the trial proceedings, too. Neither Thomas Murphy, the prosecutor, nor Lloyd Stryker, the defence leader in the First Trial, nor Claud Cross, the defence leader in the Second Trial, gave any indication at all of having even an elementary knowledge of clandestine techniques. To give one example, cross-examining Chambers about the method used to collect the documents from Hiss, have them photographed and returned, Cross extracted from him the information that he would pick up the documents at the Hiss house.

CROSS: And you got them some time between four thirty and six o'clock?

CHAMBERS: That is my recollection.

Q: And that was done during the time you were working for the Government?

A: I believe so.

Q: When you got back with the papers at night did you ring the bell?

A: I do not believe so.

Q: You don't believe so?

A: No.

Q: How did you get in?

A: My recollection is that I had a key.

Q: You had a key to what house or houses?

A: I believe I had a key to all those houses.

Q: You believe you had a key to all those houses?

A: That is right.

Q: And the key to all those houses had been given you by Mr Hiss?

A: Right.

Q: And when you came back at any time between twelve and two am you would take out the key Mr Hiss had given you, unlock the door and go in?

A: You are right.

Q: And then you would go back to Baltimore?

A: Yes, I believe that is right.

Q: When it was as late as two o'clock in the morning?

A: That is right.

Q: And then you would get up in Baltimore and get to work in Washington in the WPA at nine o'clock in the morning?

A: That is also right.

Q: And did you go by train from Washington or by car or boat?

A : I believe I went by train.

Cross then reminded Chambers of what he had testified on this point at the First Trial and at the Baltimore pre-trial, reading both passages into the record.

From the First Trial:

Q : All right. Now we come back to the key. Would you say it is to your best recollection that you did not have a key to the 30th Street house or the Volta Place house?

A : I am simply not sure. *I am quite sure I did not have one to the Volta Place house* (italics added) but I may have had one to the 30th Street.

From the Baltimore pre-trial:

Q : Now, you would get a document from Mr Hiss at five thirty, you would take it out and give it to the man on the street corner and get it back about one o'clock (am). Then what did you do with it? Go to Mr Hiss's house with it?

A : Sure.

Q : How did you get in?

A : I would have got in by ringing the doorbell, I presume.

Q : Who would answer the bell?

A : Either Alger Hiss or Priscilla Hiss.

Q : Did you stay long on those occasions?

A : I doubt if I would have stayed very long then.

Q : Well, how long?

A : Oh, perhaps for half an hour's chat. Perhaps not.

Q : At one o'clock in the morning?

A : Yes.

Q : And that was what customarily took place?

A : To the best of my recollection.

Cross then asked him if he knew that the Volta Place house did not have a door-bell, but a knocker, and drew from him the information that he had visited the Volta Place house with the

FBI on the 2nd February 1949, ie three months before the beginning of the First Trial, by which time the knocker had been replaced by a bell.

Cross used this point merely to show how Chambers had changed his story twice, thus making it a credibility test, instead of showing by it that such behaviour, two or three times a week, would be contrary to the best espionage techniques. I shall be going into this in greater detail later. However, there were several other points, which, I believe, if treated from the espionage technique angle, would have been more effective with the jury.

There were a number of points raised by Chambers – and this excludes the all important one of the documents and typewriter – which Hiss found difficult to refute. Chief among these were the old Ford roadster, the gift of the rug, a loan of four hundred dollars alleged to have been made to Chambers in the autumn of 1937 for the purchase of a motor car, and a trip to Peterboro, New Hampshire, which, Chambers declared, he had taken with the Hisses in early August 1937.

The car I have already referred to several times. To summarise, however, Chambers claimed that Hiss, on buying a new Plymouth sedan, had insisted, against his own and Peters's better judgment, on giving the car to the Party for use by a 'poor organiser out West'. Hiss said that this was not true, but that he had given the car to Chambers as Crosley.

The car had first been brought up by Chambers at the secret session of the 7th August 1948 when he had been questioned about his knowledge of the Hisses' private lives. When Hiss was questioned about the car at his secret session on the 16th August, the interrogation had gone:

NIXON: You gave this Ford car to Crosley?

HISS: Threw it in along with the apartment and charged the rent and threw the car in at the same time.

168

NIXON : In other words, added a little to the rent to cover the car?

HISS : No, I think I charged him exactly what I was paying for the rent and threw the car in, in addition.

STRIPLING : You just gave him the car?

HISS : I think the car went right in with it . . .

At the final hearing at which Hiss appeared on the 25th August, this matter of the car and its disposal occupied the major part of the proceedings. Records were produced to show that if Hiss had given Crosley the car – had 'thrown it in with the apartment' – he must have been without a motor car for three or four months, which he knew was not correct.

But worse, from Hiss's point of view, was to come. Having forced Hiss into a situation where he could only say that to 'his best recollection' he had had both cars for a time, that he remembered the Ford sitting in the streets of Washington in the snow, and that he had even been fined on its account, before he passed it to Crosley, the Committee produced records from the Motor Vehicle Bureau which showed that Hiss had transferred the title of the car to the Cherner Motor Company in Washington on the 23rd July 1936, who had transferred it to a William Rosen the very same day. They also produced the notary public, who had notarised Hiss's signature on the transfer, a colleague of his in the State Department. Though this disproved Chambers's statement that Hiss had driven it to a car-lot owned by a Communist, untold harm was done to Hiss by the incident because he maintained that he had ceased to know Crosley by July 1936.

However, Stripling, writing about the case later, concluded, 'For, in fact, though Rosen was traced and produced, and was found to have been a member of the Party until his expulsion from it in 1929, he took refuge in the Fifth Amendment, and the only thing he would say was that he did not know J Peters or Hiss.' Though the defence were later to discover that the signature on the transfer was not Rosen's, by then it was too late to do anything about it.

I believe a clue lies in the last sentence of Chambers's statement in reply to Nixon on the 7th August. '. . . Peters knew where this lot was, and he either took Hiss there, or gave him the address and he went there and, to the best of my recollection of his description of that happening, Hiss left the car there and simply went away and the man in charge of the station took care of the rest of it for him. I should think the records of that transfer would be traceable.' It fits in with my theory that Hiss left the car standing in the Washington streets, that Chambers, who had often driven the car and had been given the use of it by Hiss, saw it and took it to the Cherner Company on the 23rd July 1936, telling them that Hiss was the owner, and that someone had gone to the Department of Justice with a certificate of transfer for Hiss to sign.

For Hiss, when the incident of signing the certificate was recalled to him, remembered that the document had been brought to him while he was working at the Justice Dept., that he had signed it on the spot and had asked his colleague Marvin Smith, who was a notary, to witness his signature – an act he would hardly be likely to commit if he intended giving the car to a Communist. A significant circumstance bolstering my theory is that when the vice-president of the motor company gave evidence at the Second Trial he said that although there was no gap in his company records, there was no record of the taking over of the car by the company. This suggests to me that Chambers handed over the car to a Communist employee of the Cherner Motor Company, who made no record of the transfer, because he knew it was to be picked up later that day by another Communist. Chambers knew that Hiss had signed the certificate on that day, knew that this certificate could be traced, and knew that Hiss would be embarrassed by the whole incident. He was very right, for I think that with the exception of the documents, this car was Hiss's greatest embarrassment.

The second point was an oriental rug which Chambers had given the Hisses. It was Hiss who had first introduced the rug at the secret session of the Committee on the 16th August. Nixon had asked, 'Even though he didn't pay his rent, you saw him several times?' To which Hiss replied:

'He was about to pay it and was going to sell his articles. He gave me a payment on account once. He brought a rug over, which he said some wealthy patron had given him. I have still got the damn thing.'

When Chambers was questioned about the rug he said that it had been given to Hiss on Colonel Bykov's instructions as a token of the Soviet Union's gratitude for the help he had already given. Hiss was not to be the only recipient of a rug; Chambers was to order four. Chambers went to his friend Professor Meyer Schapiro, and asked him to order the rugs from the Massachusetts Importing Company and pay for them, and that he would reimburse Schapiro as soon as he had the funds. Schapiro agreed. At the trials, Schapiro gave corroborative evidence and his cancelled cheque for six hundred dollars – they were quite valuable rugs – was produced. It carried the date 23rd December 1936. A receipt showed that Schapiro had taken delivery of the rugs on the 29th December 1936.

As I have already said, Hiss consistently claimed that he had lost sight of Chambers in the middle of 1936. But if the rug Hiss received was one of the 'Schapiro four', this could not be true.

Hiss's recollection of the delivery of the rug was this. Chambers arrived at the 30th Street house one day in the spring carrying the rug. In the First Trial, while being cross-examined by Murphy, Hiss was in one of his rather sarcastic moods. (A short time previously, while answering questions on the payment of the gas, electricity and telephone bills, Hiss had said that he paid them. 'But supposing,' said Murphy, 'Chambers had had some long-distance charges, you would have ran [sic] after him for that?' Hiss replied, 'I would have run after him.' Pausing slightly, Murphy then said, 'You didn't mean to correct me in that way?' Hiss said, 'No, I was merely giving my testimony.' Murphy then asked: 'Is it merely your desire to use whatever correct grammar came to your mind?' Hiss retorted: 'It was merely that I was testifying in my normal speech.') Now Murphy asked him if Chambers was merely standing at the door. Hiss replied that he could not recall if it was he who answered Chambers's ringing. 'I thought you said he came to the door,' said Murphy. 'That,' replied Hiss, 'is the way he entered the house.'

Hiss went on to say that Chambers said that he wanted Hiss to have the rug as a gift. It had been given to him. As Chambers was by this time in total arrears for the rent of the apartment, Hiss took it that the rug was in part settlement of that debt.

Mrs Hiss and their coloured maid at the time, Cleite Catlett, corroborated Hiss's impression that they had had the rug while living in the P Street house. Since they did not leave this house until July 1936 according to this evidence the rug must have been given to them before July 1936. But Schapiro's evidence showed that, if it was one of the 'Schapiro four', it could not have been made until January 1937, and this supported Chambers's contention of 'late association'.

For some reason or other, the defence did not produce the rug in court. Murphy made great capital of this in his final speech to the jury at the Second Trial, putting the blame for its non-production on the defence. 'The thing to do when you are unjustly accused is to come and prove that that is not the rug. The Government can't go and subpoena rugs belonging to the defendant. . . . Bring it here. Let us look at it. Let the expert look at it. . . . He could not bring the rug in because that proves Count II' (ie that he had known Chambers in 1937). But Murphy could have challenged Hiss to produce the rug, and Hiss could not have refused without producing exactly this effect.

One wonders, therefore, just as much why Murphy did not challenge Hiss to produce the rug, as at Hiss's failure to produce it. (I have been unable to elucidate this failure.)

I believe that Chambers gave Hiss the rug when Hiss said he did, and that, therefore, it was not one of the 'Schapiro four'. No attempt was ever made to find out who received the other three. Gifts of some kind are a traditional gesture used by Russian intelligence. Alan Nunn May, for example, received gifts of whisky for divulging atomic secrets. Julian Wadleigh, who was to feature fairly prominently in the trials, certainly received a rug, though not one of the 'Schapiro four'. Chambers, therefore, may have had instructions to buy rugs before Bykov told him to purchase these four. There would be no opportunity for Bykov, or any other member of the Russian intelligence, to verify that the people proposed by them actually received the specified gifts. Chambers would know this, and being in debt to Hiss, might have thought he could stop Hiss from pressing him for payment of rent by giving him a rug intended for someone else. But it was a great pity that the rug was not produced and presented in Court to the dealer for his inspection for I believe the failure to do so, after Murphy's telling reference to it, was a significant factor in the jury's deliberations.

The third point which undoubtedly counted against Hiss was the four hundred dollar loan which Chambers said Hiss made to him when he was preparing to break with the Party and he wanted to buy a motor car. *The first time that this was mentioned was at the First Trial*; there was not a whisper of it at the Committee hearings, in the Grand Jury proceedings, or the Baltimore pre-trail. This last omission is extremely odd, for both Chambers and Mrs Chambers were ruthlessly interrogated about minute details of their private lives by William Marbury.

The four hundred dollar loan Chambers produced seemingly out of the blue in his testimony at the First Trial, when he told this story. Knowing that he was going to break with the Party soon, and fearing the consequences, he wanted to buy a car so that he could be mobile, which would help him to get away from any members of SMERSH sent to liquidate him. By this time, he already had a car of his own. The price of the new car was 812 dollars 75 cents. The trade-in allowance on his old car was 325 dollars, leaving him to find 487.75 dollars in cash. He could afford to put up 87.75 dollars himself, and he declared that Hiss lent him the balance of 400 dollars, which he had never repaid.

In support of his contention, the prosecution subpoenaed Hiss's bank account, and it was found that, in fact, a few days before Chambers bought his new car – 23rd November 1937 – Hiss had withdrawn 400 dollars. The Hisses' explanation for this withdrawal – which left only a few dollars in the account – was that Mrs Hiss was intending to make a number of purchases for the house, and that instead of drawing a number of cheques, one for each purchase, she preferred to draw the lump sum and pay cash.

As Hiss pointed out, 'We showed from our bank records other examples of withdrawals of comparable sums from the savings account to meet non-recurring family needs. For example, the following June (1938) we drew out 150 dollars, in September had withdrawn 400 dollars. The Hisses' explanation of this amount of 200 dollars. We had before this made it a practice to build up a savings account of several hundred dollars for such purposes. When we moved to Washington, the records showed,

our New York savings account was 652 dollars, which we transferred to our Washington checking account in the fall of 1935
in anticipation of larger-than-usual expenditures.'[1]

At the First Trial the defence had been taken rather off-guard
by this story. As Murphy put it in his closing speech to the jury,
the only thing they had not heard about previously was this loan,
and 'They fumbled, they dropped the ball on that one'. At the
Second Trial they did not fumble.

Cross was able to introduce the fact that the FBI had had,
under subpoena, photostat copies of all Hiss's bank statements,
and he got Chambers to admit, 'I had been talking with the FBI
every day except weekends for a matter of some months . . .'

CROSS: You say you were staying in New York and spending
practically the entire time with the FBI for a matter of
months except for weekends?

CHAMBERS: I believe that is correct.

Q: Beginning when?

A: Beginning during the Grand Jury proceedings of last – I
think it was December 1948.

Q: And extending down to what period?

A: Extending to about sometime in March I believe, of 1949.
(He later changed this to May.)

Q: And, of course, you have spent considerable time with them
since?

A: I have seen them from time to time.

Q: During that time would it be fair to say that you were spending
some five or six days a week with them?

A: Fair, I believe would be a liberal estimate.

Q: The entire day?

A: From about 10 30 in the morning until 4 or 4 30 in the
evening.

1. *In the Court of Public Opinion*, op cit p240.

Q: Over a period of three or four and a half months? (Actually five and a half months.)

A: Yes, with time out for lunch.

In another connection, he admitted, what the defence already knew, that he had been going round Washington with the FBI visiting the houses in which the Hisses had lived, and had questioned the Hisses' maids, Cleite Catlett and Martha Pope. On his own confession he spent an estimated seven hundred and fifty hours or thereabouts with the FBI mostly in their offices. He may well have had an opportunity of seeing the Hisses' bank statements, and noticing the four hundred dollar withdrawal a few days before the date on which he bought the new car, had seized on it and concocted the story of the loan, hoping to bolster with it his contention that Hiss and he had met later in 1937 – the subject of Count II – this period in which he declared Hiss had been passing him documents.

This theory receives some support from Mrs Chambers herself. Though the 'loan' was not produced by Chambers until the First Trial, the new car had been mentioned at the Baltimore pre-trial. (Chambers was not present at Mrs Chambers's examination; he was busy deciding what to do with the documents and films.) It had been paid for by Mrs Chambers and registered in her name. During a series of questions about the Chamberses' family finances she was asked:

Q: How about the automobile?

A: Mother comes in there some place. I don't know. Mother did help us out at various times. She probably gave us the money for that.

Q: Well, now, how many times did your mother give you money? That is your husband's mother, is it not?

A: Yes. That I cannot tell exactly. Mother helped us out in many ways very often.

Q : Well, now, you can give us some idea? Up to this point I have had the impression that you lived off . . . entirely what he was paid by the Communist Party?

A : Yes.

Q : Now you tell us that his mother helped him out. Now, to what extent did she help him out financially?

A : I cannot tell you that. I don't know. But in the instance of the car, for instance she did help on that.

Q : You think she gave him money to pay for that?

A : I think so. I am not certain. These things were taken care of by him, and I don't know. I can only tell you what I know.

Despite the reasonable explanation of the withdrawal of the four hundred dollars given him by the Hisses – Murphy made great play of the point in his cross-examination of Mrs Hiss – the fact that they were unable to produce any supporting evidence (who could after eleven or twelve years?) seems to have weighed with the jury. I think the business of the Ford roadster and now another motor car combined to bring the jury to give more credence to the Chambers story than to the Hiss story.

The fourth point on which the defence did not score was an alleged trip which Chambers said he made with Mr and Mrs Hiss to Peterboro, New Hampshire. The transcript of the Second Trial on the incident reads as follows :

CROSS : And where else did you go?

CHAMBERS : In 1937 Mr and Mrs Hiss and I took a trip beyond Peterboro, New Hampshire.

Q : Where did you go?

A : We went to a place where Harry Dexter White, the monetary expert of the Treasury, was living.

Q : You saw him, did you not?

A : I saw Mr White.

Q : And did the Hisses go with you that far, or what?

A : The Hisses drove me up to the entrance of the drive which ran into the property Lauchlin Curry, I believe, and they waited there in the car while I went inside and spoke to Mr White. I was with Mr White, I should think, about fifteen or twenty minutes. Then I came out. Mr White insisted on walking down the drive with me and I could not get rid of him and he obviously wanted to see how I had arrived there. Mr and Mrs Hiss had got out of the car and were standing beside it and we came alongside the car and I got rid of Harry White and went back to the car.

The background to the incident is this. Chambers said that on the 9th August 1937 – this is one of the few specific dates given by him in the whole of his testimony anywhere, which is, in itself, very suspicious – he came over from Baltimore, where he was living, to Washington and joined up with the Hisses, who were then living at the 30th Street house. (No one, either on the prosecution or defence side, ever thought to ask him why he had gone from Baltimore to Washington to join the Hisses, when the Hisses' route from Washington to New Hampshire lay through Baltimore, and it would have been simpler to have picked him up there.) The total distance to be covered was five hundred miles, and this meant that they would have to stay somewhere for the night.

Chambers said that they stayed at a tourist guest-house, Thomastown, Connecticut. They arrived there after dark, and Chambers said that he thought they registered. The next morning they went on to Peterboro, having called on Harry White on the way. The night of the 10th August they spent at another guest-house, called Bleak House. On the 11th August they motored back to New York, a distance of three hundred and fifty miles. Asked why New York, Chambers said he thought the Hisses had said they wanted to stay at a little hotel there where they had spent their honeymoon. (As a matter of fact the Hisses spent their honeymoon, a weekend only, at a farm on the Eastern Shore of Maryland.)

Challenged to explain why he remembered the date of this trip so well, he said that while in Peterboro they had all gone to a performance of *She Stoops to Conquer*.

Despite the fact that the FBI was never able to identify the tourist guest-house at Thomastown; despite the fact that the Hisses were able to prove that they had been at Chestertown, on the Eastern Shore of Maryland, during the first two weeks of August; despite the fact that the proprietress of Bleak House could not remember having accommodated the Hisses and Chambers, and produced her register in which their signatures did not occur, in support; the jury were obviously influenced by Chambers's allusion to the performance of *She Stoops to Conquer* being played in Peterboro at the time he alleged they were there. This factual touch was, I think, what tipped the balance on this point.

I am also personally of the opinion that it was another such touch which weighed heavily in the jury's considerations. It will be recalled that Chambers maintained that throughout their entire association the Hisses had known him only as Carl, whereas the Hisses maintained that they knew him only as George Crosley. Chambers was pressed on this question of name at both trials. The Committee had challenged Hiss to produce the other persons who had known Chambers as Crosley, and he failed, though he was later able to show through the testimony of a publisher of pornography that Chambers had once used the name George Crosley as a pseudonym. The publisher, Samuel Roth, declared that he had published some erotic poems written by Chambers under the name of Crosley; but this was in 1924, long before Chambers met Hiss. The defence was also able to prove – and, indeed, Chambers admitted – that at various times in his life he had used other names: Lloyd Cantwell, David Breen, Charles Adams and John Kelly.

He claimed that although the Hisses and he and Mrs Chambers had spent some time in the Hisses' houses; that the Hisses had visited their house; that they had gone on trips together; and so on; neither of the Hisses had ever asked what the Chamberses' surname was. No evidence was introduced either in the Committee hearings or in the two trials that anyone had ever seen the Hisses and the Chamberses together, or that anyone had ever met Chambers when he was actually living in the Hisses' house; a remarkable situation, for it seems to show that the Hisses were a desperately lonely couple who had no friends, which was not true. At one point in the Second Trial, Claud Cross, Hiss's attorney, was pressing Chambers on this, and so got Chambers into a corner, that more or less in desperation, so it seemed, Chambers said he had once been introduced by the Hisses, one evening while they were dining in a Georgetown restaurant, to a woman friend of theirs by the striking name of Plum Fountain. The subsequent interchange went:

CROSS : You were introduced to her?

CHAMBERS : That is right.

Q : And you can't tell what name you used?

A : That is right.

Q : Well, you know it wasn't Carl, don't you?

A : It certainly was not Carl.

Q : Was it Mr Crosley?

A : I don't believe so.

Q : Well, what name was it?

A : I have no idea, as I have told you.

Q : You wouldn't say it was not Mr Crosley, would you?

A : I think it very unlikely.

Q : But you will agree that some name must have been used?
A : Yes.

And he agreed, too, that the name was not Chambers, or Breen, or Cantwell. A little later, Cross suddenly asked him what name he had used when living in the 28th Street apartment he sub-let from the Hisses.

CHAMBERS : I have never been able to remember.
CROSS : May it have been Crosley?
CHAMBERS : It may have been.

Though he would say nothing more definite than 'It may have been' this was a virtual admission that he had used the name Crosley during the period April 1935 to July 1936. But the jury must have felt that an admission drawn from Hiss that the Hisses did have a friend with the unusual name of Plum Fountain was too circumstantial for the Chamberses' account of the meeting to be an invention.

Though time and time again, the defence were able to show that there were many flaws in Chambers's account of the private life of the Hisses, numerically these flaws were outnumbered by the correct descriptions. There were times, too, when the prosecution was able to cast very grave doubts on the correctness of the defence's rebuttal evidence. This must have weighed with the jury as well, for it does not seem to have struck them that Chambers had found sources which could have provided him with the sort of testimony he gave about the Hisses' private lives – for example, friends of the Hisses who were secret Communists – the self-confessed members of the group, perhaps – public reference books, and the FBI with whom he spent five and a half months before the First Trial.

10

The Documents and the Typewriter

The evidence of the documents and films was, on the face of it, one overwhelming declaration of Hiss's guilt. They proved, taken at their face value, not only that Hiss could be guilty of espionage, but was certainly guilty of perjury on Count II – that he had not seen Chambers after the 1st January 1937.

The documents fell into two groups:

i Four slips of paper in the handwriting of Alger Hiss.

ii The typewritten documents.

The filmed evidence consisted of photographs of original State Department papers.

i *The Handwritten Documents*

These four documents were rough notes derived from State Department documents. They were dated 28th January 1938, 2nd March 1938, 3rd March 1938 and 11th March 1938.

Documents 1 and 3 had been written on poor quality notepad paper, such as you may find on any desk for the purpose of making notes. Documents 2 and 4 were probably written – it was never shown definitely that they were – on pieces of State Department notepaper with the letterhead 'Department of State Assistant Secretary' torn off. All four bore the marks of folding.

Explaining how they came into his possession, Chambers said, 'From time to time Hiss also gave me small handwritten notes. These notes were about documents which had passed under his eyes quickly, and which for some reason or other he was unable to bring out, but which he thought were of some importance.

I would either turn over these documents directly to Colonel Bykov, or would have them photographed and then turn over the photographs.'

Hiss's explanation was quite different. (He did acknowledge that they were in his handwriting.) He was assistant, at this time, to the Assistant Secretary of State, Francis B Sayre. Documents coming into the office for Mr Sayre first of all arrived on Hiss's desk, having been put there by one or other of his two assistants. Hiss read the documents through and decided whether each document as it stood should be sent to Sayre, or whether he need not be troubled with it at all. Having reached his decision, Hiss marked the documents accordingly.

Sometimes Hiss would give Sayre oral reports on important or significant parts of dispatches and telegrams. It was customary for him to have a working-lunch with Sayre at Harvey's Restaurant twice a week, and over the meal he would discuss with his chief such documents as he thought ought to be brought to Sayre's attention, but with which he need not be bothered.

Such an arrangement was necessary, for the volume of incoming documents was heavy – often there would be in the region of two hundred telegrams a day, and Sayre, with the other duties of his office, could not be expected to read every one. Hiss did read every one, and as he read he would make notes on a slip of paper. These notes would be very brief, sometimes so brief that he could not understand them himself, and if this happened he would expand them so that when he came to Sayre, he would not fumble over the meaning. It was this procedure, Hiss declared, which was responsible for the notes being in different coloured writing.[1] After he had reported to Sayre, the

1. In Nos 2 and 3, the top part of the note was written in blue chalk, the bottom part in lead pencil. In No 4 Hiss had used blue pencil and then put in various explanatory words or phrases in lead pencil.

notes would be thrown into the wastepaper basket for subsequent destruction.

The contention of the defence was that these four documents were these rough aide-memoires made by Hiss; the contention of the prosecution was that they were notes made by Hiss for transmission to Chambers when, for some reason or other, he could not take the documents out of the office.

Document 1

M.28

Tel. from Mary Martin widow/Hugh Martin formerly employed for special work by Legation at Riga. Remember well Rubens while working for Hugh, be strict if needed, write Lib. Cong., Law Div.

This note referred to a telegram sent to the State Department by US Ambassador in Moscow, Loy Henderson.

Have received following telegram from Mary Martin widow of Hugh Martin formerly employed for special work by Legation at Riga.
(GREY) 'Remember well Rubens while working for Hugh, be strict if needed; write Library of Congress, Law Division. Signed Mary Martin.'
(END GREY)[1]

'M.28' on Hiss's note meant 'Moscow, 28th January', the date on the telegram.

1. In 1938 the State Department was using four codes – D, the most confidential, C, less confidential, B, less confidential still, A, merely confidential. If part of a telegram had been through some public process – in this case the Latvian and Russian telegraph services, it was put in another code – the Grey Code – so that the secrecy of codes D, C, B and A would not be broken.

The story behind the telegram was this. A couple travelling on American passports, known variously as Rubens or Robinson, had been arrested by the Russians. For weeks the Russians had held them incommunicado, and the Secretary of State, Cordell Hull, began to press the Kremlin for permission for US Consular officials to visit the couple. Various articles appeared in the press, and it was in response to these that Mary Martin telegraphed the Ambassador.

As this was a subject for Sayre, Hiss felt he should be informed. But at the trials Sayre could not remember whether he had seen either the original or the Hiss note.

In connection with the Reubens case, it will be recalled that Berle's notes of his talk with Chambers in 1939 (see page 145) contained the following:

NOTE: When Loy Henderson interviewed Mrs Reubens his report immediately went back to Moscow. Who sent it? – Such came from Washington.

This point was never taken up with Chambers at either of the trials, though Hiss was asked by his attorney what he knew about it, and he replied: nothing. He was not challenged by the prosecution. But unless Chambers was inventing the information he had given Berle, there must have been someone in the State Department who sent Henderson's report on the interview with Mrs Reubens to Moscow.

With regard to the Hiss note, it is quite plain that it has no intelligence value whatsoever. Even if the Kremlin could crack the Grey Code, they would have learned nothing more than they must have already known. The report of the interview is quite a different matter, however, and it is odd that Chambers should have held on to this little, unimportant note instead of producing a copy, either typed or on film, of the more valuable report.

Document 2

30 Potez - 63
A latest type
  light b p
About March 2nd US Embassy in Paris cabled that although France was permitting shipment of military supplies to China via Indo-China only to fill existing orders, it was understood that this restriction was being liberally construed. For instance the Military Attaché had learned that China had recently placed an order in France for thirty Potez-63 planes, one of the latest French light bomber-pursuit types.

This was a digest of a long telegram from the American representative in Paris, sent in two parts, on 2nd March 1938. (Incidentally, Hiss made a slip – the original read 'Naval Attaché', Hiss wrote 'Military Attaché'.)

The words '30 Potez-63. A latest type light b p' were in blue chalk. The rest was in lead pencil. This document bears out Hiss's testimony that he sometimes expanded brief notes.

The Hiss note refers only to the first part of the telegram. The information in it could have been of only mild interest to the Russians. The second part of the telegram, however, contains a passage which would have been very interesting to the Kremlin. In fact, as Hiss comments, 'In all the State Department Documents that appeared in the trials (fifty-eight pages of microfilm, papers and seventy-two documents of many more pages that were copied or summarised in the typed material) this *was the one passage of vital interest to the Russians.*[1] The Japanese army

1. *In the Court of Public Opinion,* op cit p262. The italics are Hiss's.

chiefs realised that today the Japanese people are worked up to a pitch where they will accept any sacrifice in prosecution of war; that if this patriotic fervour is allowed to subside it will be extremely difficult to whip it up again; and that therefore advantage should be taken of the situation to strike against Russia. Furthermore, these military chiefs are convinced that they will be able to wage a successful war against Russia while holding the Chinese in check on their flank with little difficulty. My informant added that this was also the view of many French military officers.'

The implications of the omission of this passage are almost too apparent to need setting out. Had Hiss prepared this note for Chambers he could not have left out this vital paragraph.

Document 3

3
Chatfield N A
whether decided escalate or not would not change plans for cruisers this year and in any case new battleship would not be laid down before end of current year
(Written in blue chalk)
March 3. Johnson US Chargé at London cabled that Lord Chatfield had told Naval Attaché that whether escalation was eventually decided on or not he would not change his plans for cruisers this year and in any case new battleships would not be laid down before the end of the current year.
(Written in lead pencil)

This referred to a telegram sent on the 3rd March 1938 by Mr Herschel Johnson, US Chargé d'Affaires in London. It had a mild interest for the Russians, who might be interested to know that the British were intending to keep to their cruiser construction schedule for 1938, but were not going to lay down any new battleships that year.

Much was made of the fact that Hiss had practically written out this note twice. He explained that often a day or two elapsed between his receiving the telegram and reporting to Sayre, and the first part did not contain all the relevant facts. In any case, since the first part contained the information interesting to Russia, why bother to write it out twice?

Document 4

Mar 11. Gauss US Consul at Shanghai cabled that military observers estimated that over 7,000 reinforcements with considerable quantities of heavy artillery had landed at Woosung during past 2 weeks. Over 50% believed destined for the Southern Tsinpu front, the rest to be distributed between Wuhu, Hangchow and along the lines of communication.

This was written in blue chalk with additions made in lead pencil. It referred to a telegram sent in Grey Code and *en clair* on the 11th March 1938 by the US Consul in Shanghai, which he repeated to Hankow and Peiping. It would have been of interest to the Russians, but not vitally so.

The one striking question about these four notes is: if Hiss made them for Chambers for onward transmission to Moscow, he must have been genuinely mad to have given them in his own handwriting to someone who could – though a practised courier would not – have lost them. It would have been the rashest kind of act for a man involved in espionage. Admittedly Hiss, if he was guilty of spying, had not been trained in espionage security techniques, but the most ordinary common sense would have told him that he was laying himself open to discovery, however remote the chance might be. No man in his position would take such a risk.

ii *The Typewritten Documents*

The typewritten documents consisted of sixty-five typed pages all produced on the same typewriter, allegedly an ancient Woodstock belonging to Mrs Hiss, with the exception of one document, which a prosecution expert witness was to say was typed either on a Royal or an Underwood typewriter. The composition of these papers is very interesting.

It will be recalled that in explaining why these documents had been typed, Chambers had said that Bykov had decided that there must be an increase in the documents transmitted by Hiss, and that to increase this flow some should be typed in the intervals of Chambers's visits. Bykov told Chambers that some of the documents should be copied verbatim when this seemed desirable, but that others could be summarised.

As Hiss so rightly points out in his book: 'The typed pages included some verbatim copies of official papers, including cables. They also included a number of summaries of documents, or brief quoted excerpts. There was no rational classification which would explain why this differing procedure was followed by the typist . . . lengthy as well as short cables were copied verbatim.

'On the other hand, short as well as long cables were summarised. In other words, cables of comparable interest and length were summarised or elaborately copied in full quite arbitrarily. . . . Another arbitrary feature of these papers was that some pages contained several summaries or excerpts in full, while others contained only a few lines of the same kind of material – brief summaries of cables of the same or closely following dates being put on separate pages. Again, some copies placed date, salutation, and signature as in a facsimile reproduction of the original; others had an informal summary of the date, place of origin, address and sender and then quoted exactly the full text of the message. . . . And in content the documents selected and the passages chosen for excerpting were not of a kind likely to have been of special interest to the Russians.'[1]

One of the most striking features of the sixty-five typed pages was that *twenty* of them were taken up with a verbatim reproduction of a State Department paper subtitled *Need for New Policy in Economic Development of Manchukuo*. It contains many columns of figures and a description, in very great detail, of the warehouses of a Manchukuo company. It was a dull document from any point of view, and practically worthless as an espionage effort; by which I mean that the Russians would find more than a brief summary of its main conclusions all that was necessary and would deplore the time and effort spent on copying it verbatim.

According to State Department records the original of this strange document had been in Sayre's office from the 16th February to the 11th March 1938. During these twenty-four days, Hiss must have had ample opportunity to have taken it from the office. In this period Chambers would have called for documents three times, or at least twice. Why then go to the trouble of copying it verbatim by typewriter? It just does not make sense.

The one document that was not typed on the Woodstock typewriter was based on originals which did not pass through Hiss's office at all. This was Government Exhibit No 10, and was a nine-page summary of the very delicate relations between Japan and the United States as a result of the bombardment of the American gunboat *Panay* by the Japanese in 1937. The date of the original document was January 1938. State Department records tended to show that it went only to the Far Eastern Division.

1. *In the Court of Public Opinion*, op cit pp269 and 270.

But there was one other document which, though typed on the Woodstock typewriter, was also shown by the records to have gone only to the Far Eastern Division. This was Government Exhibit No 13, a verbatim report of an interoffice memorandum which dealt with some newspaper reports concerning a Japanese official who was on his way to America with the task of raising three hundred million dollars.

About Exhibit 10, Chambers at first insisted that he had got it from Hiss. When it was pointed out that it had been typed on a different typewriter, he said he thought he may have got it from Harry Dexter White of the Treasury (by now dead); and finally, when it was shown how very unlikely it was that White would have had access to the original, he lamely claimed that he 'believed it was given to [him] by Mr Hiss', but could offer no explanation why it should be typed on a different typewriter.

iii *The Filmed Documents*

These consist of fifty-eight pages of photographed documents. Most of them dealt with American negotiations for a trade agreement with Germany. They originated in the Trade Agreement Section, and since trade agreements were part of Sayre's interests were passed to his office, where Hiss had access to them.

Now in the Trade Agreement Section Henry Julian Wadleigh worked. Wadleigh had been named by Chambers in his talk with Berle in 1939, and he was to admit that he was one of Chambers's sources for documents. He gave evidence at both trials, and at the Second Trial he testified that he had passed so many documents to Chambers that he could not be absolutely sure about specific documents. He could not be sure that he had not given the Manchukuo report to Chambers, but he did identify a number of documents which he could, and probably did, pass out.

In relation to the Manchukuo report, since Wadleigh had

access to it and was passing papers to Chambers, it is of very significant importance to note that Wadleigh was never instructed by Bykov or anyone else to increase his output by typing documents. How was it, then, that it came to be copied on Mrs Hiss's Woodstock typewriter? Chambers did not testify that he had himself asked Mrs Hiss to copy it. And it has to be remembered, too, that Mrs Hiss though she had taken a typing course at college was by no means an expert, whereas the layout of the Manchukuo document was so intricate that it could only have been copied by an expert typist.

To support the contention that Wadleigh did pass at least one of the filmed documents to Chambers, one of the documents had been photographed from a carbon copy. In the typing, the typist had written *division* for *divisions*. In the original which went to Sayre's office and was handled by Hiss, the missing 's' had been added in ink. The correction, however, had not been made on the carbon photographed by Chambers's photographer, Felix Inslerman of Baltimore. When the prosecution suggested that a carbon might have gone to Sayre's office as well, the defence produced a former State Department official, who deposed that at that time it had not been customary for a carbon as well as the original to be sent to Sayre's office. The carbons were kept on file in Wadleigh's office.

But there were other documents that refuted Chambers's contention that they had all come from Hiss. In his closing speech to the jury at the Second Trial, Hiss's attorney said: 'I call to your attention Exhibit 11. Exhibit 11 is a summary or excerpt from sixteen underlying State Department documents. In other words, you had to have sixteen documents or informative copies of sixteen different cablegrams, to have written the four pages that make up Baltimore Exhibit 11. No 2 on this list did not go to Mr Sayre's office. Now, if No 2 did not go to

Mr Sayre's office and wasn't available to Mr Hiss, how in the world could he have typed the full four pages of Exhibit 11? Whoever did it had to have all of the underlying documents . . .

'I will take another one, Exhibit 42. Forty-two is only two paragraphs. The second did not go to Sayre's office, which would mean if you count up the underlying documents, I think about twenty out of some seventy-two.

'Now the significant thing about this schedule is that an informative copy of all these documents that form the basis of these Baltimore typewritten documents either went to Trade Agreements, where Wadleigh was stealing papers, or the Far Eastern Division from where we knew the Baltimore Exhibit 10 was stolen . . .'

Against this, the prosecution set the point that some of the documents were dated after Wadleigh had been transferred to Turkey. Anyway, there was the typewriter, sitting there before them in the court. They had heard the experts say that the documents had been typed on that very typewriter – and who had produced the typewriter? The defence itself.

iv *The Typewriter*

The history of the typewriter is a very interesting one.

Mrs Hiss's father, Thomas Fansler, an insurance broker, had been the original owner of the machine, and had given it to his daughter. Mrs Hiss could not recall exactly when she took possession of it, but said that she certainly had it in 1933. This was shown to be the case, because the prosecution produced a letter which she had written on the machine on the 30th January 1933. It was also certain that she still had the machine in May 1937, for the prosecution also produced a letter applying for admission to a course at the University of Maryland, dated the 25th

May 1937, which was written on it. Note, it had been in their possession when Chambers had lived in the 28th Street apartment.

By 1937, however, the typewriter was practically worn out, according to the Hisses. Hiss says in his book that in 1948 both he and Mrs Hiss were quite unable to remember how or when it was disposed of.

Naturally, when Chambers produced the typewritten documents, the FBI set up one of the most intensive searches ever. If the typewriter had been the Boston Strangler it could not have been searched for more diligently. No fewer than thirty-five special agents combed Washington alone – as Mr Stryker commented, 'They shook down the city of Washington to a fare-thee-well' – but they could not find it.

Nor could Hiss's investigators find it either, until one day in the spring of 1949, Mike Catlett went to Donald Hiss, and told him he had heard there was a search for a typewriter and that he might know where it was. (Mike was the son of Cleite Catlett, the coloured maid who worked for the Hisses when they were living in the P Street, 30th Street and Volta Place houses; that is, from April 1935, to some time after the 29th December 1937, though her employment had not been continuous.) Donald Hiss took Mike to see Edward McLean, one of Hiss's attorneys, who told him to do what he could to trace the typewriter. Mike went to work, and after many leads, eventually traced the machine – Woodstock No 230099 – in the possession of one Ira Lockey, who said he had taken it in payment for a removal job he had carried out.

It was Perry (Raymond) Catlett, Mike's younger brother, who had remembered that the Hisses had given them an old typewriter, with a number of other cast-offs, at the time of one of the Hisses' moves. The great point about the date of the gift of the typewriter was that if the Hisses did part with it when they moved to the Volta Place house, on the 29th December 1937, they could not have typed Chambers's typewritten documents on it in the first three months of 1938. The prosecution, therefore, made a great play of the date, but at the First Trial could not shift Mike Catlett from his dating of the gift by the Volta Place move.

Between the trials, however, the FBI, by Perry's account, put him through a grilling about the typewriter, which ended with his signing a statement, in which he had apparently said, 'I can't remember whether they gave me it before or after they had moved to Volta Place, they could have lived in Volta Place for several months before they gave it to me.' Confronted with this when he took the stand, Perry declared, 'I did not tell [the FBI agent] that they gave it me after they moved in Volta Place. That is a mistake. He wrote that himself.' But the damage was done. When it came to making a choice of whom to believe between the FBI and a self-exposed muddled-headed coloured boy . . .

In her testimony Mrs Hiss maintained that she gave the machine away because it was no longer in working order. The keys stuck and the ribbon became mussed up. But on this occasion Mrs Hiss did not show up very well, because she seemed to have some difficulty in describing what was wrong with it. When Murphy asked her why she had not had it repaired, she could not produce a really satisfying answer.

However, there was a good deal of evidence to support her contention that the machine had been practically a wreck. Perry Catlett declared that the keys jammed so badly when he received it that it was hardly usable. A Sergeant Roulhac, brought all the way from Alaska, testified that when he was living with the Catletts the typewriter was kept in a junk room, and anyone who felt like a bit of fun could bash away on it, though without much result. He had done so, and he had seen Perry do so, and Perry's girl-friend.

Presently the Catletts parted with it, and Edward McClean's investigation showed that it had passed through a number of hands before it eventually came to Ira Lockey. Lockey testified that he saw it sitting out in a yard in the rain in 1945. His daughter was learning typing, and since during the war it was impossible to buy typewriters, he had asked the then owners, for whom he had carried out the removal, if he could have it in payment for his work. After his daughter married, she had no further use for the typewriter, and his son took it. The son let his small daughter 'peck on it some . . . but she never did much with it because the keys would stick on it. That is just where it stayed, because no one ever used it – it was in such bad condition'. In fact, as soon as he had got it, he realised he had not got much of a bargain, 'it was in such bad condition that I didn't think it was worth-while to have it repaired'.

Now, bearing this evidence in mind, there was one strange thing about the Woodstock 230099 produced in court. Mr Murphy made a dramatic gesture and called an FBI man to sit down at the typewriter there in the courtroom before judge and jury, and asked him to type a few lines. Without any difficulty whatsoever the agent rattled off a line or two of typing *on a machine allegedly in such bad condition* that it had to all intents and purposes been abandoned by its last owner.

Only one expert was called to testify about the vital question of whether or not the typewritten documents and the Hiss Standards – as the letters admittedly typed by Mrs Hiss on her Woodstock were called – were typed on the same machine; and he was a Government expert, named Feehan. With an almost melodramatic display of apparatus, the chief of which was a number of greatly blown-up letters from the Standards and the

Chambers documents, he declared that in his opinion both Standards and documents (except the odd-man-out) were typed on the same machine.

The defence seemed to be as ignorant of the techniques of comparing documents as the House Committee – and the defence – had been about the techniques of espionage. For Lloyd Stryker did not cross-examine Feehan, nor call in defence experts in rebuttal; and what is even more remarkable at the Second Trial, Claud Cross behaved in exactly the same way, and this despite the fact that at this trial Murphy radically changed his strategy and instead of concentrating on 'guilt by association', concentrated on the evidence of the documents.

In February 1967, Dr Meyer Zeligs, a Californian psychiatrist, published a book called *Friendship and Fratricide*,[1] a psychiatric study of the case. It created quite a furore in America and was harshly attacked by one or two eminent reviewers. The book was the result of six years' close study of Hiss (from personal contact), of Chambers as revealed in his writings and his behaviour and what he said to the Committee and the trials, and questioning of everyone he could find who had ever had anything remotely to do with the two men or the case. In connection with the defence failure to call their own experts, and with the more extraordinary failure of Stryker and himself to cross-examine the Government expert, Mr Cross wrote to Dr Zeligs, 'I wanted to cross-examine Mr Feehan, but my associates advised against it and I followed their advice. I could never understand why Mr Feehan did not have someone type from the Woodstock typewriter in the courtroom and make his comparison with the Baltimore Document. Instead, in rebuttal Judge[2] Murphy had a typist type something with the Woodstock typewriter in the

1. Andre Deutsch, London, 1967.

2. Mr Murphy is now a judge.

courtroom marking the typing as exhibits, and then in his argument told the jury that they did not need an expert; that they could tell for themselves whether the typing just made was the same as the Baltimore documents. He practically requested them to send for the typewriter as soon as they got in the jury room, which they did. As to the examination of Mr Feehan, my judgment then, and now is, that I think an examination of all of his working papers would be illuminating.'[1]

Despite the fact that the defence had shown that Hiss could not have had access to some of the documents (which made Chambers's claim of the accessibility of the rest doubtful); despite the fact that the defence had produced the typewriter (a stupid thing to have done if Hiss knew that the documents had been typed on it); and despite the fact that Julian Wadleigh confessed to handing Chambers documents for transmission to the Russians, and the strong indications that Chambers had another 'source' in the Far Eastern Division of the State Department; the jury accepted Feehan's evidence, and this, taken in conjunction with the *doubtful* points still remaining in Hiss's defence against 'guilt by association' undoubtedly influenced them in returning a verdict of Guilty on both counts.

On the 25th January 1950 Judge Goddard sentenced Hiss to the maximum for perjury provided by the law – five years' imprisonment. Hiss immediately lodged notice of appeal. The basis of the appeal could only be that provided also by the law – in other words, only the evidence and conduct of the Second Trial could be submitted for the Appeal Court's consideration.

On the 7th December 1950 the appeal was denied. The opinion handed down, however, in the view of Hiss's legal advisers contained flaws, and though a rehearing of a case is practically never granted in America 'we felt that Judge Chase's misconcep-

1. *Friendship and Fratricide*, op cit p369.

tions about the case were so grave that we should seek a rehearing at which these misunderstandings could be corrected.' This request was also denied early in January 1951.

The Supreme Court of the United States has set very strict limits to the cases it will hear. As Hiss describes it, 'Unless an important constitutional question or the construction of a Congressional statute is involved, or unless two of the appeals courts in different parts of the country are in disagreement, or the case raises some other legal issue likely to affect numerous other cases or individuals, the Supreme Court will not pass on the case at all. . . . Despite the Supreme Court's strict limitation of its jurisdiction, my counsel and I believed that the case presented issues that warranted its review. . . . However, the Supreme Court was unwilling to review the case.'[1]

Having been on ten thousand dollar bail for fifteen months, therefore, Hiss went to prison on the 22nd March 1951.

Now, before Judge Goddard had passed sentence, Hiss had asked to be allowed to make a short statement. His request was granted and he said, 'I would like to thank your Honour for this opportunity again to deny the charges that have been made against me. I want only to add that I am confident that in the future the full facts of how Whittaker Chambers was able to carry out forgery by typewriter will be disclosed.'

That this was what had happened seemed to Hiss the only feasible explanation. At that time he had at the back of his mind and Chambers himself, or one of his agents, had typed the documents, the forgery element resting in Chambers's action in charging that Mrs Hiss had typed them; in other words that Chambers had forged not Mrs Hiss's handwriting, but her typewriting.
forged not Mrs Hiss's handwriting, but her typewriting.

What no one connected with the defence side of the case

1. *In the Court of Public Opinion*, op cit pp361 and 362.

realised at this time was that the documents need not have been typed on a typewriter that had belonged to the Hisses. This is evident in the fact that they accepted without demur the evidence of the prosecution's expert witness, calling no expert of their own. Whether the prosecution side realised that it is possible to construct a typewriter which will produce the idiosyncrasies of another typewriter so faithfully – if produced by experts in this line of business – that examination of typing done by such a machine can deceive the experts, has never been disclosed. On the other hand, there are indications that the prosecution realised that there was something peculiar about the Woodstock 230099, as I will presently show.

Hiss has described in his book how, while the appeal was being prepared, the search for new evidence went on with an even greater intensity than before. The case had been brought on so quickly after the indictment by the Grand Jury that the defence lawyers had not had time 'to follow up every lead'. Even with a Second Trial necessitated by the hung jury of the first, the time had still proved too short.

After Hiss had gone to prison these activities still continued. 'Experts in typewriters, in document analysis, in the chemistry of paper and in metallurgy made exhaustive tests.'[1] In charge of these investigations was a New York lawyer, Mr Chester Lane, whom Hiss had known at the Harvard Law School and in his subsequent career. Hiss had asked him to be his 'attorney of record' during the preparation of the appeal.

As a result of Chester Lane's discoveries, it was decided to file a motion for a new trial on the basis of new evidence. The motion was filed on the 24th January 1952, one day before the expiry of the period set under American law for such a motion to be filed. Under American law, a motion for a new trial has

1. *In the Court of Public Opinion*, op cit p363.

to be assessed by the judge who heard the case and passed sentence. In this case it was Judge Goddard. 'In spite of the effect of the new evidence which, my counsel and I were convinced, completed the demolishment of Chambers's charges, Judge Goddard denied the motion,' Hiss has written in *In the Court of Public Opinion*.[1] He has also set out there relevant extracts from Lane's affidavits submitted to Judge Goddard, and it is on these that I base my following account.

At first, Lane believed that the Hiss Standards and the Chambers documents had been typed on the same typewriter. Feehan had based his case for asserting this on typographical errors found in ten characters in both sets of papers. 'But after extended reflection it occurred to me that the method employed by Feehan and other experts rested on the assumption that if two typed documents contained a certain number of *similar* deviations from the normal . . . the laws of chance would preclude the possibility that two different machines had been used. This assumption, which doubtless is sound enough in the ordinary type of case, appeared to neglect altogether the possibility – if it was one – that a typewriter might be deliberately created, or adapted, so as to duplicate some, if not all, of the peculiar characteristics of another.'

To test whether such a duplicate machine could be produced, Lane sought out an expert typewriter engineer called Martin Tytell, gave him a specimen of typing done on the Woodstock 230099, and asked him to produce a machine – if he could – which would reproduce the idiosyncrasies of the Woodstock 230099.

After a time Tytell brought him such a machine. He declared under oath, 'I have constructed a machine which I believe meets Mr Lane's specifications. Neither I nor any of my associates

1. Op cit p365.

in the work have had any access whatsoever to the original machine [Woodstock 230099] during the course of the experiment . . . So far as I know, this is the first time such a machine has ever been made *except possibly for forgery or other illegal purposes*.[1] With the experience I and my associates have gained through this experiment I am confident that we could now create other duplicates with an even higher degree of fidelity in a fraction of the time which this machine has taken.'

Two experts in the examination of documents were now called in by Chester Lane. The first, Miss Elizabeth McCarthy, an attorney and an expert in documents for the Boston City Police Department, and for the Massachusetts State Police, declared that it was her opinion, which was 'based upon my long experience in methods of questioned document explanation, that the duplication has progressed to such a degree that an expert in this field, however highly qualified, would find it difficult, if not impossible, to distinguish between samples of the two machines'. The second expert, Mrs Evelyn Ehrlich, an expert on the staff of the Fogg Museum of Art whose specialist field was the technical examination of manuscripts and typography, stated that her opinion, after a long examination, was that 'N 230099 cannot be the same machine that typed Government Exhibits 37 and 46 – B and . . . the Hiss Standards. I base this

---

1. As I shall show presently, Mr Tytell was wrong. But this opinion given by a very expert American typewriter engineer illustrates the lack of knowledge at this time, even among experts. Hiss's defence, therefore, can scarcely be blamed for not following up such a line 'at the trial. On the other hand, as I think the reader will appreciate in a moment or two, it is very odd that the FBI, who carried out the prosecution's investigations, did not know that such machines could, and had been built, and used; and that it is suspicious, to say the least, that they did not draw the US Attorney's attention to the fact. Had Mr Murphy known this he would have felt morally bound to make his knowledge public, for in American courts as in our own, the prosecutor's duty is not to win his case by whatever methods, but to see that justice, as he sees it in a particular case, is done.

opinion upon certain differences in type impression between many of the letters in the two sets of documents, these differences appearing with such a high degree of regularity as to preclude the possibility of their being due to variations of ribbon, typing pressure and the peculiarities of operation, and being of such a nature that difference in imprint cannot be due to age or wear on the machine . . . the observable peculiarities in the type of the Baltimore Document in my opinion more nearly resemble the peculiarities in the typing from N 230099 than they do the peculiarities in the Hiss Standards which I used for comparison.'

Now, when I began to work on this book I knew that duplication of a typewriter was feasible, for I had read in H Montgomery Hyde's book entitled *Room 3603: The Secret Service Story of Sir William Stephenson*[1] : 'The FBI had no authority to engage in "special operations", so that in this sphere Stephenson operated exclusively. Among other devices which he created at this time was a small establishment within the framework of his existing organisation for the purpose of fabricating letters and other documents. It had a laboratory in Canada which was set up, with the aid of the RCMP, under cover of the Canadian Broadcasting Corporation, whose general manager at this time was Stephenson's old friend, Gladstone Murray. It was staffed by one or two experts and was called Station M. This name may have been suggested by the first letter of the surname of the officer who played a leading part in the station's activities. This was Eric Maschwitz, better known as a lyric writer ("A Nightingale Sang in Berkeley Square") and the author of several successful musical comedies (*Balalaika, Carissima*). "The operations with which I was concerned under a genius known as Little Bill were many and curious," Maschwitz has written in his autobiography, briefly and discreetly alluding to this strange

1. Farrar Straus, New York, 1965.

interlude in his theatrical career. "In them I was associated with . . . an industrial chemist, and two ruffians who could reproduce faultlessly the imprint of any typewriter on earth . . ."[1].'[2]

And a little later, 'The plan which he and his SO advisers devised in New York was to convey to the Brazilian Government a compromising letter which purported to have been written by someone in authority in the LATI head office in Italy (they chose General Liotta, president of the LATI) to an Italian executive of the company in Brazil and which would result in the cancellation of the company's concession to operate its transatlantic route . . . The experts in Station M were able to simulate exactly the style of writing paper, the engraved letterhead and form of type used by General Liotta. . . . The embossing was copied with microscopic accuracy, and a typewriter was rebuilt to conform to the exact mechanical imperfections of the machine upon which the General's secretary had typed the original letter.'[3]

I wanted, however, to prove to myself that such duplication of a typewriter was possible. So I got in touch with a skilled typewriter mechanic in England who undertook to see what he could do. To begin with, the experiment went well, but it proved to be a costly business and I had reluctantly to abandon it; however, both my expert and I were convinced that it could be done.

Nevertheless, I felt that I would still like to have the evidence of experts that such duplication could be done, and I wrote to the Chairman of the Imperial Typewriter Company, Leicester, England, and asked (a) whether he thought such duplication feasible and (b) if his firm would be prepared to co-operate with me. I produce his reply:

1. *No Chip on My Shoulder*, Herbert Jenkins, London, 1957.
2. *Room 3603*, op cit p135.
3. *Room 3603*, op cit p145.

Dear Sir,

It would certainly be possible to adjust a typewriter to produce idiosyncrasies similar to those of a given specimen. The difficulties of doing this would depend on the particular idiosyncrasies involved.

Firstly it would be necessary to determine on what machine the original specimen was written so that the particular style of type could be matched together with both horizontal and vertical spacing. It would also be necessary to match the type of ribbon used as regards grade of inking and type of wave.

Idiosyncrasies of alignment may be due to more than one cause and to determine this it would be necessary to have a fairly lengthy specimen of the writing. If these are obvious regular faults in the alignment of certain letters, it would not be difficult to reproduce these, but the faults may be caused by looseness of certain parts and unless one can determine the exact fault, it may be more difficult to reproduce the similar result.

Characteristics due to damage to the type face will not be easy to simulate as it is very difficult to reproduce such damage in such a way as to be undetectable under close examination.

There are, furthermore, characteristics which may be due to the operator but, perhaps, these are of minor importance, though from a specimen it may be difficult to decide the cause of these.

The time required to produce such a machine would depend on the nature of the idiosyncrasies and the difficulties that might be encountered in obtaining a machine of similar make and type style.

I am sorry that we could not undertake to produce such a machine for you, as to do so would require the services of one of our most skilled men for several days and the work involved would represent a high cost in the loss of normal production lost. Nor could we guarantee to produce an undetectable specimen in any particular period.

We are sorry not to be more helpful as it would, in some ways, be an interesting exercise, but I am sure you will appreciate that our business is mass production manufacturing whereas this exercise is really in the nature of laboratory work.

Yours sincerely,
R M Evans
Chairman.

To be doubly sure, I wrote to Remington Rand, London, England. I asked if the problem was capable of solution, but did not ask if Remington would take part in a practical experiment. Mr R I Falkner, the Managing Director, replied as follows:

Dear Mr Seth,

My long-service Service Manager, Mr J Jakens, reports: 'Mr Seth's notes recall to mind the circumstances which existed with regard to the construction of the typewriter which was to be used in the new trial if this had been granted. Speaking from memory, I am sure it would have been extremely difficult and certainly a matter of opinion between experts, to have been able to conclusively prove which documents had been typed on which typewriter.

In giving this opinion I am, of course, saying that forgery by typewriter is feasible. To take the specific points raised by Mr Seth, I would comment as follows:

(a) It would be possible to reproduce the idiosyncrasies of one typewriter on a "doctored" machine.

(b) Assuming that a machine of the same basic model was available, the main difficulties would be to induce the same amount of wear on the necessary operated parts to produce the characteristics. This would be essential to ensure the spacing would be identical both in the horizontal and vertical planes. Over and above this, the critical part involves the production of type faces with simulated "wear" characteristics.

(c) The results could certainly be such that a handwriting expert could be deceived unless he was, in fact, utilising microscopes and X-rays, etc.

(d) Without wishing to evade the point, it is difficult to give a time factor or how long it would take to reproduce a machine since this must depend on the age of the machine to be copied, the amount of wear it has suffered and again, whether a machine of a similar model was available to work on. Without this information one could only guess between a wide time scale of weeks stretching out to a period of some months.'

I trust the foregoing will be of some assistance but you are welcome to contact us again if we can be of further assistance.

Yours sincerely,

pp REMINGTON OFFICE EQUIPMENT

DIVISION SPERRY RAND LTD.

(Signed)

R I T Falkner

Managing Director.

But this was not the only discovery Chester Lane made in connection with the Woodstock 230099. 'I determined to make a thorough study of the authenticity of Woodstock 230099.

That study has produced results that are startling, as far as they go.' To summarise:

1 A Woodstock typewriter bearing the serial number 230099 would have been manufactured in or around August 1929 and certainly no earlier than the first week of July 1929.

2 The typeface style of the Hiss Woodstock 230099 was a style used only in Woodstock typewriters manufactured in 1926, 1927 and 1928, and possibly the early part of 1929.

From which one concludes that the Hiss 230099 is a fabricated machine.

3 The Woodstock admittedly owned by the Hisses first belonged to Mrs Hiss's father and there is evidence to show that it was in use by the 8th July 1929. Therefore this machine could not have been the Woodstock 230099.

In arriving at these conclusions, Lane had relied on information sworn to by one of his investigators, Mr Kenneth Simon. Simon had tried to locate the dealer from whom Mr Fansler, Mrs Hiss's father, had bought his machine, and this brought him into contact with Mr O J Carow, who had been branch manager of the Woodstock sales agency in Philadelphia, where Fansler had his insurance office.

(a) Carow had been interviewed by the FBI in late 1948 or early 1949 and asked to locate records of the sale of a machine of a given serial number. Carow could not recall this serial number, but he remembered telling the FBI that the machine with their serial number would have been sold in Philadelphia in November 1927 with a six months' error on either side.

(b) Carow could not say when N 230099 would have been sold because the FBI had taken away the relevant records and not returned them.

(c) Between Simon's first visit to Carow on the 23rd October

1950 and his last visit on the 18th January 1951, FBI agents had visited Carow and tried to obtain from him what information Simon had been hoping to get from him.

Nor was this the FBI's only sinister activity, apparently. The information leading to Conclusion 1 above had derived in part from an affidavit from a Mr Carlson, vice-president of the company which had taken over the Woodstock factory, which showed that a machine with only a slightly lower serial number than 230099 would have been manufactured in April or May 1929. This diverged from the information given by the Woodstock factory manager, a Mr Schmitt, who, on being asked to supply typeface similar to the typeface of Woodstock 230099, replied that such typeface could not belong to Woodstock 230099, since the machine with this serial number would have been manufactured in August or September 1929 whereas the typeface in question had been discontinued at the end of 1928.

To resolve the divergence, Simon had another meeting with Carlson and Schmitt. Carlson said his affidavit had been prepared by a clerk and that he himself was not familiar with the facts. With both Carlson and Schmitt he consulted serial number records, and as a result drew up an affidavit. When asked to sign, Schmitt said he would have to consult counsel before doing so.

Simon then asked another investigator, Donald Doud, to try to arrange for another inspection of the Woodstock records. Schmitt refused his permission.

Why did Carlson go back on his affidavit by insisting that he was not *personally* aware of the facts in it? Why did Schmitt co-operate at first, and then refuse?

As Lane said in his report, 'It is the handicaps surrounding the investigation which most require the court's attention. We search for records – the FBI has them. We ask questions – the FBI will not let people talk to us. We request access to ordinary documents in corporate files – corporate officials fear the wrath of their stockholders. We ask people to certify information in files they have shown us – they must consult counsel, and we hear no more from them. We pay experts to give us opinions – and they decline to back them up in Court because they "cannot subscribe" to anything which might support the conclusion we believe the facts to point to. And even worse, honourable and patriotic citizens who have wanted to help have been deterred by the appearance – whether or not it is a reality – of official surveillance and wire-tapping, and others who have laboured to gather information for us in the interests of justice are afraid to come forward for fear of personal consequences which might result to them from public association with the defence of Alger Hiss.'

It was these events I had in mind when I wrote in my footnote on page 199 that I tend to believe that the FBI machine was not the machine on which the Hiss Standards were typed.

Finally, a physical examination of Woodstock 230099 was made by Dr Daniel Norman, Director of Chemical Research of the New England Spectrochemical Laboratories, of Ipswich, Massachusetts. Dr Norman's subsequent affidavit reveals the following:

'1 That Woodstock type consists of a small detachable piece of metal which fits over the end of the typebar and is soldered into place.

'2 That a majority of the types on Woodstock N 230099 have been soldered onto the type-bars in a careless fashion, quite unlike the kind of soldering job done at the Woodstock factory or in a regular repair operation.

'3 That the solder used for the replacement types has a different metallic content from that used on the types which apparently had not been altered, and from that used on other contemporary machines.

'4 That the typeface metal in almost half the types contains metallic elements not present in Woodstock type metal until the date of machines of substantially later serial numbers than N 230099.

'5 That the altered types show tool marks which indicate deliberate alteration of the striking faces of the letters, as well as peculiar finish or polish, quite unlike that on types which have worn or aged normally.'[1]

These points mentioned by Dr Norman are all plainly discernible in photographs of the machine.

'At this stage of the case the Court, or the Government, may ask whether I can prove *when* N 230099 was fabricated,' Mr Laus reports later. 'I cannot. But I can say this : From 16th April 1949 when it turned up in Lockey's house, till the day it was put in evidence at the First Trial, it was in the possession of defence counsel. Between the trials it was ordered to be impounded in the Clerk's office. It was returned to the possession of defence counsel at the end of the Second Trial, and was turned over to me on or about 17th February 1950, the day I was retained as counsel. From that time until 10th February 1952, when I had it delivered to Dr Norman in Ipswich, it has been under my personal control, and no one has been allowed access to it except my immediate associates.'

Accordingly, the alteration or fabrication occurred before the machine was found by the defence. As to when it was done, there are, of course, various possibilities. One possibility with considerable logic to support it is that the initial alteration was made between the time Chambers first testified before the House Committee in August 1948 and the 17th November 1948, the day he reversed his story and produced the Baltimore Documents. The fact that between November and April neither the

1. *In the Court of Public Opinion*, op cit pp403 and 404.

defence nor thirty-five agents of the FBI could find the machine suggests that it was during this period that further work was being done on the types, in an effort to remove at least the more obvious tool marks which would betray the deception. Dr Norman's affidavit leaves no doubt that such an effort was made, and that though the result could not pass his critical examination it would have been – and in fact for nearly three years was – sufficient to deceive non-mechanical lawyers and even questioned document examiners.

The application for a new trial under US law had to be made to the trial judge. Despite all this evidence, and more besides, dealing with other points, Judge Goddard refused the application.

Alger Hiss and his advisers, as a result of these discoveries, were convinced that Chambers had doctored a Woodstock typewriter and produced the documents and films in some way they could not visualise. They were mystified, too, as to his motive. At the Second Trial, on this question of motive, they had put on the witness stand an eminent psychiatrist, Dr Carl A L Binger, and an equally eminent psychologist, Dr Henry A Murray, who tried to show 'that Chambers suffered from mental ailment of psychopathic personality of the type characterised by amoral, asocial, and delinquent behaviour, which has no regard for the good of society and of individuals and is therefore frequently destructive of both. They noted a history of theft, pathological lying, deceiving, bizarre or eccentric behaviour, false accusations, a disposition to smear, degrade, and destroy, abnormal emotionality, instability of attachments, and paranoid ideas'.[1]

Murphy practically laughed the two gentlemen out of Court. Certainly, in my opinion, their introduction to the case did the defence a good deal of harm. But Dr Zeligs's book *Friendship and*

1. *In the Court of Public Opinion*, op cit p318.

Fratricide, to which I have already referred, despite the flaws which have been criticised by expert reviewers, and the short-comings, which I, an unqualified layman, can detect, shows only too clearly that in their general diagnosis Dr Binger and Dr Murray were on the right track.

But it was not Chambers's psychopathic personality which was his prime motivator. What that was, I hope now to suggest.

II

My Version of What Happened

In the late 1920s, Russian intelligence sent to France an agent whose true identity has never been discovered. Though he was identified as a man who later called himself General Muraille, this gave no clue as to his real name. He was, however, an Old Guard Bolshevik who had suffered exile in Siberia, and had taken part in revolutionary activities before 1917. He is best known by his cover-name Paul. In 1929 he was believed to be in his middle forties.

Being an Old Guard Bolshevik, he was strongly imbued with the concept of world revolution and all his espionage efforts were devoted to clearing the path to this goal. He had no time for the French Communist Party, because in his view it was not revolutionary enough. It was this scant regard for the FCP which probably made him preserve his real identity so carefully, though it could be said that in exact antithesis to Chambers – despite the fact that Chambers used a plurality of cover-names – he was acting in accordance with the strict training he had been given by Russian intelligence.

Paul's orders from Moscow were to discover all he could about the French military situation, with special attention to new weapons. Despite his dislike of the French Party, he found that he was unable to operate without the use of its manpower. So he got in touch with Henri Barbé, the leader of the FCP, to whom he explained that he had been assigned the task of selecting likely young people for a course of Marxist–Leninist study in Moscow. Barbé agreed to help him, and put him in touch with youth organisations.

Within a short time, Paul had set up networks composed of young men he found in these organisations who were willing to co-operate. His greatest interest lay in the munitions industry centred on Lyons, from which he was successful in obtaining blueprints.

He did not, however, rely entirely on the younger generation, and it was his association with an older Communist, Vincent Vedovini, who worked as an organiser in the naval arsenal at Marseilles, that led to his eventual discovery. Having completed several lists of questions for Paul, Vedovini suddenly decided he had had enough of spying – his reasons were idealistic, for he remained a Communist – and handed the latest list to the police, with information which enabled them to identify Paul.

Paul, however, was forewarned and escaped abroad. But when he returned after a year, he walked straight into the arms of French counter-espionage. At his trial in September 1931 Paul denied he had been engaged in espionage, and when asked to explain the documentary proofs that had been turned up by the investigation and Vedovini's evidence, he claimed that he was a writer and had been merely collecting information for a novel. The Court rejected this explanation and sentenced him to three years' imprisonment. On his release, he returned to Russia and faded from the scene.

The Kremlin now summoned the French Communist Party leader, Henri Barbé, to Moscow and there tried to persuade him to take charge of espionage in France. He refused quite firmly, and within a short time was replaced by the more amenable Thorez and Duclos.

Under these two men, a system of gathering information was set up which had already proved itself in Russia, though there used for different purposes. When the Communists took over in Russia, all the old newspapers were suppressed and new ones were founded. With the old newspapers went the old journalists, and the new newspapers soon found that they had insufficient sources of information. To fill this need they produced a scheme called Workers' Correspondents (Rabcor), under which anyone who wished could send to the newspapers any item of information they thought might interest them.

A Rabcor scheme was inaugurated in France, and French workers were encouraged to send to *L'Humanité* every kind of information, especially that dealing with the French war industry. The information received was carefully sifted and all those items of particular interest to intelligence were sent to the Embassy, while the harmless ones were reproduced in the newspapers. This proved a most useful source of information, and the scheme was operated until one of the men at the top defected.

Russian intelligence has always worked on the principle that though relatively small results only may be achieved from a tremendous effort, these results make every effort worth while. Rabcor in France had shown them that ordinary workers having no premeditated espionage urge or training were able to produce here and there very valuable tid-bits of intelligence information. They had discovered that this principle could be applied to the United States official hand-outs, which were prepared by men who were so unsecurity minded that only the most blatantly secret information was omitted. The chore of wading through masses of useless material was fully compensated for by the turning up of the tiniest hint on some important subject. It might be embedded so deeply in officialism as to be almost lost, but the man who knew what he was looking for would have his patience rewarded. It seems a cumbersome and time-wasting way of going about things – but from its very beginnings Russian intelligence had ambled along with a bear-like gait, and the passage of time has never meant anything significant between the Baltic and the Urals.

Though Russian intelligence had operated in the American industrial field since 1924 – and had suffered one or two fiascos like the Counterfeit Dollars Affair – military espionage had been kept to the very minimum as part of the Russian policy of wooing United States diplomatic recognition. This was only granted after the first Roosevelt Administration had come to office in 1933. Cells and networks of the military system had always been maintained in America, so it was merely a matter of activating them once the long-sought objective had been achieved. Then they were instructed to make up for lost time; and in obedience to these instructions every conceivable method of obtaining information was utilised.

This new activity was just beginning to gain momentum in 1934 when Chambers first arrived in Washington, DC. Though, as we know, he had had works published since his student days, his literary ability had received scant notice except from a small circle of people who knew him. On the other hand, he had done a certain amount of journalistic work on the *Daily Worker* and as editor of the *New Masses*, and had there achieved sufficient experience for him to use journalism as his cover.

This was remembered when the Nye Committee in Munitions was set up and Chambers, who had come into the underground only a short time before, was sent to Washington with the assignment of getting the press hand-outs which are part of Congressional Committee procedure, and whatever other information he could. His constant approaches to Hiss show that he was hoping to wheedle out of him some unconsciously incautious snippet of information that might be useful.[1]

1. See page 93 and note the following passage from the record of the Hiss secret session with the Committee on the 16th August 1948. Having been asked by Stripling to name three people who had known Chambers as Crosley, Hiss named a Miss Elsie Gullender as one.

HISS : . . . If his first call was at the central office and he was referred to me,

Professional Soviet agents, like the Paul I mentioned at the beginning of this chapter, frequently adopted a cover that was literary in some way, for such a cover gives a very wide scope to its user. It is axiomatic of espionage technique, however, that an agent shall have enough knowledge of the cover he is using to be able to get by all but the most probing interrogation. For example, for my own operation during World War II, I assumed the cover of an Estonian seaman, who was actually living, but out of harm's way. So thorough were my superiors that I served for two months as an assistant steward on a tanker in order to get the 'feel' of the merchant seaman's life aboard, and a professional forger was extracted from Dartmoor, made up to sergeant

> Miss Gullender might remember him. She saw many, many people. If his first call was directly to me, as the press had a perfect right to come to any of us, directly, and individually, and as the legal assistant, as the counsel, I should see the press with Mr Raushenburg; and in the particular matter when I was the investigator and counsel presenting the case, I saw practically all the press.
>
> NIXON: Mr Hiss, another point that I want to be clear on, Mr Chambers said he was a Communist and that you were a Communist.
> HISS: I heard him.
> NIXON: Will you tell the Committee whether or not during the period of time that you knew him . . . from any conversation you ever had that he might be a Communist.
> HISS: I certainly didn't.
> NIXON: You never discussed politics?
> HISS: Oh, as far as I recall his conversations – and I may be confusing them with a lot of other conversations that went on in 1934 and 1935 – politics were discussed quite frequently.
>
> May I just state for the record that it was not the habit in Washington in those days, when, particularly if a member of the press called on you, to ask him before you had further conversation with him, whether or not he was a Communist. It was a quite different atmosphere in Washington then than today. I had no reason to suspect George Crosley of being a Communist. It never occurred to me that he might be or whether that was of any significance to me if he was. He was a press representative and it was my duty to give him information, as I did any other member of the press.
>
> It was to the interest of the Committee investigating the munitions industry, as its members and we of the staff saw it, to furnish guidance and information to people who were popularising and writing about its work. . . .

and set to teaching me to forge the handwriting of my alter ego. (He did such a good job that my present handwriting has more of the characteristics of my subject's handwriting than of my own pre-war handwriting.)

By adopting the cover of journalist, for which he had had some practical experience, Chambers, if he had at any time been challenged to explain why he was being so inquisitive, could have maintained that it was his journalist's natural curiosity. Moreover, as a journalist he would have been able to put questions much closer to the line of espionage than, say, a trombone player, without arousing suspicions of spying purely on account of being a journalist.

Chambers, as Crosley, set out to cultivate Hiss, believing him to be a potential source of information, treating him on the Rabcor basis that no matter how unimportant what Hiss said might appear, it could very well hold a core of value. He was delighted when Hiss offered him the 28th Street apartment for two or three months, for this gave him the opportunity to develop a closer relationship with Hiss than he could otherwise normally have done; and a closer association made greater the possibility of gleaning more information. As it happened, he also formed a personal attachment for the handsome, calm, brilliant Hiss, to which I shall refer in a later chapter.

At this time, this attempt to get information from the Nye Committee was Chambers's only underground function in Washington. Since he had not procured any worthwhile information from Hiss by the spring of 1935, he began suggesting to his superiors in the underground that he ought to receive some special training, which he knew could only be given him in Moscow. His superiors were not loth to recommend him to The Centre, because among the rather nondescript members of the American Party, he stood out, despite his many obvious peculiarities. Besides, he had acquitted himself well in the job in New York (see page 135) and showed that he would respond to training. In anticipation of making such a trip, on the 28th May 1935, he applied to the New York office of the Passport Division, for a passport in the name of David Breen.[1]

The Centre, however, took another view, and rejected him for special training, though it sanctioned his continuation in the underground. So the passport was never used.

When Hiss left the Nye Committee and joined the Solicitor-General's Office in July 1935, his usefulness as a possible source of information ended. It would have looked too suspicious, after the somewhat friendly relations that had been established, if he had cut off the association abruptly. In any case, Chambers's superiors had formed the opinion that the brilliant Hiss was bound to be promoted, and that he might be well worth contacting at a later date.

Throughout the autumn and winter of 1935-6, therefore, the contact between the two men was reduced. Chambers kept in touch, however, by going to Hiss and borrowing small sums of money. The only income he had was the pittance allowed him by the Party – always notoriously small – and he found it at times quite impossible to make it meet the demands of his family, especially as he now had to pay his rent. He made no attempt to repay these loans, and he realised that Hiss was beginning to tire of his importunity and his unkept promises to pay.[2]

1. From Second Trial transcript:
CROSS : You came all the way up from Washington . . . and signed this application for a passport, is that correct, on 28th May 1935
CHAMBERS : I believe it is.
Q : And you knew that that was a false statement to represent yourself as David Breen being born in New York City on 28th April 1900, didn't you?
A : Certainly.

2. From the transcript of the Hiss secret session with the Committee on the 16th August 1948 :

Besides his instructions to keep in contact with Hiss, he had reasons of his own (those I shall mention in a later chapter) for not wanting Hiss to refuse to see him. So when, in April or May 1936, he was given the job of delivering a rug to a Communist whom Moscow wished to flatter, realising that his superiors would never know whether he had delivered the rug to the proper destination or not, he decided to give it to Hiss, hoping that Hiss would realise its value and restore him to favour. The plan, however, misfired, because Hiss set little store by such worldly possessions.

In September 1936 Hiss joined the State Department as assistant to the Assistant Secretary of State, Francis B Sayre. The Communist underground realised that Hiss was now in an excellent position to provide information, and Chambers was questioned about his present relations with Hiss. He replied that they had rather cooled off, and he was requested to set them in motion again.

So one day, not long after Hiss had arrived at the State Department, Chambers telephoned him. Wondering how he was going to re-open the friendship, and under emotion at speaking to a man who meant something special to him personally, the only way he could think of to explain his call was to ask Hiss for a small loan. Hiss refused bluntly, and put down the receiver sharply.

The effect of Hiss's refusal to have anything more to do with him had these results:

1 He had to confess to his superiors that he had failed to make contact with Hiss.
2 He was reprimanded by his superiors for his failure.

NIXON : Even though he didn't pay the rent, you saw him several times?
HISS : He was about to pay it and was going to sell his articles. He gave me a payment on account once. . . .

3 He felt extremely bitter at this blunt rejection of his advance by a man for whom he felt a very special attraction.

For a time he smarted under the failure to carry out his superiors' instructions; the reprimand was a source of considerable resentment; and this doubled the bitterness with which he already regarded Hiss. All of this was to fester in his mind for a long time, probably throughout his entire life, or at least until the gate of the Lewisburg Federal Penitentiary swung to behind Hiss.

Chambers's superiors, however, could not afford to dispense with his services entirely for he was working as a go-between for a man called Henry Julian Wadleigh, who had become a fellow traveller, had offered to do what he could for Communism and had been passing out documents for quite a time.[1] His contact was a man called David Carpenter (real name Zimmerman) whom Wadleigh knew at the time only by his cover-name 'Harold'.

Harold had a number of 'sources' and was finding it difficult to cope with all the material they produced. It was, therefore, decided that Chambers should take over some of the 'sources', one of whom was to be Wadleigh.

Harold taught Chambers the technique of acting as go-between and then, on instructions, introduced Chambers to Wadleigh, in Philadelphia, as 'Carl'. (This was the first time Chambers used the Carl cover-name; note that it was some months after he first met Hiss.) He had not been Wadleigh's courier long when, in March 1936, Wadleigh was transferred to the Trade Agreements Section of the State Department, which widened his scope for espionage activities immensely,[2] and he made ample use of it.

At the same time, Chambers was introduced to a Communist

1. Wadleigh gave evidence at both trials, and made full admissions.

2. On his own admission he passed to Chambers over four hundred documents altogether.

cell in Baltimore controlled by Harold. But he had only slight contact with it, and it did not mean much to him.

He performed his duties as courier well, but his work did not merit his further promotion, at least for the time being.

After the Hiss rebuff, he began to form a closer association with Wadleigh, and since his behaviour with Wadleigh was contrary to all security techniques, this close association[1] was clearly not known by his superiors. It was, I believe, a compensation for the loss of Hiss's friendship, and because Wadleigh, who suffered from an inferiority complex, and was obviously impressed by his talk and his boasting, bolstered his own ego, for he was still smarting under the reprimand for finishing with Hiss. In any case, he believed himself worthy of a more important job in the underground.[2]

Chambers remained Wadleigh's courier until March 1938 when Wadleigh was posted to Turkey to assist in drawing up a trade agreement between America and Turkey. He left the United States on the 11th March 1938 and did not return until the beginning of 1939.

The Stalin Purges of 1936 and 1937 disillusioned many foreign Communists all over the world, and there were several defections of prominent espionage operators, people like Ignace Reiss, who was Resident Director controlling a network in France, and one of the most outstanding of American Communists, Juliet Poyntz, herself in the underground. The Purges did not only strike at men and women within the confines of the Soviet Union, but stretched out its tentacles abroad, reaching to the Russian controllers of

1. He and Wadleigh met for lunch or dinner at least once a week in public restaurants in Washington.

2. Wadleigh described his first meeting with Chambers thus: 'One day he [Harold] told me I was to go to Philadelphia to meet this new contact. There we met a plump little man with an air of great importance and authority.' – *New York Post* article, July 12th, 1949.

networks and their indigenous assistants. The Purge hit the American organisation.

Professor David Dallin in his comprehensive book *Soviet Espionage* has written of this period : 'The official head of Soviet military intelligence in the United States, the Soviet military attaché, and his assistant constituted the official machinery for gathering military information. Provided with the legal and technical facilities of the embassy, and supported by an extensive underground, Soviet military intelligence would have achieved much had it not been for the great purge which began about that time (1936), and soon engulfed the majority of Russian intelligence officers as well as their American aides. (According to State Department data the official staff [ranking officers] of the Soviet military attaché in Washington numbered four during 1934–6, decreased to three in 1937, to two in 1938, to one in the first half of 1939, and to none in the second half of 1939.)'[1]

With the shrinkage of the networks, Chambers's own work was bound to be affected, and in October 1937 the end came. This had been foreseen by his superiors, and with the help of two secret Communist members of the National Research Project, he obtained a post there. The post was only a temporary one, however, and terminated at the end of January 1938.

The end of his contact with the underground had been a very heavy blow to his *amour propre* and the only way he could cope with it psychologically was to pretend to himself that he had broken with the Party. To make the pretence more easy to believe, at various times, over the next several months, he called on some of the friends who had known of his Communist affiliations, told them of his break with the Party and that he was now in great danger. Among these friends was Mark von Dorn, one of his teachers at Columbia University, who had not seen

1. *Soviet Espionage*, David Dallin, Yale University Press, 1955, p415.

him for more than ten years, and another was Herbert Solow, a former fellow student at Columbia.[1]

To strengthen further his self-delusion, he behaved as if he were on the run from the vengeance of SMERSH. (He describes this in *Witness*, between pages 25 and 88.) If it was to impress anyone besides himself, it was surely his wife, whom he had not told that the underground had discarded him.

Out of a job, and without money, he looked about for some literary work. Some time in March 1938 he called on his friend Meyer Schapiro, who introduced him to Paul Willert of the New York office of the Oxford University Press, who gave him the job of translating, from the German, Dr Martin Gumpert's book *Dunant – Founder of the Red Cross*.

How he supported himself and his family after May or June 1938 is not clear, but it is quite possible that his mother helped, for she had provided the money with which he bought a house in Baltimore. Later in the year, however, he was very hard-up, for he went to the Aberdeen Proving Ground and blackmailed a former Communist, Franklin Victor Reno, into giving him fifty dollars, and a 'life-preserver' in the form of a 'Government document'.[2]

1. See Dr Zeligs's *Friendship and Fratricide*, op cit pp298 and 301.

2. *Friendship and Fratricide*, op cit p249. 'In need of money, Chambers brazenly demanded fifty dollars from Reno. Reno did not have that amount at the time. One of his former colleagues says, "We got together and chipped in to raise fifty dollars for Chambers's blackmail money. . . ." To one colleague, Herman Louis Meyer (later mathematics professor at the University of Chicago), who lived just across the hall from Reno at Aberdeen, Reno intimated that "Chambers kept asking him for something, insisted on getting from him some kind of Government document!" In November 1948 Chambers secretly testified to the House Committee that Reno had passed him "confidential military information", and in 1951 a Baltimore Grand Jury indicted Reno for fraud against the Government – he had concealed his former membership of the Communist Party. The Government did not pursue the documentary evidence Chambers produced for it turned out to be an innocuous document – the 1917 Browning machine-gun firing table – the "life-preserver" he had kept for eleven years.'

In the early months of 1938, while his delusion was in full spate, Chambers prepared an account of his activities with the Communist Party, in which he revealed all that he knew, especially about the American members. This account he put into an envelope and handed to Nathan Levine for safe-keeping. He told himself – and this was still part of his delusion – that if he met a sudden death, or died, his nephew would open the envelope and he would be revenged on the people, the haughty Americans and Russians, for whom he had worked with such devotion and who had failed to recognise his talents, or his efforts for them, and had left him to rot in poverty.

Early in 1939 he heard that Wadleigh had returned from Turkey, and in an additional effort to convince himself that he had been persecuted by the Russians, he contacted Wadleigh.

'I had not been back in the office many days,' Wadleigh said later; 'when Carl [Chambers] phoned me to make a dinner date, or perhaps a lunch date; the news he broke to me on that occasion was so shocking that I am unable to remember the circumstances . . . he told me two or three times that he had left the apparatus and the Party. . . .

'Here was Chambers's story : The authorities in Moscow were convinced that he had become a Trotskyist and that he had converted me to Trotskyism. They had ordered him to return to Moscow, clearly with the intention of executing him when he arrived, as he told it. . . .

'I realised that my underground work in the State Department was almost certainly ended, and I feared that Chambers, embittered as he was, might go to the authorities and tell them of my activities.

'Knowing that I could no longer trust this man, I feared him. . . . When we parted, Chambers said : "Well, now I am going to become a bourgeois." Then patting me on the shoulder, he added : "That's what you'll have to do, too."

'I made no comment. I just said goodbye.'[1]

'From that day on,' Dr Zeligs goes on, 'Wadleigh lived under the dread fear that Whittaker Chambers might turn him in to the authorities as a spy.'

Chambers was still very hard up and, Dr Zeligs says, 'Wadleigh next met Chambers in response to an unexpected phone call from Chambers to Wadleigh's office. Asked to identify himself on the phone, Chambers repeated several times, in a very loud, hysterical-sounding voice, that it was Carl. "He sounded desperate," said Wadleigh. "Do you want me to starve?" Chambers exclaimed on the phone and told Wadleigh to meet him "immediately" in Jackson Place. (Jackson Place is in front of the White House, and the State Department was then diagonally across an intersection from it.) Wadleigh's reaction was, "Jackson Place? Was the man completely crazy?" He imagined going there and seeing "Chambers flanked on either side by an FBI agent, all three of them greeting me with smiles". But Wadleigh hurried to the appointed spot and found Chambers waiting alone. Chambers told him he was desperate for money and asked Wadleigh to let him have ten dollars. Wadleigh had a twenty-dollar bill and a one-dollar bill in his wallet. He gave Chambers the twenty, fearing that otherwise he would be blackmailed. As he walked away from Chambers, he thought, "I hope I never never see that man again" (and he didn't, until 1948, nor did he ever get his twenty dollars back).'[2]

It was in another effort to raise money that a little later he visited Herbert Solow. The object of the visit was not merely to let Solow know that he had broken with the Party. He took

1. Quoted in *Friendship and Fratricide*, op cit p245.

2. *Friendship and Fratricide*, op cit p245.

with him an article which he asked Solow to place for him.

His utter desperation is revealed when it is known that the article he took to Solow was about his experiences in the Communist underground. Solow pointed out that the manuscript was unmarketable. 'Everything was disguised and pseudonymous', and therefore worthless. On hearing this Chambers, so great was his need, asked Solow to arrange a meeting with President Roosevelt in order that he might make a deal, 'in which he would reveal secret information of a very important nature, the possession of which would get him into trouble, in exchange for which he wanted immunity'. 'I did not know President Roosevelt,' Solow told Dr Zeligs, 'but I felt "I must do what I can". I made several abortive efforts to contact people who might lead towards the White House. I hit upon Isaac Don Levine, who was then a well-known journalist, a strong person who did not just toy with ultra-rightism. I felt Mr Levine was savvy and would not blunder. I arranged the meeting with Isaac Don Levine.'[1]

Isaac Don Levine was a strong anti-Communist who had a certain following among American rightists, and his journal *Plain Talk* had a surprising circulation.

Levine agreed to see Chambers and his articles. He was not able to do anything to help Chambers either to see Roosevelt or to market the articles. His criticism of the latter was identical with Solow's; they were too vague, did not name names – no one would look at them.

In connection with these articles, there was a feature of them which revealed how deep Chambers's obsession of his ill-treatment by the underground had gone. He had signed them with his underground cover-name, Carl, in a deliberate act to let his former associates know that they could not just wipe him off their slate with impunity.

1. *Friendship and Fratricide*, op cit p301.

It was probably most fortunate for him that the articles were unmarketable, for their publication would most certainly have directed attention to him. Very shortly after his first meeting with Levine he had a stroke of good fortune. With the help of a former friend he obtained a book-reviewing assignment with *Time* magazine. This was to be the beginning of a new lease of life, for in a short while he had been taken on to the editorial staff and was soon to be earning thirty thousand dollars a year.

Though Levine did not make any attempt to market Chambers's articles, he did not forget him, and not long after their first meeting he took Chambers to see General Walter Krivitsky, a defecting Resident Director, who had sought asylum in America. Chambers claims in *Witness* that it was Krivitsky who revealed to him the name of the man who had been his Russian contact – Colonel Boris Bykov. In fact, Bykov and Chambers never met, for the simple reason that Chambers's position in the underground was not of sufficient importance for him to have contact with such a high-ranking officer as Bykov would have been.

In early September 1939 after the signing of the Ribbentrop-Molotov Pact, Levine felt that now was surely an auspicious moment to try to bring Chambers's information once again to the notice of the Government, and this time he was more fortunate. He was put in touch with Adolf Berle, Assistant Secretary of State, who agreed to see Chambers, and Levine accompanied him to the interview. In fact, Chambers was now reluctant to go, and Levine has described that he 'took him by the arm' to Berle.

Now, Chambers, since his early days in the Party, had made it his private business to learn as much as he could about the Party members. This curiosity was an extension merely of a general curiosity, which far and away exceeded the curiosity of normal individuals. Not only did he learn as much as he could about the Party – and after he had joined it, the Communist underground in Washington – he went to very great pains to discover personal details about the lives of the people whose names he heard mentioned. He was, in fact, his own Index.[1]

To give one illustration of Chambers's achievement in this respect. In an article in the *New York Post* (1st July 1949) Wadleigh describes how he and Chambers were once discussing Charles Darlington, Wadleigh's superior, and he was amazed by Chambers's inordinately wide-ranging knowledge about Darlington's career and background. 'When I asked Chambers, "How come you know so much about Charlie Darlington?" Chambers answered, "Well, we naturally like to know about a person who is your room-mate so we have made inquiries from our friends in the State Department and that is how I got the information." '[2]

1. One section of the Russian intelligence organisation is known as The Index. It contains a vast collection of biographies about everyone who might, even very remotely, be of use at some time or another, to Soviet espionage. Besides information about parentage, place and date of birth, education and academic achievements, career, family details, friends, and of the usual items which might be useful in gauging the background and intelligence of the subject as a potential agent, his relations with his employers, his financial circumstances (how much he earns, whether he owns a motor car or a house, and so on), his debts (most important), whether he is a good family man, if married, or a philanderer, whether married or single, if he drinks, and how much, if his wife has any influence on his actions, and all the 'dirt' that can be raked up about him. The main object is to discover weaknesses as well as strengths, since weaknesses may be played upon, or used as blackmailing weapons to induce a reluctant collaborator to collaborate.

2. It is just conceivable that the information had come from The Index, though I personally doubt it, since Chambers was too low in the hierarchy to need such information.

There are men who do have this insatiable curiosity, and the lengths to which they will go to satisfy it are extraordinary. My close friend, the late Gilbert Harding, whom I knew intimately in the days before he became famous as a television star, was such a man.

Harding was my assistant at the BBC for a time, and once as we left the office after a night shift – this was in 1940 – he asked me to accompany him to Somerset House. I declined as I was tired and wanted to get home, but I was

From his 'private information service' he gave Berle the names and particulars of men in the upper echelons of the Government which I have reproduced in Berle's notes on page 141. He named Wadleigh, who was involved in espionage, but who was the odd-man-out in the list, and he named Alger Hiss. These two he added for very personal reasons – revenge; in the case of Wadleigh because he was envious of his English Public School and university background, and yet despised him for his feeble achievements; in the case of Hiss because Hiss had spurned his friendship and had been the cause of his being reprimanded. The inclusion of Donald Hiss's name was to add to Alger Hiss's hurt, which he hoped would result from the official investigations into his information. (This particular scheme eventually misfired, for the House Committee and everyone else concerned accepted, without reservation, Donald Hiss's denials of ever having been a Communist or of engaging in espionage activities.) He mentioned Priscilla Hiss, too, for two reasons – to deepen his revenge on Alger Hiss, and to appease his jealousy of Mrs Hiss, who was as close to her husband as he had longed to be.[1]

curious enough to ask why he was going to Somerset House. 'I want to look up the birth certificate, the marriage certificate of X,' he said, naming one of our superiors, 'and his father's will.' 'What on earth for?' I asked. 'I just want to know about those things, that's all!' Gilbert replied.

In fact Gilbert and Chambers must have been very much alike in some ways. 'During the forty-odd years of his adult life Chambers crossed the paths of many different kinds of people. Some were blinded by his brilliance of mind; others he enticed by fluency of language, extraordinary knowledge, or dramatic talk about his unusual personal experiences,' Dr Zeligs writes in *Friendship and Fratricide* (p236) and he might have been describing Gilbert Harding's effect on various kinds of people. In fairness to Gilbert, however, I must say that Gilbert did not lie on Chambers's colossal scale – if he lied it was generally for effect – he was fastidious in his person and dress, and he remained faithful to his homosexual instincts.

1. When I was in New York, I wrote to Mr Adolf Berle asking him to be kind enough to grant me an interview. Unfortunately Mr Berle did not reply to my request, but if I had had the pleasure of meeting him, some of my questions would have been, 'Can you still recall how Chambers introduced the names of

To Berle he could not accuse those he named of espionage, for if he did, the consequences of such a serious charge would most probably recoil on his own head, and he was as fearful now of the US authorities as he was of the Russians and what they might do when they discovered what he had done – as they certainly would. He merely said that his nominees had been Communists or fellow-travellers, and in describing the Ware Group that it was an underground conspiratorial group.

Because the United States Government took no overt action, Chambers believed that any action that might have been taken was blocked by Roosevelt. (He continued to believe this, for he stated it as fact in *Witness*.) In fact, after Berle had spoken directly to the President, the matter was passed to the FBI, but their investigations could find nothing to support Chambers's charges. (By this time Wadleigh had given up his espionage activities in his dread of being exposed by Chambers.)

Though no official record exists of it, he claims that the FBI did visit him in his office at *Time* in 1941. He says he telephoned Berle to ask his permission to tell the FBI agents what he had told Berle two years previously; and he says Berle gave his permission.[1]

A day or two after this alleged visit from the FBI, Chambers was appointed a senior editor of *Time*, with thirty thousand dollars a year. He now regretted ever having told Levine what he had; he regretted even more his talk with Berle. He told Herbert Solow that he was prepared to let bygones be bygones.

the Hiss brothers? In your notes as produced in the trial transcript, with the exception of the note about Loy Henderson's interview with Mrs Reubens, the two Hiss names and Priscilla's are last on the list. Did he seem to add them as after-thoughts? I ask, because I am puzzled why he did not include them under the State (Department) heading?'

1. This is another question I would have liked to put to Mr Berle, 'Did he recall this telephone conversation?' – for I can find no record anywhere that he was ever asked. But perhaps I have missed it.

With a salary now larger than a Cabinet minister's, Chambers invested in a farm at Westminster, Maryland. He had always had a yearning to farm, and, in fact, in the spring of 1937 he had bought what was euphemistically called a farm, but which was little more than a smallholding, not far from the farm he now purchased. (His mother had helped with the purchase money in 1937.)

Chambers's desire to let bygones be bygones referred not only to his revelations to Berle, but to his whole past in the Communist Party. He made desperate attempts to cut himself off from his scandalous earlier way of life, and among the measures he took was to be baptised into the Episcopal Church. For two or three years he was left in peace, and it was not until March 1945 that he was next visited by a Government official, Mr Ray Murphy, a security officer in the State Department.

Chambers was shocked by the re-emergence of interest in his story, but he was tied to it, and he could not retract without getting deeper into trouble with the American authorities. In his statement to Ray Murphy on this occasion, and in a second statement he made to Murphy in August 1946, he also had to stick to what he had told Berle, for obvious reasons.

The reason for Murphy's resuscitation of the matter derived from political moves put in motion by the opponents of the New Deal to disparage the New Dealers. One of the main objects of the attack were the ardent young men who had helped to make Roosevelt's plan a reality. Prominent among these architects of the New Deal was Alger Hiss.

As Dr Margret Boveri has put it in her impressive book *Treason in the Twentieth Century*,[1] 'America more than any other Western country has suffered a profound crisis of confidence in the last four decades. The pendulum has swung from unsuspecting

1. English trans Macdonald, London, 1961, pp24 and 25.

confidence to hysterical suspicion with remarkable violence and speed. During the 1920s, Communists and Socialists (apart from the famous "Red Scare" of the Wilson administration), enjoyed a period of benevolent toleration. During the 1930s it became "chic" in the expensive flats of New York millionaires to sympathise demonstratively with the Reds. It was the era of the so-called "Parlor Pinks." In colleges and universities it was almost a matter of intellectual honour to be Left Wing. The student generation of the 1930s to which Alger Hiss belonged had been very young during the self-satisfied reactionary 1920s. Appalled by the destructive effects of the economic collapse, they saw in Roosevelt and his New Deal the opening phase of a gigantic social revolution. For the first time in American history, scholars and intellectuals enjoyed the favour of those in high places, and found positive responses to their schemes and ideas almost everywhere. Without disagreeable detours through political apprenticeships, they went directly to Washington. Many of them came from the Harvard Law School where reigned the unconditional liberalism of Justices Holmes, Brandeis and Frankfurter – men who had fought for freedom of speech, even unpleasantly radical speech.'

A tactic of this attack on the New Dealers was a smear campaign that these men, including Hiss, were Communists.[1] The FBI remembered Chambers's accusation against Hiss as far back as 1939. Naturally any investigations they might make must include him, and since they had now been able to uncover information that appeared to show that at least some of Chambers's accusations had substance, they were going more deeply into matters. Not only that, Chambers, as a self-confessed member of

1. For a succinct and lucid account of the background of these events, the reader can do no better than refer to the introductory chapters of Alastair Cooke's book *A Generation on Trial*.

the Communist underground, must be a very useful source of information on a subject about which the FBI themselves were still strangely ignorant – the organisation and operational methods of Soviet espionage.

But there was soon to be another reason for Murphy's interest. In 1945 a woman called Elizabeth Bentley went to the FBI and confessed to them that she had been a Communist underground agent who, like Chambers, had been a courier between a Washington network and the Russians. Unlike Chambers, however, she had become a really important operator, whose work had impressed the Russians so much that when in 1944 Anatoli Gromov had replaced Vasili Zubilin, ostensibly as First Secretary at the Russian Embassy, but actually as Resident Director of the American networks, he presented Miss Bentley with the Red Star in recognition of her services to The Cause.

By this time, however, she was becoming more and more disillusioned with the network and the leadership of the American Communist Party, particularly with Earl Browder, the American leader. This disillusionment increased until in August 1945, after much heart-searching, she went to the FBI and told them all she knew – and it was a story that knocked Chambers's into a cocked hat.

For more than a year she worked secretly with the FBI who naturally checked her information. It was a long task, for she named eighty contacts, thirty-seven of whom were in the Government service. It was she who first named Harry Dexter White. Chambers claims in *Witness* to have known Miss Bentley well, and according to him they had another common 'target' besides White – George Silverman. Only some did Miss Bentley accuse of espionage, but these represented six espionage groups, the leader of one group being Nathan Silvermaster. Some, like Lauchlin Currie, whom Chambers also claimed to have known, and who was one of the President's special assistants, denied all the charges, was as straightforward as Donald Hiss at his interrogations and nothing was ever proved against him. Miss Bentley, however, did not name Alger Hiss.

When the Department of Justice had had time to consider the reports of the FBI and other security organisations, it convened the New York Grand Jury to investigate the charges of espionage within the Government, and when Miss Bentley appeared before it, though its proceedings were supposed to be secret, the information reached the ears of the House Committee, who subpoenaed Miss Bentley to appear before it, fixing the hearing for the 31st July 1948.

Naturally, Russian intelligence knew of Miss Bentley's defection, and of her long stints with the FBI. In other days she would have been liquidated by SMERSH in the quickest possible time, but in recent months something had happened that had made them vary this procedure.

One of the chief criticisms of Roosevelt, not only in his own country, but abroad, had been that he had been too soft in his dealings with Stalin. From various eminent sources, including Churchill, it is apparent that Roosevelt believed that he – and he alone – could handle the formidable Russian leader. Indeed, Yalta and more besides were seen as appeasement of Communism.

The death of Roosevelt in April 1945 brought to the head of American affairs Harry S Truman, a very different character from Roosevelt, with very different ideas, which were not long in becoming apparent. For within a few weeks Truman was telling his Secretary of State to let Stalin know that America would not acquiesce in the formation of a Soviet-controlled Poland, nor join the United Nations if Russia insisted on her interpretation of what the veto should be.

Throughout the remainder of 1945 and through 1946 it became clear to all who could apprehend these things that a breach had been sprung between America and Russia, and that it was visibly widening with each week that went by. Any lingering hope that the breach might be closed was shattered on the 12th March 1947, when President Truman made in Congress a declaration of what has become known as the Truman Doctrine. He proclaimed, in effect, that the world was divided into two camps, the democracies and the totalitarian states; and he declared America's intention to fight totalitarianism wherever it might be found.

Two days before he made this speech, a Conference of Foreign Ministers had opened in Moscow to try to settle various outstanding questions left over by the Allied victory in Europe. As a result of the speech, though the Foreign Ministers – and this includes Molotov – tried their best to carry on as though Truman had remained silent, they found their work impossible and broke up.

In the ensuing months, the Russians took Truman at his word, and worked hard at consolidating their position in Eastern Europe, and succeeded, the first moves being the conclusion of trade agreements with Bulgaria, Czechoslovakia, Hungary, Yugoslavia, Poland and Rumania all between the 10th July and 26th August. In November, the Cominform issued a statement which reiterated the Truman Doctrine from the opposite standpoint.

The setting up of the Marshall Plan, and such actions as that taken by the French and Italian prime ministers, who dismissed the Communists in their governments, were retaliatory acts by the democracies. As a matter of fact, the democracies had no other course open to them but to support the Truman Doctrine, for they needed money to rehabilitate their war-shattered countries, and America was the only country able to supply it. So the world plunged headlong into the Cold War.[1]

By the spring of 1948 the Cold War was in full swing and in June Stalin launched his latest move in it – the Berlin blockade.

Stalin's chief enemy in the Cold War was the man who had really started it all, and who had won vital preliminary rounds with the Marshall Plan – President Truman. 1948 was Presidential Election Year, and Truman was due to come up for re-election. Though it was proclaimed by the pundits that Truman did not stand a chance of winning, Stalin was not averse to doing whatever he could to make the failure as certain as possible. Though he did not realise it at the time that he made his decision and issued his instructions, Stalin had a great ally in the Republican-dominated House Committee on Un-American Activities.

The news of the appearance of Elizabeth Bentley before the New York Grand Jury that reached the ears of the House Committee also reached the ears of the Kremlin. Since 1945 the spy-rings which Miss Bentley had denounced had lost the greater part of their usefulness, and could be cast off. The only consideration in the problem of what to do with Miss Bentley was how far she might have compromised Soviet espionage techniques. A brief assessment of her activities was reassuring. She had never been trained in Moscow, and the techniques she had used had been the amateur – if successful – ones taught her by her chief, Jacob Golos. Soviet espionage, therefore, had nothing to fear from her revelations.

If she could, and indeed by her testimony she undoubtedly would, create a crisis of confidence among the American people

1. This very brief summary of events, though it suffices for my purposes, may fail to convince some of my readers. To them, and indeed to all who are interested, I recommend *From Yalta to Vietnam*, by David Horowitz (MacGibbon and Kee, London, 1965, Penguin Special 1967).

in their leadership by the revelation that successive Democratic Administrations over the past sixteen years had allowed Communist spies to infiltrate the Washington corridors of power, and for nine of those years had had the information and had not acted on it, then the wrath of the nation would surely be turned on the present Democratic leader, Truman. This would be bound to have a serious effect on his being returned to power. Anyway, it was worth trying. There was nothing to lose. So the fiat issued from the Kremlin that nothing was to happen to Miss Bentley.

This kind of operation is one that appeals to Soviet espionage, and they entered into it with the enthusiasm of a starving man entering a banqueting hall. During the consideration of what could further be done to make the operation more successful, The Index came forward with the reminder that Whittaker Chambers had, way back in 1939, included Alger Hiss among those in high places whom he had denounced as Communists.

Thus Alger Hiss's subsequent career had been even more brilliant than his earlier career, which had first attracted The Centre to him and whom they had set Chambers on to catch, and he had failed. Hiss had been an adviser in Roosevelt's delegation at Yalta, it was even said that Roosevelt had thought highly of his advice; he had certainly thought highly of Hiss's talents, for he had confirmed the suggestion that Hiss should be the first Secretary-General of the United Nations. If a man of Hiss's distinction could even be suspected of having been a Communist, it would do much to aid Elizabeth Bentley's unconscious effort to cause confusion in the minds of the American people, and react even more sharply against Truman's chances of re-election.

The Index further reminded SMERSH that Whittaker Chambers was still alive – no action had been taken against him for much the same reasons that no action had been decreed against Elizabeth Bentley; he had been really insignificant, compared with her – and that, in fact, he had been interviewed by American security officers. It was likely that he would be called to testify, if Bentley's case came out into the open.

This was agreed, and an agent contacted Chambers and told him – if he wished to avoid unpleasant consequences – that if he were not called to give evidence, he was to volunteer, and that in any subsequent proceedings he was to concentrate on Alger Hiss. There had never been any indication that Chambers had been at any time an especially brave man, but, in any case, he needed little persuasion. Though a decade or more had passed since Hiss had spurned his special friendship, it still rankled. But even more importantly, the operation appealed to his delight in the conspiratorial;[1] and, though he was no longer an active Communist, it was a sop to his peculiar *amour propre* to be chosen for the role, for it would wipe out his failure to recruit Hiss in 1936. He had also an additional cause for pleasure – he hated the New Deal and by association all that the Democrats stood for,[2] and would like to see nothing better than Truman defeated. So with the burden placed squarely on his shoulders, he took the stage.

The Russian plan succeeded, at least in its first phase. As Miss Bentley stepped down from the witness stand at the close of her evidence on the 31st July 1948, before the House Committee, McDowall thanked her for her courage in daring to brave a 'walk through the shadow of publicity'. In truth, she had to be courageous for the resulting publicity was stupendous.

1. Dr Zeligs has given examples of Chambers's indulgence in conspiratorial attitudes; and a close friend of Chambers, Mr Duncan Norton-Taylor of the *Time-Life* organisation, confirmed this to me over luncheon in the Universities Club in New York, in the autumn of 1966.

2. See *Witness*, pp 472 and 473.

Truman himself saw through the Russian ruse, though he got his attribution wrong. After he had read Miss Bentley's testimony he called a press conference at which he declared that the hearing had been arranged by the Republican Party in order to drag 'a red herring' across the campaign trail.

I have deliberately omitted all mention of the hysterical atmosphere in which the House Committee hearings of the Chambers-Hiss affair took place chiefly because the Republican Party's part in the business is no part of my case.

In a footnote on page 792 of *Witness*, Chambers has written, 'Senator Nixon's role did not end with his dash back to the United States to rally the House Committee when the microfilm was in its hands. His testimony before the Grand Jury that indicted Alger Hiss[1] is a significant part of the Hiss Case.

'Throughout the most trying phases of the Case, Nixon and his family and sometimes his parents, were at our farm, encouraging me and comforting my family. My children have caught him lovingly in a nickname. To them, he is always "Nixie", the kind and the good, about whom they will tolerate no nonsense. His somewhat martial Quakerism sometimes amused and always heartened me. I have a vivid picture of him, in the blackest hour of the Hiss Case, standing by the barn and saying in his quietly savage way (he is the kindest of men), "If the American people

---

1. 'Nixon announced this same day that he would personally take the pumpkin films to New York for the grand jury. He said that he would answer any questions that "will assist them in bringing to justice those who fed this information to Chambers".' (See p190, *In the Court of Public Opinion*, Hiss.)

'Also on the 13th, Nixon appeared before the grand jury. I do not know what he told the jury. Certainly his views as to what the jury should do (indict me) and should not do (indict Chambers) were by this time well known. His mere appearance powerfully reinforced these exhortations, and I do know that just before testifying, he repeated his views to the press, saying that "the indictment of Chambers for perjury without anybody else would constitute a whitewash because it would be impossible to bring out the truth regarding other people".' (See p190, *In the Court of Public Opinion*, Hiss.)

understood the real character of Alger Hiss, they would boil him in oil".'

The press also behaved in an absolutely irresponsible way. There is no law in America prohibiting newspapers from commenting on a case while it is *sub judice*, and according to their bias, the various newspapers and journals slanted their presentation of the evidence and produced commentaries that pre-judged the case before the testimony had been heard. Even the pro-Hiss papers did Hiss's cause harm. In addition, the House Committee behaved outrageously, by leaking what had gone on in secret sessions, and new evidence that had come in before it was heard in public session.[1] As a result the trials took place in an atmosphere of public near-hysteria, if not full-hysteria.

But for all the apparent success of the Bentley and Chambers hearings, the Russian ruse failed. President Truman was re-elected early in November.

Since the pressure had to be kept up until polling day, it was necessary for Chambers to give Hiss an opportunity to sue him for libel.

It will be noted that it was not until after the results of the election were known that Chambers suddenly introduced espionage and the documents. Up to that time he had adhered to his story to Berle in 1939, that the Ware Group was merely a conspiratorial group, and again and again throughout the Committee hearings and even on the opening day of the Baltimore pre-trial he insisted that the group did not engage in espionage. (See pages 122–126.)

With their plan misfiring, it was all the more important for the Russians to sustain their attack on Truman. Anyone else might have been content to acknowledge failure and retire;

---

1. For an excellent impression of the atmosphere, I would again refer the reader to Alastair Cooke's *A Generation on Trial*.

this is not the Russian way, however. Thus they instructed Chambers that Hiss must be shown to have committed espionage or at least be suspected of it.

There was only one way to drive this home – by the production of documents. They told Chambers they would produce the evidence for him. But when they came to review the film that had come via Chambers, they realised that none of the documents could be 'proved' to have emanated from Hiss and only from Hiss.

The man in charge of the operation in SMERSH was a Colonel Mikhail Shpigelglas. He was one of SMERSH's star products and had a record of organising forgeries for Stalin's nefarious purposes. Shpigelglas at once saw that to make certain Hiss was irrevocably tied to some of the documents, documents would have to be forged in such a way that Hiss or someone connected with Hiss had prepared them. There was a typewriter in every American home like the Hiss home. What could Chambers tell them about the Hiss typewriter when he had stayed in the Hiss home?

An agent was sent to Chambers with these urgent inquiries. The meeting took place in the Maryland farmhouse.[1] When Chambers heard what the agent had come for he recalled that he had used the Hiss typewriter which had either been left in the 28th Street apartment when he was the tenant, or during his stay at the P Street house. Could he produce these specimens? If he could have a few moments, he thought he might be able to. Excusing himself he went down to the basement study.[2] In a

1. In *Witness* Chambers tries to explain away strangers calling at the farm who might have been seen. On page 752, he writes, 'Rumours that Hiss investigators were prowling around the farm had reached us. I believed there was no length to which these people would not go . . .'

2. Chambers was an inveterate hoarder of papers and his own writings. After he died, his friend, Duncan Norton-Taylor, was asked by Mrs Chambers to go

few moments, he returned with one or two pages of typescript. The agent looked them over, asked a few questions to make sure that these were the pages typed on the Hiss machine, was assured and hurried away.

For an organisation such as SMERSH's[1] it was an easy matter to identify the machine on which the specimen pages had been written. The following day an expert in adapting typewriters from the SMERSH laboratories in Moscow, accompanied by an assistant, flew in to Washington. He brought with him a Woodstock typewriter of the period required, which the methodical organisers of SMERSH had in stock – SMERSH has an almost complete collection of all the typewriters that have ever been produced in Europe, the United States, Japan and the British Dominions, from 1924 onwards – and went to work. Having inspected the typescript and compared it with a specimen from the Woodstock he had brought with him, he discovered that he had a formidable task before him, though not a hopeless one. The majority of the letters would have to be 'doctored', and the only way to do so satisfactorily would be to remove them, adapt them and replace them. Time was short and they would have to work fast.[2] He had been told that while the reproduction of the script should

through his papers and produce a posthumous volume of Chambers's writings. This, after a great labour of love, Mr Norton-Taylor did, and produced *Cold Friday*, which was published by Random House, New York, in 1964. In his Introduction to *Cold Friday* (pxiii) Mr Norton-Taylor has written, 'In time, Esther Chambers steeled herself to go down to the basement study. There were a half-dozen cartons and a briefcase filled with letters and fragments of writing – some of them typed, some of them still in his difficult handwriting.' And on page xvi, 'From the cartons in the study came chapters, paragraphs, written and re-written – fragments, excursions, luminous beginnings sometimes without endings, enigmas sometimes without answers.'

1. With all modesty may I refer the reader to my book *The Executioners: The Story of SMERSH*, Cassell, London, 1967.

2. See Dr Norman's report on page 207, regarding the carelessness with which the types had been soldered on to the typebars on Woodstock 230099.

be as perfect as possible, the documents did not have to be absolutely perfect; sufficiently good enough to cast doubts on Hiss's innocence if they did not completely deceive the experts.

A selection of filmed documents had also arrived from Moscow together with the original of one document and the four Hiss handwritten notes, which one of the State Department sources had extracted from the wastepaper basket where Hiss had thrown them after use, and which, because of their small size, had been passed on as they were.[1]

As soon as the typewriter was ready the typing began. It was a rushed job, but relays of typists finished it in time.[2]

In the meantime, Chambers, since being pressed by Marbury to produce documents on the 5th and 6th November, had been wondering how to explain, if asked, where he had found them, for he had excused his failure to produce them by saying he had not 'explored all the sources where some conceivable data might be'. (This was his counsel's explanation of the 6th November.) During these considerations he suddenly remembered the envelope he had left in 1938 with Nathan Levine and which contained the account of his dealings with the Communist underground in which he had 'named names', so that if he were murdered or should die, he would be avenged on the Party, which had treated him so badly – in other words what he called his 'life-preservers'. He did not know whether it still existed, but

1. 'Or, as these [handwritten notes], would have been available to others (officials other than Wadleigh, charwomen in the case of handwritten notes if thrown into the wastebasket, messengers in the case of the telegrams) had someone else passed them to Chambers?' (See *In the Court of Public Opinion*, op cit p193.)

2. The Hiss Standards and the documents, while compared for type idiosyncrasies, do not appear to have been compared for 'typist's handwriting', eg consistent errors and overtyping. This point seems to have been overlooked by the defence, and was not introduced by the prosecution.

if it did this would be just the thing. He rang up Levine to find out. He did not ask Levine outright if the envelope were still in existence, he asked him to have his 'things ready for him' when he called next day, and when Levine did not query his use of 'things' he understood that the envelope was available. As he turned it over, it appeared to him a god-send, for he could produce Levine to corroborate his story of the envelope.

On the 13th November he received news that the forged documents were ready. The Russians had decided that it would be unwise for another agent to call at the Maryland farm, and when he said that he was going to New York, it was arranged that he should pick them up there, before going to Levine's. The procurement of the envelope he had to play by ear, and providence seemed to be with him when Levine picked up the dustpan and brush and went back to the bathroom, where the envelope had been concealed. He slit open the envelope to make it look as if he had inspected the contents while Levine was out of the room. He would not have to show the contents to Levine. He was practically certain Levine, who was a lawyer, would not pry. Once again, fate played into his hands. As Levine replaced the dustpan and brush, he asked if Chambers had found what he was looking for.

'My answer was more to myself than to him. "Good God," I said. "I did not know that this still existed." '[1]

Going back on the train to Maryland, Chambers went to the toilet, tore up the contents of the envelope into tiny pieces and flushed them down the lavatory, little by little at intervals. Then he put the papers he had received from the Russians into the envelope and tucked the spools of film in with them.

Arrived home, while his wife was putting the children to bed, he examined the typewritten documents. They had done a good

1. *Witness*, op cit p736.

job with the typing, but his heart sank, not when he read the documents, but when he saw the dates on them. Every single one of them bore a date from the first three months of 1938; and ever since he had seen Berle, right down to the 5th or 6th November, he had consistently maintained that he had broken away from the Party 'in the fall of 1937'. He had underlined this by the stories he had woven about imploring Hiss to break away, too, about Christmas 1937, the toy rolling-pin Christmas present, and the episode when, having called on the Hisses, he had imagined they were going to murder him.

Someone in SMERSH had seriously erred. It was going to be extremely difficult to explain the sudden switch he would have to make if the papers were to do what they had been manufactured to do – convict Hiss (falsely) of espionage. Even after he had surrendered the documents to his lawyers, the thought of it worried and depressed him. For a time he wondered whether Moscow might have done this deliberately, to humiliate him again. Rather than that, he would kill himself.[1]

Through Marbury's intense interrogation of Mrs Chambers he decided to take a chance and to try to fight it out. It had been his own idea to divide the cache of material between his lawyers and the Committee. His motive for bringing the Committee into it he describes in *Witness* as follows : 'No act of mine was more effective in forcing into the open the long-smothered Hiss Case than my act of dividing the documentary evidence against Hiss [into two parts] . . . it was my decisive act in the Case. For when the second part of the divided evidence, the microfilm, fell into the hands of the Committee, it became impossible ever again to suppress the Hiss Case.'[2]

At the same time, however, there was a moment when it

1. See *Witness*, p746.
2. Op cit p742.

seemed to spell utter disaster. The Committee having received the films naturally had them examined to determine the date of their manufacture, and the Eastman Kodak expert reported that they had been made in 1945. Nixon told him this terrible news.

'I walked out of the broadloom and heavy oak hush of his [Nixon's] office into the teeming Wall Street crowds. "God is against me", I thought.'[1]

Later in the afternoon he learned that the expert had corrected his former opinion. That kind of film had been made in the 1930s, discontinued and then, in 1945, brought back into production.

The relief of this news was almost too much to bear. What if more mistakes were to be discovered? That night he made preparations to kill himself if he should ever find himself threatened. He bought two tins of a cyanide compound which, when used in a certain way, gave off a deadly gas.

Though everything seemed to be going well – except that he still had to face the problem of changing the timing of his break from 1937 to early 1938 – he fell into a fit of deep depression (he was subject to such fits) and decided it was all not worth it, so he would kill himself. He made an attempt to gas himself that night at his mother's house in New York, misused the cyanide compound, and got nothing worse than a bad headache.[2] This experience seems to have had a cathartic effect on him, for he now went into the ordeal with new determination to see it through, his old resentment against Hiss boiling up and adding fuel to the determination.

The results we know.

SMERSH played one more hand. Hearing that a search was being made for the Hiss typewriter, and having no difficulty in keeping

1. *Witness*, op cit p768.

2. See *Witness*, op cit, pages 770, 771, 774, 775

track of Mike Catlett's searches on behalf of Mr McClean SMERSH took one jump ahead of him when he got on the trail of the coloured removal man, Ira Lockey. Nor was it difficult for an expert agent to switch the Hiss-Lockey machine for the SMERSH-doctored Woodstock 230099.

Supporting Evidence

Having set out the foregoing theory it is incumbent on me to put forward if I can evidence of actual fact that will give my argument the force of logic. I have given such evidence in relation to a few points as I have developed my argument. I will give briefly below my remaining supporting evidence for the salient points of my theory.

No articles from the Nye Committee

I base my version of Chambers's contacting of Hiss on the Nye Committee on the fact that Chambers produced no articles on munitions based on the material he received from Hiss in this connection. The Library of Congress could find no articles that could conceivably have been written by Chambers on the subject of American munitions.

Hiss's last sight of Chambers

Hiss maintained that he had his last sight of Chambers in July 1935. This is supported by the fact that when he moved to the Solicitor-General's Office on the 1st August 1935 he was of no more use to Chambers as a potential source of information.

The Breen Passport

David Breen, whose name Chambers borrowed for his false passport acquired when he hoped to be going to Moscow, had been born on the 28th April 1900 and had died at the age of three and a half. Chambers describes in *Witness*[1] how J Peters obtained

1. Op cit pp355 and 356.

fraudulent birth certificates. He had organised two teams of researchers. One team studied the dates of birth of children in the Genealogical Division of the New York Public Library, the other the deaths of children. When it was discovered that a child died in infancy, using the dead child's name, Peters wrote to the Board of Health requesting a photostat copy of the birth certificate. With this copy Peters would then apply for a passport.

This is a common Russian espionage practice. Compare the false passport which the Russian spy best known as Gordon Lonsdale obtained in Canada. There had been a real Gordon Lonsdale who had been born on the 27th August 1924 at Kirkland Lake, Ontario, Canada, and had died before he was thirty. Posing as Lonsdale, this Russian spy obtained a copy of the real Gordon Lonsdale's birth certificate, and with it obtained a Canadian passport.

The fact that there had been a real David Breen substantiates Chambers's claim to have been connected with the Communist underground, and his description of how J Peters supplied the necessary birth certificate, tallying as it does with normal Russian espionage practice, confirms his actual contact with the underground.

On the other hand, the story he tells in *Witness* (pp253–7) does not pass muster. It was contrary to Soviet practice to set up in a country an apparatus composed of foreigners to that country. This was particularly true of England where the Aliens Regulations made life quite difficult even for bona fide innocuous foreigners. Besides, during the 1930s there was practically no Soviet espionage activity in Great Britain. This is a fact of espionage history.

Chambers's story is further discredited by the fact that Maxim Lieber, who was supposed to have provided him with a cover-job, firmly declined to confirm this claim, on Chambers's own admission.[1]

The Rug

The rug was first introduced into the affair by Hiss himself. On the 16th August 1948 at the secret session he said, in answer to Nixon, 'He was about to pay [the rent] and was going to sell his articles. He gave me a payment on account once. He brought a rug over which he said a wealthy patron had given him. I have still got the damned thing.'

If Hiss had really received the rug from the Russians and knew where it came from, he would surely never have volunteered the information.

The rug was, I believe, an attempt by Chambers to win Hiss's gratitude and incidentally to prevent his pressing for the rent of the apartment. Chambers said that when he handed over the rug he took it in Silverman's car to a certain spot and then handed the rug over to Hiss.

Why this strange arrangement when he claimed to be making frequent visits to the Hiss house? Silverman never confirmed this story.

The 1936 Telephone Call

My authority for this is Dr Zeligs's book.

'Money was, according to Hiss, the cause of the termination of his brief relationship with George Crosley. Hiss told me that, to the best of his recollection, his last contact with Chambers as Crosley was a telephone conversation with him sometime in the fall of 1936, after not having seen him for some time. As Hiss best surmised the call, Chambers wanted to borrow another small sum, Hiss realised that he would be sponged on again, reminded

1. *Witness*, op cit p355.

Crosley that he had not paid what he owed him, and told him that he did not want to see him again.'[1]

Chambers's Jealousy of Zimmerman (Carpenter)

'There was only one thing that Carpenter and I ever agreed on – we disliked each other at sight', Chambers writes in *Witness* (p384) and goes on to paint a picture of Carpenter in the most scathing terms. He then goes on, 'For Carpenter was envious, and I know of no way to deal with envy except to run away from it. Much worse, he was afraid of me, and there is almost no way to deal with that. He was afraid of me in general. Specifically, he was afraid that I had come to take over his kingdom.'

One does not need to be a trained psychologist to read between the lines here, Chambers's own assessment of his own worth. The whole passage in *Witness* (pages 384 and 385) is redolent with this.

Chambers Never Met the Ware Group

I base my assumption of this on several points. He stated both to the Committee and in *Witness* that the men who composed the Ware Group were each head of a cell, and that they met together regularly.

It is contrary to established conspiratorial practice for the heads of cells to know one another, except in the most exceptional circumstances. Classic Soviet clandestine practice accentuated this point always.

Chambers, by his own description, was engaged in espionage activity and his role of courier, though important, by traditional espionage practice gave him no other status, which is a lowly one in the espionage hierarchy. There is absolutely no conceivable reason why he should ever come into contact with the group,

1. *Friendship and Fratricide*, op cit p231.

which later evidence showed did exist, but never contained more than four members – Ware, Abt, Witt and Pressman.

Harold's (Carpenter's) Sources

'There were those connections. One of them worked at the Bureau of Standards . . . the third member of his trio was . . . Henry Julian Wadleigh.'[1]

Chambers himself omits the second source.

Chambers's Behaviour During his Break with Communism

The admissions which he made to the Committee during the trials and in *Witness* demonstrate conclusively that his was not a genuine break with Communism, and the actions he did take – eg going to Florida – are ridiculous in comparison with the activities he indulged in otherwise, namely :

1 He applied for a scholarship for his daughter to a Baltimore school in the name that was on his Party card – Whittaker Chambers. (Source – Baltimore pre-trial depositions)

2 He made several trips to New York in broad daylight. (Sources – Committee hearing transcripts and both Trial transcripts) Compare *Witness* p39

3 He bought a house in Baltimore in the name of David Chambers. (Source – *Friendship and Fratricide* p440)

The Gumpert's Translation

Every writer on the Hiss-Chambers case has commented at some length on Chambers's sudden switch from autumn 1937 to the 15th April 1938 and according to his partisanship had tried to explain it.

One of the most conclusive pieces of evidence for putting the real date in 1937 is that provided by the files of the New York

1. *Witness*, op cit p385.

office of the Oxford University Press. Chambers always claimed that he did not receive the commission until May 1938. Mr Chester Lane, however, in presenting his report on 'New Evidence of Fraud and Forging', prepared after Hiss had gone to prison, describes letters from the OUP to Chambers dated in mid-March 1938, and one from Chambers, in his handwriting, dated the 3rd May in which he says, 'I have not been at Mount Royal Terrace for more than a month', which in effect means that he had been in hiding on the 2nd April 1938 and therefore out of the Party by then, and this being so he could not have received from Hiss the last State Department message in the Baltimore documents. This message was dated the 1st April 1938 and arrived at 7 45 on that day, and therefore could not have been distributed until the 2nd April, a Saturday. If Chambers had visited Hiss for material on the 2nd April he would have had the original of this message available, and there would have been no need to type it.

Further, the OUP files and the files of Pearn, Pollinger and Higham, the literary agents dealing with the Gumpert's manuscript, show conclusively that the *last* batch of the manuscript was posted to Chambers on the 18th March.[1]

'Life-Preserver'

I base my conclusion that the Baltimore Documents had not lain in the Levine envelope for ten years as Chambers claimed, on Dr Norman's report on the stains on the envelope.

'. . . the envelope in which Chambers said the document had been kept is most peculiar in itself; its observable stains, both outside and in, and the condition of its flap, and of the two parts of the label which presumably once sealed it, pose questions which defy logical explanation'. From this Dr Norman declared

1. See *In the Court of Public Opinion*, op cit pp391 and 392.

he would show 'that some of the Baltimore Documents cannot have been kept in that envelope; they are devoid of the stains and pressure marks which they would have had to show if they had been in the envelope. . . . That the absence of stains and pressure marks on the Baltimore Documents cannot be explained by the presence of other protective material, since the envelope could not have held all these and the microfilms, too.'

In a footnote Lane adds, 'I have myself examined the envelope and seen in it markings which might well have been made by the cylinders of the undeveloped microfilm. There is another marking made apparently by the presence of a squarish box or carton approximately three by three inches. This mark, from its shape and size, cannot be the mark of Chambers's "little spool of developed film"; and therefore even the "pumpkin papers" microfilm may well not have been in the envelope.'[1]

The main argument against the typing of the documents described by Chambers – aside from these specific conclusions – is, of course, the stupidity of the whole arrangement. Chambers was trained in photography. The prosecutor brought this out in the Second Trial:

MURPHY : You have photographed documents?

CHAMBERS : I have.

Q : And how did you do that?

A : How the photography is done?

Q : Yes.

A : A Leica camera is attached to a stand which is collapsible and has to be set up, and a table of the calibrations used to figure out the proper height of the camera above the documents which are being photographed. Special lights are then focused on the documents, at a certain exposure, which depends, as

1. *In the Court of Public Opinion*, op cit pp409 and 410.

I recall it, in part on the nature of the ink or pencil on the document that is there used.

Q: How long does it take to develop a film?

A: I seem to recall that it took about from five to eight minutes to develop film on the hydroquinine bath. Then the film is fixed in another bath. After that it is washed and subsequently sponged and dried.

What was then to prevent Chambers from keeping the equipment at the Hiss house and photographing the material there and developing elsewhere? This would have entailed only one visit to the Hiss house instead of two, one of which was in the middle of the night.

Apart from the fact that the visits to Hiss's house were contrary to all security practice, especially such frequent ones, the night visit was particularly outrageous from the espionage point of view. I have visited Volta Place. It is a quiet narrow Georgetown street, with houses directly opposite the Hiss house. People in these opposite houses must have noticed the frequent visits of the slovenly dressed Chambers; and particularly they must have been aware of the strange night visits, for since he had no key, he had to summon the Hisses, and this by knocker, because there was no bell. The whole arrangement is too foolish to be credible.

Wadleigh, who admitted that he was told by the Russians he was expected to produce more, was never asked to type documents. Why only the Hisses?

More Than One Typist

Mr Lane also had had the documents examined by Miss McCarthy and Mrs Erhlich, the experts in this field, with a view to detecting whether the typewritten documents had been typed by Mrs Hiss. As a result they were prepared to come into court and demonstrate:

'1 That the Baltimore Documents were not typed by one person, but by two, and probably more, and that therefore Priscilla Hiss cannot have typed them all, as Chambers said she did.

'2 That Priscilla Hiss did not type any of the Baltimore Documents.

'3 That neither Priscilla nor Alger Hiss made the pencil corrections on the Baltimore Documents.'[1]

Other evidence to support the fact that Mrs Hiss did not type the documents at the 30th Street or Volta Place houses – and she would not have dared to attempt to do so anywhere else for fear of discovery – came from the next-door neighbours.

Chambers claimed that the typing of documents had begun in August or early autumn of 1937. At this time the Hisses were living at 1245 30th Street. I have also inspected this house personally. It is a semidetached framehouse, and the party-walls are so thin that voices can be heard through them and that so clearly it requires only a slight conscious effort to identify conversations.

During the time that the Hisses lived there, that is, from the 1st July 1936 to the 29th December 1937, their next-door neighbours were a Mr and Mrs Geoffrey May, who came forward and testified at the trials.

MAY : Well, after a few months our relations were quite informal and we would drop in when we felt they would be interested in visitors. We were very close neighbours . . . and one of our windows overlooked the entrance to their house. We could not help seeing visitors occasionally as they would enter.

. . . . . .

MAY : As nearly as I can remember I would probably leave the office about five and get home about five thirty or a quarter to six.

1. *In the Court of Public Opinion*, op cit p109.

Q : What did you observe with reference to the time that Mr Hiss generally got home when you were living there on 30th Street?

A : I would say that State Department hours are slightly later than other hours . . . it seems to me he (Hiss) would come home later than I would by fifteen minutes or half an hour probably.

. . . . .

Q : Were the walls of the house where you were living, 1243, rather' thin so that you could hear noises in the other apartment?

A : They were inconveniently thin.

. . . . .

Q : Did you ever hear any typewriter being used in the Hisses' apartment when they lived there?

A : I don't recall having heard any typewriting in their house while they were living there.

Q : Did you hear such typewriting in their house while a subsequent tenant was living there?

A : Yes; a subsequent tenant was a newspaper columnist and he used a typewriter a great deal.

Q : And you could hear the typewriter in your apartment?

A : To my own inconvenience; yes.

Chambers claimed not only to have visited the 30th Street house but to have stayed there. Yet neither Mr or Mrs May ever saw him.

If he had gone there in the middle of the night, and sometimes stayed talking, as he claimed, the odds against the Mays not hearing him would be very short indeed. Yet, neither ever heard anything of these nocturnal visits.

The Mystery of Colonel Bykov

I do not believe Chambers ever met Colonel Bykov, or anyone so high-ranking as the chief of Russian military espionage in America, for these reasons:

1 He learned Colonel Bykov's real name for the first time from General Walter Krivitsky, in the presence of Isaac Don Levine. Chambers did *not* first describe his contact and from that Krivitsky recognised and named him – it happened the other way round. In his evidence before the House Committee, Isaac Don Levine testified '. . . and the most astonishing thing that developed that night was the identification of the man who is now known in the press under the name of Colonel Bykov. That occurred in my presence. Mr Chambers, I believe, did not know him under that name. He simply described a very high top-secret officer of the Soviet secret service in this country under an alias . . . First, Krivitsky described him as a man with singular, reddish eyes. He was small, had red hair, came from Odessa, and described him as a very dangerous man.'

The description Chambers always used subsequently practically word for word. According to Chambers, Bykov had so little English, they always conversed in German. The Russians never send non-English-speaking personnel to English-speaking countries.

2 Chambers claimed to have introduced Wadleigh to Bykov, and did, in fact, introduce Wadleigh to someone, someone who was using the cover-name Sasha. Wadleigh described Sasha, whom he understood to be Chambers's 'boss in the apparatus', as having only one arm, and without red hair. Chambers, when questioned on the point, insisted that Bykov had both arms.

3 If the man whom Chambers called Bykov was the head of the Russian organisation in America, he was certainly the most incompetent of secret agents. His behaviour as described by

Chambers – the meals in restaurants, and particularly the one he is supposed to have had with Hiss – is the absolute antithesis of how a trained agent would behave. Yet Krivitsky, who had known the real Bykov, described him as 'a very dangerous man'.

On this point alone, I would reject Bykov as a figment of Chambers's imagination. Certainly he had a Russian contact, but he would be much lower in the hierarchy. Only very rarely would the chief of an organisation meet a courier.

Hiss a Communist

At the House Committee hearings, a Louis Budenz gave evidence. Budenz was another defector, and had once been editor of the *Daily Worker*. He independently corroborated much of Miss Bentley's story. At one point he was asked by Stripling : 'Do you know Alger Hiss?'

BUDENZ : I do not know him personally, but I have heard his name mentioned as a Communist.

NIXON : Will you go into detail, Mr Budenz?

BUDENZ : At that time (1940–41) Dennis said to me, explaining why he had to call on this man, that people like Alger Hiss, Nathan Witt and Edwin Smith . . . could not be called upon as they had been in the past to aid the Party . . . because they themselves were under a certain cloud; that is to say, that all the people in governmental positions in Washington who were friendly to the Party or under Communist discipline were in difficulties at that time. . . .

NIXON : You are absolutely certain Alger Hiss's name was mentioned?

BUDENZ : Oh yes; I recognised Mr Hiss's name before it was here mentioned publicly; that is, I know that his name was mentioned along with Nathan Witt and Edwin Smith, so far as I recall.

NIXON : Mr Budenz, did you ever tell the investigation agencies of the Government about Mr Hiss's reputation in Communist circles?

BUDENZ : Yes, sir; I told the FBI . . . within the last year – no, it may have been a year and a half ago.

NIXON : Mr Budenz, is it possible that when Mr Hiss was referred to in Communist Party circles as being under Communist discipline, that it was simply a case of the Communists claiming as their own a person whom they considered to be a liberal?

BUDENZ : There is a very definite distinction. That is, the Communists did refer to those under discipline in a different manner from the way they do those just friendly to them. . . . Of course, there is a remote possibility that Mr Hiss's name might have been used incorrectly. My impression was that Mr Hiss was equivalent to a member of the Communist Party. The phrase Communist Party member so far as I refer to it was never used, but that he was under Communist discipline and he was associated with Nathan Witt and Edwin Smith.

As Congressman Rankin commented when Miss Bentley gave similar reasons for saying that Lauchlin Currie was a Communist, 'This is a smear by remote control.' Budenz was not asked to repeat his evidence at the trials.

At the Second Trial, however, Murphy produced a Mrs Hede Massing, a well-known Communist and one-time wife of the Austrian Communist leader, Gerhart Eisler. She claimed to have met Hiss in 1935 at the house of Noel Field in Washington. During a conversation with Hiss she said to him, 'I understand you are trying to get Noel Field away from my organisation into yours,' to which Hiss replied, 'So you are the famous girl that is trying to get Noel Field away from me?' She said, 'Yes,' and he said, 'Well, we shall see who is going to win,' to which she replied, 'Well, you realise you are competing with a woman,' and then she could not remember whether she or Hiss had said, 'Whoever is going to win we are working for the same boss.'

In rebuttal the defence produced a Mr Rabinavicius, a former high-ranking Lithuanian diplomat, who had volunteered to give evidence. He described how he had heard Mrs Massing recount another version of this story at a party. Later he asked her whether Hiss had said he was a Communist or a member of the underground, and she had said, 'No, he did not tell me. He did not have to tell me. I knew he was. . . . One *apparatchik* understands, realises who is another *apparatchik*.'

The facts are that Noel Field left the State Department on the 1st July 1936 and Hiss did not join until the 1st September. At the party described by Rabinavicius, Mrs Massing had said that when she asked Field to join her *apparat* he had said, 'Why should I, we have such an organisation in the State Department.' Since Hiss and Field were not contemporary at the State Department, this makes nonsense of Mrs Massing's story.

This was the only witness called to corroborate Chambers on this point. In 1950 a Nathan Weyl wrote a book called *Treason*, in which he devoted a chapter to the Hiss case. In this chapter he wrote, 'If he was a secret Communist, he hid the fact superbly. . . . Throughout the two arduous trials he underwent, Hiss cut an impressive figure. . . . Alger Hiss avoided testimony with intellectual overtones. . . . To him, apparently, every former Communist was a traitor. There were no shadings.'

On the 19th February 1952 Weyl gave evidence before the Senate Internal Security Committee. A former Communist, he claimed to have been a member of the Ware Group, where, he said, he had met Pressman, Kramer, Abt, Collins and Hiss. Weyl had met Hiss there more than five times, describing it as a Marxist study group.

To the anti-Hiss party this evidence of Weyl's has constituted proof of Hiss's guilt. But how can this testimony be reconciled with what he wrote in *Treason*? Moreover, when he appeared before the House Committee in 1943, he had made no mention of Hiss. All of which nullifies his testimony.

On the other hand, Lee Pressman gave evidence before the House Committee in 1950, waived his constitutional privilege, and confessed that he had formed a group in Washington in 1935 (as Chambers claimed). During this evidence he said, 'I do know and I can state as a matter of knowledge, that for the period of my participation in that group . . . Alger Hiss was not a member of the group,' whose other members he identified as Nathan Witt, Kramer and Abt, the seven-membered group described by Chambers as the Ware Group.

Chambers mentions this testimony of Pressman's twice in *Witness*, on pages 335 and 346. In neither reference does he directly allude to the fact that Pressman said that to his knowledge Hiss was *not* a member of the group. He accuses Pressman of forgetfulness 'on most other relevant points, so that his testimony fell far short of the full facts'.

Shpigelglas

Mikhail Shpigelglàs had been an outstanding student at Moscow University under the Rectorship of Vyshynsky. He had set his mind on entering Russian intelligence and rejected Vyshynsky's offer of an assistant Readership when he graduated.

To attract the attention of the intelligence authorities he wrote a thesis on William Wickham, chief of British intelligence in Europe in the last decade of the eighteenth century. Wickham was one of the most brilliant secret agents Great Britain has ever produced, and outstanding among his exploits was his bringing about the downfall of the French Republican general, Pichegrue, in 1797.

This he did with the help of an unmitigated rogue, a typical Chambers character, called Comte Maurice de Montgalliard. The main feature in the operation was a document, later discovered to have been concocted by Montgalliard, purporting to be an account of the history of Pichegrue's treacherous activities against Napoleon, untrue from beginning to end. This document, in a passable forgery of the handwriting of the Comte d'Antraigues, the French Royalist representative in Venice, came into the possession of Napoleon by the machinations of Montgalliard. As a result Pichegrue was arrested and imprisoned, and later committed suicide.[1]

Shpigelglas was recruited into Russian intelligence and received rapid promotion. He was deeply involved in the framing of the Red Marshal Tukhachevsky by means of forged documents in 1937, which resulted in the Marshal being shot by Stalin.[2]

As a result of his role in the Tukhachevsky affair, Shpigelglas was promoted Colonel. He also played a part in the preparations for the assassination of Trotsky in 1940. After the war he became one of the outstanding high-ranking officers of the Ninth Section of the Special Division of the Second Directorate for Positive State Security (SMERSH). At the time of the Hiss case he was in a position of considerable influence in SMERSH.

The common denominator of the Pichegrue and Tukhachevsky

1. See *Wickham Correspondence* I, pp478 and 501, FO Swit 20 *Wickham to Grenville* 8th March 1797.

2. Consult (i) *The Tukhachevsky Affaire*, Victor Alexandrov, Macdonald, London 1963.

    (ii) *The Secret Front*, Wilhelm Hoettl, Weidenfeld and Nicolson, London 1953.

    (iii) *German Military Intelligence*, Paul Leverkuehn, Weidenfeld and Nicolson, London 1954.

affairs – the forged documents – and Shpigelglas's interest in the one and involvement in the other, and his high rank in SMERSH at the time of the Hiss case, are, I suggest, not without significance.

The Special Relationship

During my version of what happened I have dropped hints from time to time about a special relationship which existed between Chambers and Hiss.

When I first began to consider my theory in detail, I could fit everything into place except one point: Why had Chambers named Hiss to Berle in 1938? At this time I did not know about the telephone call which Hiss had from Chambers in the autumn of 1936; and as I cast about for a motive I came upon a poem of Chambers's which Mr Stryker had read into the record at the First Trial. It was called *Tandaradei*, and was written in 1926, round about the time of his brother Richard's death. It ran –

Tandaradei

All that I can have at all
Is your body; all I can feel,
As our bodies precipitate and fall,
Is the stretch of your body. I would kneel
If I could touch more than the small
Back of the head of the heavy face you conceal.

In my breast – with its little hard eyes,
Like little hot lead–moulds, pressed
Into the soft of my breast. My straying hand tries
To gather in the mould of the rest –

How the shins taper out of the thighs,
And end in the broad fresh-wedge of the foot at its best.

But all my hand can encompass and possess
Is the tine spinal-coils in your neck, and the ribs that drop
So fearfully into the cavity when you press
On me your heart that seems, at moments, to make full stop,
As your sap drains out into me in excess,
Like the sap from the stems of a tree that they lop.

And, as you draw your limbs like a pale
Effulgence around me, I must
Have them drawn into me – as you fail
And begin to leave me. You shall be a hand thrust
Into my flesh; your hand thrust into me impales
My flesh forever on yours, driven in through the body-crust.

As you stir the coil of your spine; and you stir to collect
Your limbs from me; as we fall
Away bodily; as we are wrecked
On each other; as we call, as we call
To each other unanswered – I shall never let you recollect
Your heavy limbs from mine at all.

Expanded,
And the body well
Again; the long superabundant singleness ended.
The old shell
In hand again, mended,
And sound and resonant with the deep iron nerves of a bell.

Body – sound –
With the swell
A bell makes – ringing out from the glow of my body makes
on the dark around.

Whole-mended
Again, I may sound
The triumph of my ringing flesh that knew to set itself free and
be mastered expended.

Now I am right
In what I offended,
I may go forth again, again unmastered, into the light.

The homosexual implications of the poem struck me immediately, and I wondered whether Chambers had ever made homosexual advances to Hiss – who was a strikingly handsome young man and who, I imagine, must have been very attractive to homosexuals – and had been rebuffed. If this had been the case, then it would supply a very potent motive for revenge in whatever form that revenge might take. I recalled Chambers's description of Hiss. 'When seen from behind he had a "mincing" gait,' he told the Committee, and this seemed to me to suggest that Chambers was trying to convey to the Committee his dislike of Hiss on account of the homosexuality which 'mincing gait' implied, and in view of his own preoccupation with homosexual intercourse in *Tandaradei*, I thought that perhaps fearing that a homosexual past might be raked up, by implying that Hiss was a homosexual he was setting up a defence in advance, against any such accusation.

In *A Generation on Trial*, Alastair Cooke has broadly hinted at some rumours going round at the time of the case that one or both men had been involved in a homosexual relationship.

Chambers had clearly heard these rumours, and refers to them with some vehemence in *Witness*, implying that they were the invention of Hiss partisans. When I met Alastair Cooke to discuss the case, he said that there had been some pretty unpleasant stories in circulation, but nothing conclusive had ever been discovered against either men.

I still had not solved my problem when I met Mr Hiss. I asked him pointblank if Chambers had ever made a homosexual pass at him. The forthrightness and firmness of his No make it impossible for me to suspect his veracity on this point.

Then suddenly something connected *Tandaradei* in my mind with Chambers's brother Richard. I read and re-read the passages in *Witness* referring to the brother, and it seemed to me that there was some underlying, unexpressed feeling for the brother that I had previously missed, and I wondered if the Chambers boys had ever been homosexual lovers. On pondering this, I realised that it did not help me much except in establishing Chambers's homosexual tendencies.

During our three months in New York while I was carrying out my researches, my wife and I formed the habit of walking in Central Park before lunch on Sundays, when the weather was fine, which it almost always was. On one of these strolls we came upon a couple of teenage twins, a boy and a girl. They were holding hands and completely immersed in one another, and as I watched them, thinking of the difficulties towards which they might be heading, out of my memory came a case involving a brother and sister of which I had personal knowledge.

The brother had been a year or two younger than the sister, and he had developed extremely strong sexual desires for her. Because of the incest-tabu, however, he had kept these desires in check. 'I used to go almost crazy wanting her,' he told me, 'but I realised I mustn't because she was my sister.' He put off marriage on this account until his middle thirties, and when he did marry, the woman he chose was the same age as his sister and physically resembled her. The marriage, however, could not be consummated because of his impotence, although he did not suffer from organic impotence since up to the time of his marriage he had achieved sexual relief by masturbation and had had occasional successful intercourse with girls younger than himself. After marriage he was able to masturbate, and after divorce he had successful intercourse, but always with younger girls.

This made me wonder whether Chambers might have had homosexual longings for his brother but was inhibited from trying to fulfil them because of the brother relationship, ie the operation of the incest-tabu. Supposing this were true, how did it affect the Hiss-Chambers combination?

On checking I discovered that Hiss was only a year younger than Richard Chambers would have been had he lived. Moreover, he closely resembled Richard Chambers in temperament and outlook. Would it be possible for Whittaker Chambers to have developed homosexual longings for Hiss but because of Hiss's role of brother-substitute, had been inhibited from expressing them in the same way that my incestuously desirous brother had been from consummating his marriage because his wife resembled his sister, and had in effect become his sister-substitute?

I had heard on the grapevine that Dr Meyer Zeligs had made a study of the Hiss-Chambers case purely from the psychiatric point of view, and I wrote to him posing my question. He replied that if I could wait until his book were published I would find all my answers there.

I was so excited by this, that I wrote to Dr Zeligs's publishers and asked them if they could supply me with an advance copy of the book *Friendship and Fratricide*. I must acknowledge here my deep appreciation to the Viking Press for making an advance copy available to me.

In the book I did, indeed, find the answers to my questions. Dr Zeligs had delved deeply into Chambers's past. He did have homosexual tendencies. Dr Zeligs produced evidence from one man of an overt homosexual act by Chambers and he confirmed that Chambers had been homosexually attracted to his brother. He cited the poem *Tandaradei* as one item of the evidence among many, to support this. He also confirmed my suggestion that Hiss in every respect was for Chambers a substitute for his brother Richard.

Appreciating the suspicion with which psychiatrists are regarded by some laymen – and with jealousy by their fellow psychiatrists – when I came to write my book I decided not to rely on Dr Zeligs's findings alone, and submitted my problem to two eminent English psychiatrists, without revealing to them who were involved. I submitted two questions to them:

1 My case of the incestuously motivated brother and his fate, and asked if, in their opinion, the same could happen in a brother-brother relationship, and whether a man who had homosexual longings for a brother could have such longings for a man who reminded him strongly of his brother, and be inhibited from expressing his longings with the brother-substitute?

2 An interpretation of *Tandaradei*, and an answer to the question: Was it possible to tell from the poem whether the poet and his subject had had physical homosexual relations?

A consultant psychiatrist at one of the largest mental hospitals in the British Isles reported:

'The conclusion which you draw from the case you quote is probably quite valid and the analogy is also (theoretically) valid. You must remember, however, that many people inhibit, consciously, homosexual feelings because of their social implication, guilt about them and so on, and it is not *necessary*, therefore, to postulate a homosexual attachment to a brother to explain the inhibition or suppression of a homosexual attachment to another man who may resemble the brother; or to put it in psychiatric jargon, who is subconsciously identified with him in the "patient's" mind.

'It is an attractive argument and could be right – that is, it is not theoretically wrong.

'I do not regard the poem as positive evidence that there was any actual homosexual relationship between the man and his brother. Poems are often fantasy or descriptions of fantastic happenings, and even a more realistic description of homosexual acts would not give any evidence of an actual physical relationship between the two. I can say quite definitely therefore that it is not possible from the poem to deduce whether there was any physical relationship between the two or not.

'I would agree that the poem *Tandaradei* appears to describe a homosexual act and I suspect one in which the writer is the passive partner. Various references suggest this. His reference to his nipples pressed "into the soft of my breast"; the reference to the "sap" draining into him, and of his hand thrust into him "impales my flesh on yours", etc. . . .

'The anatomical descriptions I must say I find rather puzzling. I did wonder, however, if the descriptions of the hand "encompassing the spinal coils of the neck" suggested a position of mutual fellatio; but I think this is probably farfetched. However, I do agree that this poem is a description of a homosexual act in which the writer is the passive (feminine) partner.'

My second psychiatrist is a consultant at a well-known London clinic and has an extensive private practice.

His answer to my first question was:

'This is quite possible. I have recently had two patients who had homosexual longings, as you express it, for a brother, but have been inhibited from making sexual advances because of the relationship. Both had found brother-substitutes and both had wanted to have physical relations, but were prevented because of the resemblance of the substitute to the brother.

'With regard to the poem, the writer was clearly a man of exceptionally strong homosexual instincts. The whole poem is a description of a homosexual act. The second stanza describes the fore-play of the act but expresses a measure of disappointment, as if the poet, who is here playing the passive role, had hoped for a more satisfactory response.

'The third stanza describes an act of reciprocal fellatio; the popular description is sixty-nine.

'The fourth stanza seems to switch from fellatio and its culmination, to anal penetration. The hand here means the phallus; the implication being that in the sexual act the phallus takes over the functions of the hand as it searches out the erogenous zones in fore-play and finds the ultimate erogenous zone in anal connection.

'This is clearly a description of a repeated homosexual act at, so to speak, the same session. "The old shell in hand again" is a reference to the re-stimulated penis; and the poet clearly finds the second encounter more rewarding than the first.

'Bearing in mind that the poem is not necessarily a description of an actual physical act, but may be fantasy, it is nevertheless possible to say that the sexual desires of the poet for his subject are exceptionally strong.

'It is not possible to determine definitely from the poem whether the poet and the subject engaged in an actual physical relationship. But there can be no doubt at all of the intense sexual desire of the poet for his subject.'

Dr Zeligs goes at great length into the relationship of the

Chambers brothers, and if I, a layman, have interpreted him correctly, he is not only supported by my two psychiatrists but makes it abundantly clear that my 'lover-scorned-revenge' theory is not only possible, but probable here.

Conclusion

I have called this book *The Sleeping Truth*. Only two sources can ever unravel the mystery – Alger Hiss, by confessing that Chambers's charges were well-founded; the Russians, who would have to disclose every detail of Hiss's treachery backed by incontrovertible proofs.

The reader will by this time have discerned my own belief in Hiss's innocence. This being so, I also believe that we already have the truth – Hiss's declaration of his innocence.

I am only too conscious of the fact that I have *proved* nothing. But I do sincerely believe that something like what I have described actually happened.

As Lord Jowitt showed all too clearly in his analysis of the case, even at the time the doubt surrounding Hiss's guilt was of such proportions that had he been tried in an English court, he must have been acquitted.

When I met Alger Hiss one of the things about him that impressed itself on me was his utter lack of bitterness. This, I suggest, is yet another pointer to his innocence, for no man can have gone through what he has gone through, and not be bitter without being a man of outstanding character.

A man of such character, I maintain, could never be a traitor.

Montgalliard and the Pichegrue Affaire

Comte Maurice de Montgalliard was a member of an impoverished noble family in Languedoc. He had been a student at the Royal Military College at Sorrèze, a gentleman-at-arms and eventually an officer. He resigned his commission in 1784 after two campaigns in Martinique, and returned to France, where, poor as he was, he managed to invade the most exclusive social circles. This he achieved by becoming the sycophant of the absentee Archbishop of Bordeaux, Monsignor Champion de Cicé, one of whose wealthy god-daughters he married. A friendship with Jacques Necker, the Minister of Finance, also assisted his upward progress. His real name was Roques, and he had no claim to the title which he bestowed upon himself.

When the French Revolution became imminent, Montgalliard offered his services secretly to King Louis XVI and, according to his own account, was chiefly concerned in the preparations for the King's fruitless flight. Though listed as an aristocrat, somehow he managed to avoid arrest and the guillotine. One says 'somehow', but it would appear that he bought his security by becoming the secret agent of Robespierre, for in May 1794 he arrived at Austrian headquarters, where he was accepted as Robespierre's personal envoy. While there, he made the acquaintance of the Duke of York, who suggested he should visit London. In London he was received by the Duke of Gloucester, and by the Prime Minister, William Pitt, and fêted as a French aristocrat who had survived the Terror. It is thought to have been Pitt's suggestion that he should return to the Continent, but from whatever quarter it came, it was certainly backed by worthwhile financial considerations, for he agreed. Within a short time he had made friends with Prince Louis-Joseph de Condé, commander of the French Royalist Army in exile.

The French Royalists were in extremely straitened circumstances, and in order to relieve their situation Montgalliard suggested to Condé that he should return to England to try to negotiate a loan. Condé agreed, and to Montgalliard's surprise he was able to return before long with sufficient funds to meet all the back pay of the Royalist army, plus 500,000 livres, plus a credit account of 3,500,000 livres to be devoted to secret services. Montgalliard's commission was heartening, but he saw an even rosier prospect opening up before him if he could persuade Condé to give him control of the secret services. To this the Prince also agreed.

Montgalliard's first great plan was designed to bribe General Pichegrue, the most illustrious of the Republican army commanders – Bonaparte was still only halfway up – into betraying his army and bringing it over to the Royalist side. The chief difficulty lay in approaching Pichegrue, who was closely guarded and surveilled by three representatives of Directory – political commissars. Montgalliard decided that he could not be his own agent (on account of his reputation) and chose for this role an ambitious little man, a bookseller and publisher in Neuchâtel called Louis Fauche-Borel.

The offer made to Fauche-Borel, if he succeeded and the monarchy was restored, was a million louis, directorship of the Royal Press, the Inspector-Generalship of the Libraries of France, and the Order of St Michael; if he failed, he would receive a thousand louis – all of which is an indication of the cut Montgalliard himself expected to take. Fauche-Borel accepted these terms, and was given 7,200 francs for his travelling expenses.

Fauche-Borel was a natural agent, and managed to establish contact with Pichegrue, but unfortunately he aroused the General's distaste to such a degree that Pichegrue was driven to telling his aide, 'The next time that gentleman calls, you will oblige me by having him shot.' The representatives of the Directory had also by this time become aware of Fauche-Borel's machinations, and they ordered his arrest as a spy for the émigré and foreign enemies of France.

The Directory's awareness of Fauche-Borel's role had, in fact, been engineered by Montgalliard. The Comte had directed that his agent should channel all negotiations through him, having it in mind that a portion of the funds which the bookseller would need could in this way stick to his own fingers en route.

But Fauche-Borel disregarded this instruction and dealt directly with William Wickham, the British Chargé d'Affaires in Switzerland, who provided the money in his true role of Chief of the British Secret Service in Europe, a role which he filled brilliantly. The discovery of this 'betrayal' gave Montgalliard a *mauvais quart d'heure*, for he saw himself being deprived of what he considered his fair share of commission, and to counteract this loss he made post-haste for Venice, where he sought out Lallemont, the Minister for the French Republic there.

Very soon he was deep in a game of triple deception. To Lallemont he poured out the story of the attempt to bribe Pichegrue, and Lallemont was so impressed that he suggested that Montgalliard ought to go personally to Napoleon with the story, saying he would provide letters of introduction.

From Lallemont, with the possibility of gaining the ear of Napoleon, Montgalliard hurried hot-foot to Monsieur d'Antraigues, who, though a member of the staff of the Russian Minister, acted as the representative of the Pretender, Louis XVIII. He told d'Antraigues that he had access to Napoleon, and suggested that he might be able to bring him over to the Royalist cause if the financial bait offered were large enough.

The story now becomes rather complicated, for mixed up with it are the diabolical machinations of perfidious Albion, which are not at all easy to disentangle.

First, the British plan had been to win Pichegrue to the Royalist cause, as Montgalliard had suggested. But according to a letter from Wickham to his friend Charles Grenville, dated the 8th March, 1797,[1] soon after Montgalliard had arrived in Venice in 1796, the rumour was rife in all the capitals of Europe that it had been Wickham who had betrayed the plot to the French Republic. Wickham denies this and tells Grenville that it was Montgalliard who betrayed the plot.

But, second, how much is Wickham's denial worth? For it is known that when Montgalliard heard of Fauche-Borel's contact with Wickham, in an attempt to blackmail Wickham into dealing with him, the Comte threatened that unless Wickham paid him £500, he would divulge the Pichegrue plot to the Directory. If Wickham really had wanted to win Pichegrue to the Royalists, he would surely have paid out this modest sum, at the same time that he saw that Montgalliard was rendered harmless. Instead he flatly refused to consider the proposal, which seems to indicate to me that he wanted the plot to become known to the Directory, since he could be sure that Montgalliard would carry out his threat if his blackmail were not paid.

What is fact, is that the story of the plot did reach the Directory and Pichegrue was recalled and retired: the worst that could be done to him in the absence of firm evidence of the plot.

But to return to d'Antraigues, who was not unlike Montgalliard in character. D'Antraigues had been in constant touch with Francis Drake, who had first been British consul at Genoa,

1. *Wickham Correspondence* I, pp478 and 501, FO Swit 20.

and then British Minister to Genoa and Milan, and who was one of Wickham's most skilful agents.

Having received Montgalliard and heard of his plan to bribe Napoleon, d'Antraigues consulted Drake. As a result of this he refused to become involved with Montgalliard. But Drake had a use for Montgalliard.

When the French troops entered Venice early in 1797, Drake urged d'Antraigues to put himself out of reach of the Republican forces. D'Antraigues refused, and left with dignity in company with the Russian Minister. On arriving at Trieste, however, he was arrested by General Bernadotte, as the result of 'information received'. He was taken to Milan, where he was interviewed by Napoleon, and placed under open arrest.

Meanwhile, at the instigation of Montgalliard, d'Antraigues's despatch-box was searched. In it was found a document, purporting to be in d'Antraigues's handwriting, which described the plot to bribe Pichegrue. In fact, the document had been forged by Montgalliard at the instance of Francis Drake.

The document was taken to Napoleon, who at once sent it to France. On the strength of it Pichegrue was arrested on the 4th September 1797, tried for treason and convicted. He managed to escape to London, but after a time was persuaded to return to France, where he was again arrested, and committed suicide in the Temple prison.

D'Antraigues also escaped from French custody and made his way to Austria, where he firmly denied that he had written the document which had been used to bring about the downfall of Pichegrue.

Montgalliard was rewarded by the Directory, and though a proscribed aristocrat still, was allowed to live openly in France. From being a Royalist, he became one of the most ardent Bonapartists. But he fell on bad days through his own extravagance, and in 1810 was imprisoned for debt. From prison he wrote to the Minister of Police offering his services in any capacity. By the Emperor's orders his debts were paid and he was granted a pension of 14,000 francs in return for becoming a political spy. With the Restoration of the Bourbons, he tried to insist that he had been Napoleon's captive and that at heart he had always been a Royalist. But the Royalists did not believe him, and thereafter he faded out of the picture.

The British role in this unsavoury incident is difficult to determine, and the British Government's motives even more so. Until further research may prove me wrong, my theory is that the whole affair was organised, not to win the support of the leading soldier of Republican France, but to cause the greatest political confusion within the ranks of the Directory. In effect, to bring about exactly the same situation in eighteenth-century France as the Hiss case was designed to bring about in twentieth-century America.

The Tukhachevsky Affaire

Marshal Mikhail Tukhachevsky represented the nearest approach to military genius produced by Russia in the twentieth century. A former officer in the Imperial Army, at the Revolution he threw in his lot with the Bolsheviks. Appointed commander of the First Red Army on the Volga front in 1918, when he was barely twenty-five, his promotion was rapid and his influence on the future development of the Red Army considerable.

The Red Army emerged from the early struggles of the Soviet Union 'a vast, straggling, loosely organised force, resembling an overgrown partisan army, with few common factors binding it together in the way that discipline and tradition bound the professional armies of the Continent'.[1] The first task, therefore, of the new leaders, insofar as the defence of their country was concerned, was the organisation of a new army capable of fighting a modern war. The discussions were long, the debate many-sided, the details of which need not be entered here. But even when the broad outlines had been decided upon, the actual practical work of creating an army along the lines laid down was somewhat impeded by the rivalries of differing schools of military thought.

One of the urgent problems facing the architects of the new Red Army was the formation of an officer corps of sufficient intellectual ability to understand and execute the principles of modern warfare. It was a matter of education, and this was

1. J M Mackintosh in chapter 5 of *The Soviet Army*, ed B H Liddell Hart (Weidenfeld and Nicolson, London, 1956) p52.

practically out of the question owing to the lack of trained instructors. Until this lack had been removed, progress could only be slight.

However, the picture was not quite so black as it might appear at first sight. After the First World War, Russia and Germany had reached an agreement by which, in return for facilities to practise armoured and chemical warfare, Germany undertook to receive Russian officers in the Berlin military academies.

The Russians returned home impressed by German efficiency and discipline, the adoption of which they urged upon the creators of the new Red Army. These officers, a comparatively small group, found a champion in Tukhachevsky, the Deputy Commissar for War, and it was entirely due to his leadership and vision, supported by their drive, that a modern Russian Army began to emerge.

But though the aims of those responsible for this new army were being successfully achieved, all was not yet well, for their relationship with the Party was so strained that there was soon to be serious conflict between them. The basis of this conflict was a deterioration in the morale of the peasant soldiers, brought about by the collectivisation of land policy. The professional soldiers, ie the commanders, urged some modification of this policy, but the politicians, driven by their fear of Stalin, refused all but a few minor concessions.

Stalin was now approaching the climax of his attempt to seize supreme and absolute power. In 1936 he revealed the method by which he was determined to achieve this personal hegemony – the elimination of all those whom he considered to be his political enemies. This year saw the First Great Purge.

In the state of mind in which Stalin was, there is little wonder that he should see in the attitude of the Red Army leaders towards the politicians a plot to overthrow him. Marshal Tukhachevsky, now Commander-in-Chief, was an open opponent of Stalin in the councils of the Central Committee. *Ipso facto*, therefore, in Stalin's view he must be the ring-leader of the plot. In any case, Tukhachevsky was so popular with the people that he could legitimately have represented a threat to Stalin's position had the opposition broken out into an actual struggle. So Stalin summoned Yezhov, chief of State Security (NKVD), and ordered preparations to begin for the liquidation of the Marshal.

Tukhachevsky was so popular a figure that any plan to eliminate him – apart from blatant murder – would have to be directed towards discrediting him. A military leader can be discredited in only two ways: his military leadership can be found defective; his patriotism can be placed in doubt. Since it was patently impossible to fault Tukhachevsky's military leadership, it was his patriotism that would have to be attacked. He would be accused of treason in plotting with Nazi Germany to overthrow the Soviet regime.

Such an accusation would have to be supported by proofs which would fool the world. Witnesses were no use, for already the world was proclaiming that witnesses in Russian spectacular trials were being compelled to give false evidence. The proofs would, therefore, have to be in the form of documents, which would have to be forged.

SMERSH, the Ninth Section for Terror and Diversion, was the agency to carry out such an operation; but Yezhov had his doubts about the ability of SMERSH's present leadership to carry it out with the required finesse. Casting about for a man who possessed the requisite finesse, Yezhov came upon Colonel Mikhail Shpigelglas, the second deputy chief of INO, the Foreign Division of Russian intelligence.

Shpigelglas was a well-educated man, a graduate of the Faculty of Letters of Moscow University. On being awarded his diploma he was specially congratulated by the Rector, Andrei Vyshynsky, who later achieved notoriety as the prosecutor of the Purge trials, and a very dubious fame as the Foreign Minister who always said *Niet* at the United Nations.

Vyshynsky suggested to him that he should stay on at the university as a licensed university reader. Shpigelglas declined courteously, explaining that he believed he might be able to serve Russia better by becoming an official. To support his claim he wrote a thesis on William Wickham, chief of the British Secret Service in Europe, in the late eighteenth century. (See Appendix I.) It was on the basis of this study that Shpigelglas was taken into the INO and subsequently became one of its outstanding members.

Now, in Paris there was an organisation of Russian émigrés known as ROVS, whose objective was the overthrow of the Soviet regime. The chiefs of ROVS had always been objects of SMERSH's interest and in 1930 they had liquidated ROV's chairman, General Kutyepov. Kutyepov was succeeded by General Miller, who had not long been *en poste* when Hitler came to power in Germany.

The accession of Hitler and his opposition to Communism split ROVS down the middle. The younger elements now wished to switch their support from England and France to Nazi Germany, a policy opposed by Miller and his supporters.

Miller's appointment had been opposed by a General Skoblin who worked assiduously for the chairman's removal and his own appointment. Secretly he organised the revolt of the younger generals, but Miller proved to have more powerful backers than Skoblin's group of generals, and soon Skoblin realised that he would have to seek other means of achieving his goal.

Eventually he hit upon the plan of winning Nazi support by offering himself to them as a spy. Some time previously he had been introduced to Heydrich, of the Nazi security organisation, the Sicherheitsdienst. He now decided to go and see him with his offer.

He did not go empty-handed, but took with him a copy of a ROVS intelligence report on a recent secret visit to France by Marshal Tukhachevsky, the object of which had been to sound out a possible Franco-Russian alliance against Hitler. Heydrich was delighted, for the report gave him a weapon against his rival, Colonel Walter Nicolai, chief of German military intelligence, who was trying to persuade Hitler to drop his opposition to Communism. From now on, Skoblin became deeply involved with Heydrich.

But besides furthering his ambition, he had one other very pressing need – money. He had married a woman of great beauty who had made a name for herself in Imperial Russia as a singer of so-called historical songs. At the Revolution she had been married to a penniless ballet dancer, and when Dzerzhinsky, then organising the Russian intelligence services, was looking for someone to carry out a special task for him, he approached her and she consented to work for him.

She was still on the Tcheka payroll when she was arrested by Skoblin's forces with her husband. Skoblin fell in love with her at first sight, persuaded her husband to divorce her and married her himself. That had been in 1920.

In drawing up his plan for the downfall of Tukhachevsky, Shpigelglas decided that he would need the help of the Nazis. He therefore required an agent who had contact with the Nazis, and when on probing more deeply he discovered Skoblin's relations with Heydrich, the name rang a bell. Consulting the Index, he found that Madame Skoblin had once been a Tcheka agent and he felt sure that a little pressure would probably be enough to co-opt the General into his plans.

The bait he offered Skoblin was the removal of General Miller and his own succession to the presidency of ROVS. To this he added the prospect of a large sum of money. Skoblin fell for both.

What Shpigelglas required from Skoblin was that Skoblin should impress upon Heydrich that Tukhachevsky was a powerful enemy of the Third Reich and must be removed. The best way of achieving this would be to hand to Stalin 'proofs' that Tukhachevsky had been plotting with commanders of the Wehrmacht, and Stalin would do the rest. But the 'proofs' would have to be so good that they deceived everybody. Witnesses were no good; the 'proofs' would have to be documentary. He, Skoblin, would make himself responsible for getting the 'proofs' into Stalin's hands, but he could explain to Heydrich how he would do it. He had contacts in Czechoslovakia, who would pass the 'proofs' as authentic documents to President Benes. Benes would be advised to send them on to Stalin, and coming from the greatly respected Benes, Stalin would have no doubt about the truth of the allegations against Tukhachevsky.

It was a complex scheme which only a man of Shpigelglas's complex mind could produce. He had to rely on Skoblin to a very great extent for its success, but he believed he had judged his man correctly.

And indeed he had! Heydrich was completely convinced by Skoblin's description of Tukhachevsky's danger to the Third Reich; and he liked the General's suggestion for getting rid of him. He could not act, however, without the consent of Hitler and Hess, and this meant taking Himmler and one or two others into his confidence. The Führer's consent was forthcoming, and Heydrich got down to particulars.

In various departmental files there were letters from Tukhachevsky. They were mostly bread-and-butter letters written after visits to the Wehrmacht on official occasions. There were, therefore, samples of the Marshal's signature at hand, samples of the typing of the letters, and samples of the Russian Army's official notepaper.

With the help of the Russian expert Behrens, 'reports of the state of the Red Army, its armament and other interesting intelligence' were concocted. A difficulty arose with regard to the typewriter. Skoblin undertook to produce a Russian machine which would simulate the writing of Tukhachevsky's machine perfectly. Shpigelglas naturally helped him to honour this undertaking. German forgers were engaged to add the signatures.

That the plot worked is history.

And, to my mind, the most interesting feature of the story, apart from Shpigelglas's diabolical plan, is the fact that until he died at the hands of members of the Czech Resistance, in a suburb of Prague in May 1942, 'Butcher' Heydrich used to boast that it was he alone who was responsible for depriving the Red Army of its leadership when Operation Barbarossa was launched. For with Tukhachevsky died:

Three Marshals of the Soviet Union out of five.

All eleven Deputy Commissars of Defence.

All the commanders of the military districts.

The heads of the naval and air forces.

Thirteen out of fifteen army commanders.

Fifty-seven out of eighty-five corps commanders.

A hundred and ten out of a hundred and ninety-five divisional commanders.

A hundred and eighty-six out of two hundred and twenty brigade commanders.

But returning to Shpigelglas's role in the affair, it was bold, audacious and successful. In comparison, the framing of Alger Hiss was child's play.

Index